# Banking and Money

**David King**

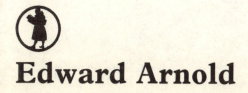

**Edward Arnold**

© David King 1987

First published in Great Britain 1987 by
Edward Arnold (Publishers) Ltd, 41 Bedford Square, London WC1B 3DQ

Edward Arnold (Australia) Pty Ltd, 80 Waverley Road, Caulfield East,
Victoria 3145, Australia

Edward Arnold, 3 East Read Street, Baltimore, Maryland 21202, USA

**British Library Cataloguing in Publication Data**

King, David N.
  Banking and money.
  1. Banks and banking
  I. Title
  332.1′024339    HG1601

  ISBN 0–7131–6516–2

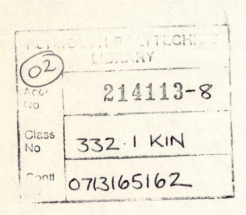
Text set in 10/11pt Plantin Compugraphic
by Colset Private Limited, Singapore
Printed and bound in Great Britain by
Biddles Ltd, Guildford and King's Lynn

# Contents

|   | Introduction | vii |
| 1 | From barter to banks | 1 |
| 2 | Financial claims | 22 |
| 3 | The elements of a banking system | 44 |
| 4 | Controlling the money stock – the basic principles | 69 |
| 5 | Controlling the money stock when last resort lending is done indirectly | 95 |
| 6 | International aspects of money | 113 |
| 7 | The main financial institutions in the United Kingdom | 137 |
| 8 | Monetary control in practice | 165 |
|   | Bibliography | 187 |
|   | Index | 189 |

# Introduction

There are many textbooks which discuss banking and money, so what is the case for adding another? The answer is that this book is not like the others and seeks to fill a gap which they have left.

Broadly speaking, the existing books can be divided into three groups. First, there are those books which appear at first sight most like this one: these are books which require little previous knowledge of economics and contain discussions of money and financial intermediaries. However, the other books of this nature are almost invariably written primarily for students taking professional examinations in banking. The present book is written for students in economics. The different clientele results in far more than a small difference in emphasis. For instance, the economics student will find here an extensive discussion of how the authorities can seek to alter the money stock and interest rates – a discussion focused on diagrams illustrating the demand and supply curves for money – but he will not be distracted by an extensive description of all the different financial intermediaries in the UK. Again, references in this book to foreign countries hinge on how transactions between different countries affect their money stocks and interest rates, not on how one country's institutions can be compared with another's.

Secondly, there are the introductory textbooks to economics as a whole, or perhaps macroeconomics as a whole, which give a necessarily rather brief coverage of some of the material covered here. The problem with these texts is that their brevity makes it very hard for the student who has read them to understand what actually happens in the UK. He is likely to believe that the supply of money is perfectly inelastic with respect to interest rates, and that the authorities typically seek to alter interest rates by altering the money stock; and he is unlikely to see any reference to the effects on the money stock and interest rates of discount houses, wholesale banks, international money flows, non-bank financial intermediaries or Euro-dollars.

As a consequence, he will be at a severe disadvantage when he comes to the third group of books which comprise specialist books written by monetary economists on various aspects of the subject. These books tend to take for granted that banks will try to create more money if interest rates rise, that the UK money stock is most often controlled by altering interest rates – rather than the other way round – and they talk in terms that assume the reader has gone way beyond the introductory texts.

It is the purpose of this book to fill the gap between the second and third groups of books just mentioned. I hope that it will be of value to the general student in economics who wants to pursue banking and money to a level beyond that of the general textbooks in order to relate the economics to the real world. And I hope it will be of value to the student who intends to specialise in monetary economics by providing a starting point that will help him to understand more fully the specialist literature that he will encounter.

Chapter 1 outlines both why and how money has developed and it shows briefly how banks can create money. Before discussing banking systems more fully, in Chapter 3, I digress in Chapter 2 to explain the various main types of financial claims. Chapter 4 outlines the main ways in which the money stock can be controlled. It does so in a simplified situation – to be found in most countries but not in the UK – where central bank lending at last resort is done directly to the clearing banks rather than indirectly via the discount houses. Chapter 5 shows how the analysis must be adapted when such lending is done indirectly; in fact, the effects of the UK arrangements are to make the discussion rather more complex, but not to invalidate any of the methods outlined in Chapter 4, so students who so wish can omit Chapter 5. Chapter 6 considers the implications of international money flows, focusing on how far they constrain the ability of a country's monetary authorities to determine its own money stock and interest rate level.

The last two chapters, like Chapter 5, are directed particularly towards the UK. Chapter 7 outlines the main financial institutions, explaining that there is a greater variety than has been noted in earlier chapters. Chapter 8 outlines briefly the development of monetary control in the present century, and explains why controlling the money stock is not quite as simple in practice as it was made to sound in Chapters 4 and 5.

To prevent confusion, I would like to draw attention to one item of terminology. I have used the term the 'money stock' to indicate the quantity of money that there is in the country at a particular point in time (though as Chapter 8 explains there are actually several different measures available). This concept is popularly referred to as the 'money supply'. The problem with the popular term is that the amount of money in a country is generally determined by the intersection of a demand for money curve and a supply of money curve, and it seemed to me best to use the term the supply of money to relate to the whole supply of money curve, not to the amount of money found at the particular point on the curve where it intersects the demand for money curve.

I have five types of debt to acknowledge. First, I would like to thank the Bank of England for permission to reproduce the copyright material taken from the *Bank of England Quarterly Bulletin*. Secondly, I am grateful to Mr A.C. Storrar from the Accountancy Department at the University here for very helpful discussions about balance sheets. Thirdly, I am very grateful to my colleague Mr R. Shone for reading part of the text, to my colleague Professor C.V. Brown for reading most of the text, and to my former colleague Dr P.E. Earl – now at the University of Tasmania in Hobart – for reading the whole text. Their comments were invaluable, and while I naturally accept full responsibility for all outstanding errors, I take some consolation from the fact that there are a good deal fewer errors than there would have been without their help. Fourthly, I am indebted to Mrs S. Hewitt for preparing all the diagrams ready for publication and for her help with the index and proof-reading. Finally, I am pleased to thank Mrs A. Cowie for typing the original manuscript and for incorporating subsequent alterations with her usual – but incomparable – care and efficiency.

Stirling
May 1987

# 1

# From barter to banks

## Introduction

Production and exchange are perhaps the two most important aspects of economic activity. Production is obviously necessary for man to live, even in a primitive community where it may consist primarily of creating a supply of picked fruit or skinned and cooked animals ready to eat. Exchange is important because it can facilitate much higher living standards all round. This chapter is concerned chiefly with the ways in which exchange may take place, for the development of money and of banks was largely a result of attempts to make exchange easier. However, it is worth starting by considering briefly the three main reasons why exchange may be beneficial.

First, some families, tribes or nations may have access to some commodities which are unavailable elsewhere. Some of the earliest exchanges probably reflected the desires of Stone Age communities to acquire useful or decorative items they previously did not possess, such as flints and cows, or pretty shells and semi-precious stones. Students who have encountered some international trade theory will recognize that such communities would be seeking to acquire items in which they had both a comparative and an absolute disadvantage. In return, they would have to offer some other items in which they had both a comparative and an absolute advantage (unless, of course, they sought plunder as an alternative to exchange).

Secondly, even where an individual, family or community can produce a wide range of items for itself, and so be largely self-sufficient, it is generally beneficial for them to concentrate on producing the items where their production is relatively efficient, and then to seek to trade these in return for items where they are relatively inefficient. As a result of such trading, people will concentrate their production on items where they have a comparative advantage. This situation is discussed at length in an international context in international trade theory, but it applies to much smaller production units than countries. Consider, for instance, a primitive village with three adults, and suppose the first is relatively good at killing wild animals for meat, the second at growing vegetables, and the third at producing cloth. Each adult might initially seek self-sufficiency in all of the items mentioned, but if instead each adult were to specialize in the item where he was relatively efficient, then they could raise their total output; and by suitable exchanges they could each end up with a greater quantity of all items than they had before they specialized. The process of specialization can be taken further to create, for example, the division of labour found in an assembly line. In his book *The Wealth of Nations* (1776; 1964 edn, Vol. 1, 5), which is the foundation of later classical economics, the Scottish economist Adam Smith gave a pin factory as an example of the division of labour. In this factory, one man drew out the wire, another straightened it, a third cut it, a fourth pointed it, a fifth ground the top ready to receive the head, another put on the heads (themselves made by others), whilst others finished the pins and packaged them. In a factory with just 10 specialist makers, Smith claimed that an astonishing total of 48,000 pins could be made in a day; but had the workers sought self-sufficiency in all items, and so turned only occasionally to pin-making, then each might have taken a whole day to make just one pin when one was required. Of course, each worker in the pin factory could be seen as seeking to exchange his highly specialized labour for part of the fruits of the team's production.

Thirdly, even if all the individuals in a particular community had similar skills, they could well do better to eschew self-sufficiency, for at times group activity could prove much more productive. For instance, hunting may be more successful if pursued by teams of sufficient size to surround the prey, and building may be easier if large groups can move heavy stones. In this sort of situation, where there are what are termed economies of scale, each participant could again be seen as seeking to exchange his labour for part of the team's production.

# Barter

The most primitive way of organizing exchange is by barter or direct swapping. It is possible that the earliest form of barter was done in silence whereby one party to a deal would come to an open space, lay out the goods they wished to part with and then retreat (Morgan, 1965, 10). The other party would then approach and lay out what they were prepared to offer in exchange, and then also retreat. The first party would now return to inspect the second party's offer. If they were satisfied, then they would pick up the offer and go back home; if not, then they removed some items from their own offer and retreated to see what response the reduced offer received. The tendency for silence was probably encouraged by language problems and also by the fear resulting from an absence of a legal framework for life in general and exchange in particular.

The most frequently cited difficulty with barter is the requirement for what is known as a double coincidence of wants. If a citizen from what is now Afghanistan wanted to exchange some newly-mined lapis lazuli for a horse, then he would have to find someone seeking lapis lazuli who wished to dispose of a horse. Some time could be spent searching for such a person. Life would be much easier if there was some commodity which all people were willing to accept in return for what they had to sell. One such commodity might be cloth. In this case, the citizen with the lapis lazuli might find one person who would buy it from him for cloth, and then find another person who would take some cloth in return for a horse. The cloth here would be acting as money, or as a medium of exchange, and would remove the need to find a single individual anxious both to buy lapis lazuli and sell a horse.

The widespread acceptance of cloth, or some other form of money, as a medium of exchange would be particularly useful in facilitating trade in items which cannot be divided up. For instance, a man might wish to sell a cow and buy some goats. Even if he found another man wishing to buy a cow and sell some goats, there would be a problem if the general feeling was that one cow was worth two and a half goats, for in this case it could prove impossible to negotiate a precise double coincidence of acceptable swaps. One solution would be to swap two cows for five goats, but the first man might not have two cows he wished to part with and the second might not have five goats he wished to part with. Now if the first man was given some cloth for his cow, then he could either return some of it in exchange for two goats, or return all plus a little more for three, and the problem would be readily removed.

# The functions of money

It is clear that money greatly helps exchange to take place by acting as a medium of exchange and so avoiding the need for double coincidences of wants. Indeed, being a medium of exchange is generally considered to be money's primary function, and later chapters will focus on the question of deciding what items should be regarded as money by considering which items are generally acceptable as mediums of exchange. However, money has two other attributes which also help to make exchange easier in a money economy than it is in a barter economy. In particular, money can act as a unit of account and as a store of value, and these two functions will be taken in turn.

One problem with barter is that bargaining could be time consuming. Consider an economy with just four commodities, horses, lapis lazuli, cows and cloth. A man might have to discuss the price of horses in terms of lapis lazuli today, the price of horses in terms of cows or cloth tomorrow, the price of cows in terms of cloth or lapis lazuli the next day, and then the price of lapis lazuli in terms of cloth the day after that. It can be seen that with just four commodities in an economy, there would be six different price ratios which could be discussed. With N commodities, there would be $N(N-1)/2$ price ratios. This is because each of the N commodities needs a value in relation to all the remaining $(N-1)$ items; it might seem that there therefore need to be $N(N-1)$ ratios, but the number of ratios is actually half of $N(N-1)$ since, once cows have been related to, say, cloth, then cloth has automatically been related to cows. This formula can be used to show that in an economy with, say, just 100 commodities, there would be as many as 4,950 ratios. Suppose, though, that cloth became generally accepted as a medium of exchange. In this case, there would be only three price ratios in a four-commodity world, such as cows, horses and lapis lazuli in terms of cloth. With N commodities, there would be just $(N-1)$ ratios, which would mean a mere 99 ratios with 100 commodities. By using cloth here as a *numeraire*, or standard of measurement, fewer ratios would need to be discussed. In turn, conventions about values would be more easily established, thereby facilitating speedy exchanges.

An interesting example of a *numeraire* was cited by Crowther in 1940 (p. 14) who claimed that goats acted as one at that time in parts of East Africa, so that 50 bananas were worth one goat, five bushels of corn were worth two goats, a young and comely wife was worth six goats, while a hunting-knife was apparently worth 10 goats. In more developed economies, the standard of measurement function of money is generally termed the unit of account function. This is because it also enables the values of such diverse matters as sales of goods, labour employed and raw materials used to be made in terms of one item and, as a result, it enables all these items to be shown on one account; of course, accounts can be drawn up for individuals, governments and other organizations as well as for firms. A related use of money as a measure, or unit of account, is that it also serves as a standard for deferred payments whereby it can be used to quantify the amounts which must be paid at a future date when loans must be repaid.

It was noted earlier that one advantage of a monetized economy is that an individual can sell a commodity to one person for money, and then use the money to purchase a different commodity from someone else. The sale and the purchase might occur in quick succession, but they might instead occur some time apart. When there is a significant time gap, then the money can be said to be acting as a store of value. Money is by no means the only way of storing value, for it is possible to store value in a stock of goods (such as axes) or by purchasing securities (as discussed in the next chapter) but this property is a useful one which adds to money's ability to facilitate exchange and so specialization. For example, people will be encouraged to devote their efforts to producing crops, such as strawberries, or large items, such as houses, if they can receive occasional large sums of money which can then be spent slowly as and when desired on unstorable items like fresh food and services. In a barter economy, anyone producing such items would have to accept occasional large receipts of various commodities; these commodities would then have to be stored and then swapped in small amounts at future dates in return for purchases of fresh food and services. This would be a cumbersome process.

Despite the advantages of money, barter did not disappear in prehistoric times as some texts imply. In Norman times in England, for instance, most households would have used little money. The majority of households were largely self-sufficient, and presented some of their output to the lord of the manor in return for the use of some of his land and for accommodation. Money would have been used by them on rare occasions, though it would have been more important in the lives of the few rich people. Even today, barter is still to be found. Examples of small-scale swaps can be found in households; for most people devote much of their productive activity to providing services about the home, and implicitly make contracts with others in the home whereby one member may at times do the cooking and shopping for all if another does the washing-up and gardening for all. The contracts are complex, and much domestic friction is attributable to some household members feeling that others offer too little in return for what they are given! Small-scale bartering can also occur between households, for instance between children, while more substantial swapping occurs when people trade-in an old car in part payment for a new (or newer) one.

Examples of large-scale swaps occur at the level of international trade, particularly in deals between Western countries and non-Western countries (see Tschoegl, 1985). For instance, after the OPEC oil price rise in 1973, many European countries arranged swaps of items such as nuclear power stations and military goods in return for oil, chiefly in an effort to assure themselves of oil supplies but perhaps partly to strengthen their negotiating position in the future. Also, Western countries sometimes give the capital equipment and technology needed to build a factory to an East European country in return for some of the factory's output once it is in operation; and Western countries sometimes sell goods to East European countries on terms which oblige the exporting countries to use some of their receipts in making purchases from the Eastern countries concerned. Deals such as these appeal to East European countries when they are short of the Western currencies generally needed to pay for goods from the West. The deals also help to get round the problems which arise if Eastern currencies are over-valued by their governments in relation to

Western ones, for over-valuation means Eastern countries may find it easier to swap their goods in the West in individually negotiated deals than to sell them at the high prices determined by official exchange rates.

# The early development of money

It is appropriate to see money as something which has developed, albeit at different rates in different countries, rather than something which emerged overnight. This development can be seen by considering some of the items which have served as money. One item, which was probably in use in various places from Homeric times to the present century, was cattle. The obvious disadvantage of cattle is that they would be suitable only for large transactions, and they were probably confined chiefly to dealings in land, slaves or wives. The citizens of the Pacific island of Uap used stones up to 12 feet across for many centuries. These had a high value, and they were used only rarely, for instance in the settlement of inter-village conflicts. One feature of them which may have appealed to some citizens was the fact that they could be ostentatiously displayed with little risk of theft! But a more significant problem with these would be the difficulty of transport. However, continued use of these stones was perhaps made possible only by the smallness of the island.

It is clear that it is an advantage if money is reasonably portable, which is much the same as saying that it should have a high value to size ratio so that it is easy to carry enough to purchase valuable items. It is also helpful if money is divisible, that is available in small pieces, so that it can be used for modest transactions as well as big ones. A further desirable characteristic of money, if it is to be an effective store of value, is that it should be reasonably durable, a point which might seem to argue against using cattle unless it is remembered that cattle can breed more cattle. A more serious disadvantage of cattle is that they vary, so that a slave who was worth four young fat cows might be held to be worth eight older skinny ones. This point implies that some time-consuming discussion would be needed with each transaction using cattle. It is clearly desirable to use for money items which do not vary significantly. However, a more important quality for money than any of these is that it should command confidence, and hence widespread acceptance. In large measure this means that money needs to have a fairly stable value, for people will not want to store units of money whose value might fall, and hence they will not want to accept payment in such money. In practice, stability in value tends to arise where any growth in the stock of money is subject to some reasonable control or limit.

In view of these desirable properties, it is not surprising to find that some of the items with the longest and widest use as money include cowrie shells, which were probably used for thousands of years in the Far East and which were valued also for their ornamental and magical qualities, and precious metals, which have been widely used in Europe and other parts of the world, perhaps for a shorter time-period. The fact that cowrie shells, silver and gold have always been prized for their own properties, and so have some intrinsic value of their own, doubtless helped them to become established as important types of money, for it tended to raise their value to size ratio and it tended to reduce the risk of holding them as a store of value, since people knew that if these items ever ceased to be generally accepted as mediums of exchange then they would still have some value.

It should be stressed that when shells and metals became accepted forms of money, then they acquired a value in exchange that far exceeded their intrinsic value. The point is that their value became determined chiefly by the modest amount of them there was in relation to the number of people wishing to use them as money and the extent to which they wished so to use them. In today's world, some pieces of paper which are used as money have a high value, but this is entirely because they are in limited supply and not at all because they have a high intrinsic value (which they don't). Stored shells or precious metals would actually have lost much of their value if they had ceased to be used as money, for then the demand for them would have fallen greatly. An example of this point in recent times is given by Crowther (1940, 23) who observed that the tendency for countries to cease using silver in their coins in the period 1870–1940 resulted in the 1940 value of silver in relation to gold being one-sixth of what it had been in the earlier year.

In comparison with the cowrie shell, metals had two major disadvantages as money. First, they had to be exchanged by weight, so that weighing (often, perhaps, with dubious scales) and cutting were frequently needed, whereas shells changed hands by tale, that is simply by counting the required number. Secondly, the purity of metals could vary, so that anyone accepting an allegedly pure metal had always to be on the lookout for impure alloys using cheaper metals. One advantage of using iron as money, as opposed to other metals, is that a given weight of something alleged to be this metal could not profitably be faked by using impure alloys because iron itself is the most abundant and cheapest metal. Julius Caesar mentioned that iron was being used as money in Britain when he visited it, though some later authorities have doubted whether it was (Morgan, 1965, 17). However, the abundance of iron would also have given rise to a major difficulty of using it as money, for it would have caused a low value to weight ratio and hence have led to huge chunks changing hands in all non-trivial transactions. It was the relative scarcity of other metals, notably gold, silver and copper, but also bronze and lead, which made them more satisfactory as money; and it was to reduce the problems of weighing and impurities that these scarcer metals began to be issued in coins of standard weights and composition and hence of standard value.

## Coins

It is not certain when the first coins were made, chiefly because it is hard to be sure of the date and use of archaeological finds of objects which might have been coins. However, it seems certain that there were coins before 1000 BC in China and by 800 BC in Asia Minor. The earliest coins may have been made by merchants, for they would have benefited most by their introduction, and early mints were probably private enterprise establishments where people could bring bullion and have it processed into more convenient coins. A charge, or seignorage, would be made by the mint, and such charges would create the earnings of the mint. Of course, it was always desirable that private mints should be bound by law to issue sound coins, and it was perhaps to avoid the need to police these laws, as well as a desire to acquire the seignorage, that governments tended to seek monopoly powers over minting. They did not always succeed, and as late as the seventeenth century there were, for example, dozens of mints in Germany and Poland.

Morgan (1965, 13–15) has noted that the first European coins were made from a gold-silver alloy called electrum. Silver coins appeared at some stage in the eighth century BC, gold ones in the sixth and bronze ones in the fifth. Copper coins were not much later. In England, William the Conqueror found a situation in which the main coin was the silver penny whose silver content was such that 240 contained one pound weight of silver. He established his main mint at the Tower of London and adopted a standard fineness for the silver of 925 pounds of pure silver in 1000 pounds of metal, a standard known as 'sterling silver'. Gold coins were first minted in England by Edward III, but they were never common, principally because even the smallest gold coin would have been too valuable for most transactions. Copper coins were first introduced into England by James I.

Although the use of coins made precious metals much more convenient to use as money, there were still some problems. One obvious one was the possibility of forgers producing coins with less precious metal content than they were meant to have. Naturally, forgery tended to be subject to stiff penalties. But coins also had two less obvious problems.

First there was clipping and sweating. The object of coins was to indicate that they contained specified amounts of metal and could then be exchanged by tale instead of weight. Ready acceptance by tale encouraged citizens to remove some of the metal either by clipping the coins round the edges, or by putting a whole lot of coins in a bag and shaking it for some time so that friction between the coins caused some metal dust to collect at the bottom of the bag. Any metal acquired from clipped edges or metal dust could be sold, perhaps on bullion markets. For centuries the chief deterrence to such activities was the fear that adulterated coins might not be accepted at their face value, but would be weighed once again. In 1529, Francis I of France had to pay 12 million escudos to the Spanish in ransom for his two sons, who had been exchanged for him as hostages after his capture in battle; it took four months to check the coins he produced, and 40,000 were rejected by the Spanish as being below standard (Vilar, 1976, 173). Morgan (1965, 18) claims that an effective remedy to clipping was to produce coins with a milled edge, an idea devised by a Frenchman, Pierre Blunden, who came to England in 1649, but put into practice only from 1663. The remedy seems to have taken some time to work for Smith (1776; 1964 edn, Vol 1, 177) claims that clipping and sweating continually increased until 1695.

A second problem with coins was the possibility of official debasement. To understand this, it is necessary to recall that the earliest coins were intended to contain a specified amount of metal of a specified purity. The face value of the coin would thus reflect the bullion price of that metal on the bullion markets (apart from any seignorage which, in modest amounts anyway, could be seen a payment for having bullion converted into well-recognized usable coins). However, it would always be tempting for governments and other mint-owners to issue substandard or debased coins made of an impure alloy, and then use the precious metal saved to make some new coins for their own use. Governments, in particular, would be tempted to issue debased coins in order to settle their own accounts. Once debased coins appeared, sound ones were liable to disappear. Their owners might seek to have their store of them converted into more numerous debased ones at the hands of a forger; or they might hoard them, in expectation that there would soon be more coins around in total, now that the precious metal content had fallen, in which case there was likely to be a rise in prices in general, and hence a rise in the price of precious metal too, so that their old pure coins would soon be sellable on the bullion market for more than the face value which they had as money. In short, there would be a case of Gresham's Law whereby bad money drives out the good, though Sir Thomas Gresham's observation of this effect in 1558 was certainly not the first time it had been noted.

The trouble with debasement is that while it helps a government to increase its purchasing power over goods and services currently produced, it reduces the purchasing power of other citizens who are typically confronted with rising prices. The most commonly cited rulers who did profit from debasement are Nero and Henry VIII. Perhaps the main deterrent to other rulers was the fear of the unpopularity that they would incur if they drove up prices by replacing relatively pure coins by a greater number of debased ones in order to acquire some for their own expenditure. Indeed, Elizabeth I sought to improve the silver content of the coinage, and in 1776, Adam Smith (1964 edn, Vol. 1, 24) noted that the English pound still had about one third of its original silver content. This reflected far less debasement than had occurred in Scotland and France, where the relevant fractions were one thirty-sixth and one sixty-sixth; and much of the loss in England was attributable to the occasions when sovereigns had called in all the old clipped and sweated coins and replaced them with brand new ones of the original size but with no more silver than they had when collected in. However, the coins most noted for retaining their intrinsic value were the gold bezants of the Byzantine (or Eastern Roman) Empire which were a symbol of stability from the time when it split from the Western Roman Empire until it was attacked by the crusaders in 1204.

To set against these problems, it is tempting to suppose that a great advantage of using coins would be the possibility of having coins of different metals circulating simultaneously. This would be useful because it would mean that there could be a variety of coins of roughly similar size yet different values, hence facilitating transactions of widely differing amounts. However, there was a problem in trying to have coins made from more than one metal. To see this problem, consider first the situation with one metal. Suppose the mint offers one silver shilling coin, containing almost half an ounce of silver, for each half ounce of silver brought to it. In this case, the growth in the number of coins would depend chiefly on the growth in the amount of silver available to the country's citizens, and if this were slower (or faster) than the growth in the demand for money then prices would tend to rise (or fall) in relation to silver. However, the mint would never be reluctant to exchange one silver shilling for half an ounce of silver.

Next, suppose the mint wanted an additional more valuable coin made of gold and found that, on gold bullion markets, an ounce of gold was fetching 40 shillings. It could readily introduce a new gold sovereign coin, worth 20 shillings, containing almost half an ounce of gold. However, problems would arise if the bullion price of gold in terms of silver altered. Suppose it fell to 30 shillings an ounce following a glut of gold from newly-opened mines. The result would be a tendency for people to cease using their silver coins as money. For with every 30 one-shilling coins they had, people could buy an ounce of gold on the bullion market and then demand two gold sovereigns at the mint with the same purchasing power as 40 shillings. In short, there would be another example of Gresham's Law where, in this case, the now relatively more valuable or 'good' silver would be driven out by the now relatively cheap or 'bad' gold.

It follows that, in practice, precious metal coins will be predominantly of the metal where the mint offers the higher price relative to the bullion market. In England, silver held sway as a currency against gold until the eighteenth century since the mint tended to over-value silver in relation to gold. Towards the end of the seventeenth century silver became scarce (relative to the demand for money) and golden guineas were minted to help maintain an adequate money stock. Soon silver became even scarcer and so relatively under-valued by the mint. In an attempt to improve the balance, the mint reduced the price it would offer for gold so that the value of the gold guinea was reduced from 30 shillings at one stage to just over 20 at another. In 1719 its value was fixed at 21 shillings on the advice of Sir Isaac Newton, who was Master of the Mint as well as a mathematician and scientist. With this value for the guinea, the mint would actually offer £3 17s 10½d (about £3.89) for an ounce of gold. This value was maintained even when guinea coins were replaced by sovereign coins worth 20 shillings, and indeed it persisted until 1931. However, this gold value implied a low mint price for silver, so the usage of coins containing silver gradually declined. Later, so-called silver coins were introduced for small denominations (as were copper ones), but they have a negligible metallic value. No doubt their widespread acceptance was encouraged by the fact that paper money of even less intrinsic value was already in circulation, and this must now be examined in the context of the development of banks.

# Early banking activities

From earliest times, banks have performed a wide variety of functions, and their development has differed from one country to another. There were certainly institutions in ancient Greece and Rome which undertook dealings in foreign exchange and accepted deposits for safe-keeping. Some of these institutions were located in temples, though one set of money-changers in the Temple in Jerusalem was driven out by a famous visitor who felt such secular activities should be conducted elsewhere! These early bankers probably made most of their income out of foreign-exchange dealings, for there was a wide array of different coins around, and there was fair scope for profits for the knowledgeable. Their association with temples may have had something to do with the fact that these buildings often had secure stone-walled strong rooms where the bankers could keep the stocks of coins belonging to them. In addition, they kept some deposits of coins entrusted to them by their owners for safe-keeping. It seems these banks also indulged in money-lending, though usually they lent their own money, rather than money entrusted to them on deposit. It is possible, too, that such early banks agreed to transfer deposits between depositors so that they could effect payments without having to withdraw their coins. Certainly later Roman banks undertook such transfers.

Banking in Western Europe declined along with the Western Roman Empire, and then re-emerged in the Italian cities, perhaps a little before AD 1200. These Italian banks performed broadly the same functions as the late Roman ones, though lending was at best a sideline since the Roman Catholic Church proscribed usury. It is worth stressing that the objection to usury, that is lending in return for interest, arose in early times when, perhaps as a result of a bad harvest, food prices soared and the poor had to borrow to pay for food, for it was felt unethical to help them with anything less than an interest-free loan. As time passed, and more and more loans were sought by merchants to expand their businesses, so the blanket proscription seemed less appropriate. Even so, lending for interest was not given much legal sanction in England until after Henry VIII broke from the Roman Church, and indeed the laws against it were not finally repealed until 1571.

Of course, laws against usury did not prevent it altogether. One interesting way of avoiding the laws has been outlined by Kindleberger (1984, 39). This could be used by anyone or any institution concerned with international transactions and it involved bills of exchange. More is said about bills in the next chapter, but in essence a bill of exchange is created when a trader, on making a purchase, does not give money to the seller but instead gives him a piece of paper, known as a bill, on which is written a promise to give the holder of the bill a specified sum of money on a specified future date known as the bill's maturity date. Of course, the seller would generally want the promised sum to be a little more than the value of the items sold so that he would get a return (or, in effect, interest) as a result of allowing the purchaser to defer his payment. In medieval times, however, bills were of little use in internal trade since a seller could not charge interest and so would get no benefit from waiting for his money. However, bills could be used in trade between areas using different currencies.

Suppose, for example, that a London merchant made some purchases in Florence and gave the Florentine merchant a bill made out in sterling instead of giving him coins. The Florentine merchant might then use the same bill to make a purchase in nearby Lucca, and the merchant there might later use it to buy something from a dealer in Oxford. The Oxford dealer could secure his money in due course by demanding that the London merchant honour his obligation to pay money to the holder of the bill on the maturity date set out on the bill. Now three people, in Florence, Lucca and Oxford, presumably held on to the bill for a while, and so between them they effectively lent money to the London merchant who was able to acquire the items that he purchased some time before he had to part with any money. The three people who lent would not have charged interest explicitly, but they could have done so in effect by choosing suitable exchange rates in deciding how much money the bill was worth in each deal. Because exchange rates were uncertain and volatile, it would be very difficult to show that usury had occurred. It should be emphasized that although traders might have been able to use certain bills with certain merchants, no individual bill would have been generally acceptable as a medium of exchange and so bills would not really be classified as money.

However, despite such dodges, and despite the relaxing of laws on usury in much of Protestant Europe at least, lending remained something of a sideline of banks for some time. One of the most celebrated banks, that in Amsterdam, was set up by the government there to ease the problems caused to trade by attempts to exchange coins of various qualities from different mints. Traders could open deposits at the bank by placing their coins there, the size of their deposit being affected by the pedigree of the coins concerned. Thereafter, though, they could deal with other traders by asking the bank to transfer deposits of 'bank money' with no further trouble. A number of other public banks were set up with similar objectives. Generally these banks were expected to refrain from lending, but generally they succumbed to the temptation. The Bank of Amsterdam got into difficulties after making loans to the Dutch East India Company in the 1780s, and it subsequently found itself unable to meet all the demands for coins from those of its depositors who wished to take some out. It was eventually wound up early in the following century.

Meanwhile, important developments in banking had taken place in seventeenth-century England. There is a tendency to suppose that the main event was the evolution of many goldsmiths into banks, but while many banks evolved it is not entirely clear how many of them began as goldsmiths. However, goldsmiths were certainly well suited to perform one role of banks, namely the safe-keeping of coins (as well as other valuables) because they had secure strong rooms. Morgan (1965, 23) notes that the first recorded deposit of money at a goldsmith's was in 1633. The practice doubtless became more common after 1640, for in that year Charles I confiscated the gold and plate which people had deposited for safe-keeping at the Royal Mint in the Tower of London. Although this booty was eventually returned, the event would clearly have encouraged depositors to look elsewhere.

However, the circumstances that really caused an explosive growth in the banking activities of the goldsmiths, and indeed in banking altogether, was the development of a situation in which anyone holding deposits of coins with them could then very readily use the money in their deposits to make purchases without actually having to withdraw their coins. To understand this development and its importance, it is useful to use some illustrative balance sheets. Accordingly, it is also useful to have some understanding of what a balance sheet shows.

# Balance sheets

The illustrative balance sheets used for banks in this chapter – and most of those that follow – omit, for simplicity, some of the items that would appear in the balance sheet of a real-world bank. In order to appreciate fully what a balance sheet shows, it is necessary to consider one which has no omissions. This section considers the balance sheet for a non-bank company, but the same principles apply to the balance sheets of all business concerns, including banks (and, indeed, to all other concerns such as households or clubs). Broadly speaking, any balance sheet seeks to show for a particular moment in time the value of all the concern's assets, and also to show how the money was raised to pay for those assets. The most common items appearing in company balance sheets are shown in Table 1.1 which relates to a hypothetical company.

**Table 1.1**   Balance sheet for a hypothetical company on 31 December 1986

£

| Liabilities | | | Assets | | |
|---|---|---|---|---|---|
| Creditors | | | Fixed assets | | |
| Debentures | 50,000 | | Land & buildings | 280,000 | |
| Loan from bank | 20,000 | | Plant, machinery & | | |
| Loans from trade | | | vehicles | 220,000 | |
| creditors | 30,000 | 100,000 | Fixtures & fittings | 30,000 | |
| | | | Investments | 20,000 | 550,000 |
| Capital & reserves | | | Current assets | | |
| Share capital: | | | Stocks & work in | | |
| Ordinary shares | 150,000 | | progress | 25,000 | |
| Preference shares | 100,000 | | Loans to trade | | |
| Profit & loss a/c | 200,000 | | debtors | 20,000 | |
| Revaluation reserve | 50,000 | | Cash in hand | 100 | |
| | | 500,000 | Bank deposit | 4,900 | 50,000 |
| Total | | 600,000 | Total | | 600,000 |

The right-hand side shows the value of the company's assets under two main headings, 'fixed assets' and 'current assets'. In general, fixed assets are items which the firm is likely to want to retain for at least one year and will use to earn money. Mostly they comprise land and buildings, plant, machinery and vehicles, and fixtures and fittings, but the company may also have some investments in the form of securities which are discussed in the next chapter. (It should perhaps be emphasized that Table 1.1's inclusion of investments in securities under the heading 'fixed assets' accords with the definition of fixed assets laid down for balance sheet purposes by the UK Companies Act of 1981; but such investments would *not* be included as fixed assets in the definition of fixed assets generally used by economists.) Current assets include stocks of raw materials and finished goods and, for some firms, work in progress (which comprises partly-finished products such as houses under construction) as well as outstanding loans to trade debtors, who may have been supplied products on credit or account, along with petty cash, or cash in hand, and money in the firm's bank deposit.

The left-hand side indicates the main ways in which money can be raised to pay for these assets. In effect, it can be found by borrowing, or from the firm's owners, or out of the firm's profits. The items headed 'creditors' reflect outstanding borrowing, and these items really are liabilities in that they must eventually be repaid. Debentures are a form of security (discussed in the next chapter) but the firm may also borrow from the bank or from trade creditors, who may have supplied raw materials on credit or account. Broadly speaking, share capital is the money raised from the firm's owners when they bought shares (again discussed in the next chapter) whilst the profit and loss account item reflects the total profits the firm has both made and retained in its life-time in order to acquire assets; thus this item reflects total profits retained in the firm's lifetime retained to finance expansion, that is total profits after deducting payments such as taxes on profits to the government, interest to those from whom it has borrowed and dividends to its shareholders.

Now, if all the firm's assets still had the same values that they had when they were originally bought, then it would be possible to record those historic values on the right-hand side, and it would be possible to record outstanding loans from creditors on the left-hand side along with the money raised from shareholders and total retained profits; and the totals on each side would balance since the left-hand side would show how much money had been available while the right-hand side would show where it had gone. However, some assets will not have their original values.

On the one hand, the monetary value of the firm's land and investments may well have risen since they were purchased. In the case of land a rise could be a result of inflation, and in the case of investments a rise could occur if the other firms in which this one has bought some shares had done as well. Now the assets side of a balance sheet seeks broadly to show the present value of the concern's assets – rather than the original historic value – so any gains such as these are included on the right-hand side by recording estimates of these items' current values. To make the left-hand side balance the right-hand side it is necessary for the left-hand side, too, to include the gains to the firm by buying items whose value has risen. This inclusion is done by introducing on the liabilities side an extra item called the revaluation reserve and showing against this item the value of all the relevant gains.

On the other hand, the value of some investments may have fallen, and some loans on the assets side may in practice cease to have any value if they have become 'bad debts' – that is if the people to whom they were made are clearly unable or unlikely ever to repay them. Any adjustments to the assets side for these reasons can be offset by suitable downwards revisions to the revaluation reserve on the liabilities side. Also, the value of the firm's plant, machinery, vehicles, fixtures and fittings will generally have fallen (perhaps to zero in the case of many items purchased years ago) as a result of wear and tear and obsolescence. These losses are allowed for in the right-hand side by estimating for each item the total fall in value, known as depreciation, and deducting it from the item's original cost to give an estimate of its current value, and then entering amounts which show the total present value of these assets rather than their total historic values; of course, any item which has lost all its value as a result of depreciation will then be ignored altogether on the assets side. The left-hand side is made to balance by allowing for the whole of this depreciation in the profit and loss account entry, so this entry actually shows total retained lifetime profits after deducting depreciation as well as after making the other deductions noted earlier. Lifetime is more interesting in the case of buildings, for their value may have been both enhanced by inflation and reduced by depreciation. The right-hand side shows their present value, while on the left their enhancement is included in the revaluation reserve and their depreciation is allowed for in the profit and loss account entry.

Now although the terms in a balance sheet are carefully defined so that the total assets and liabilities must be precisely equal, there is no reason why there should be a balance between the value of any one or more groups of assets and the value of any one or more groups of liabilities. However, this chapter, and several which follow, will give some illustrative balance sheets for banks and other financial institutions which cover only those assets and liabilities which are most relevant to their financial activities, and these balance sheets will assume that the totals of these selected assets and liabilities do exactly balance. This is done for simplicity, and it is not a very serious simplification; for in practice, the value of the excluded items (such as share capital or land and buildings) is typically very small in relation to the items shown as far as these financial institutions are concerned.

# Early banks

Consider a bank in early days when lending for interest was not prohibited. Such a situation would apply, for example, to Roman banks and also to English banks in the seventeenth century. Suppose that coins alone are generally acceptable as a medium of exchange, so that the stock of money possessed by a country's citizens can be defined as the total value of the issued coins in that country, that is to say, the total value of all coins except for new ones in mints awaiting issue. Suppose, next, that a large number of citizens decide to deposit some of their coins at banks or goldsmiths for safe-keeping. The balance sheet for one such concern's banking operations at noon on a particular day might be as shown in Table 1.2. Its liabilities equal the £1,000 worth of deposits made there, which can be regarded as similar to money lent to it, at least inasmuch as these deposits must be repaid when depositors so require. Its assets are given by the £1,000 deposited coins, rather like the cash in hand which was regarded as an asset for the firm in Table 1.1.

Now each bank could find many coins being deposited every day and many being withdrawn every day as its various depositors receive and spend money on their transactions. Accordingly, the bank in Table 1.2 could find its assets and liabilities varying by the day, or even by the hour, though at any moment in time its assets and

**Table 1.2**   Balance sheet (1) for early bank

|  |  |  | £ |
|---|---|---|---|
| Liabilities |  | Assets |  |
| Deposits | 1,000 | Coins | 1,000 |
| Total | 1,000 | Total | 1,000 |

its liabilities would always be equal to each other. However, it might well find it always had a fair number of coins to hand. On this basis, it might be tempted to make loans from time to time.

Suppose, for example, that shortly after noon on the day concerned in Table 1.2, a merchant asks the bank for a loan of £50. He might wish to borrow this for one year, and offer to pay it back with £2 interest in a year's time. The bank might agree to make the loan, in which case it would lend him £50 worth of coins and end up with the balance sheet shown in Table 1.3. Notice that liabilities have not altered, for the bank would still have to give £1,000 to its depositors if they all demanded their coins. On the other hand, the bank could now lay its hands on only £950 worth of coins, but its assets now include also a loan of £50 which should eventually be repaid (just as the assets of the firm in Table 1.1 included loans made by it·to trade debtors). If all went well, then the merchant would repay his £50 in one year. This repayment would not change the bank's total assets or liabilities, any more than his borrowing £50 did, but it would alter the composition of its liabilities at the moment of repayment, for it would raise the coins figure by £50 and cut the loans figure by £50. The merchant might even keep to his word and produce £2 interest. This may be supposed to be used by the banker to help meet the costs incurred in employing staff and using buildings, and it will be ignored as far as his balance sheet is concerned.

**Table 1.3**   Balance sheet (2) for early bank

|  |  |  | £ |
|---|---|---|---|
| Liabilities |  | Assets |  |
| Deposits | 1,000 | Coins | 950 |
|  |  | Loan | 50 |
| Total | 1,000 | Total | 1,000 |

Now the making of the loan had the important consequence of putting the banker at risk. From the moment he made one loan, he put himself in a position where he would not have been able to pay all his depositors in full if they had all simultaneously demanded coins. Shortly after the Table 1.3 position arose, for instance, he might have found all his depositors arriving and demanding £1,000 worth of coins between them whereas he had only £950 to give. Had this occurred, the banker would have been declared bankrupt, and he would have had to go out of business. For this reason, these bankers would always seek to maintain a prudent ratio of coins to loans, though the interest attainable on loans would always tempt them to imprudence.

It should be stressed that no matter how many loans were made, the money stock would stay put at the value of the country's issued coins, for only coins could be used as a medium of exchange. However, an interesting point, which will be referred to in later chapters, is that the amount of spending power which the country's citizens might reckon they had at their disposal would rise as a consequence of the loans. In the case illustrated by Table 1.3, for instance, the merchant taking out the £50 would clearly and rightly reckon his spending power had risen by £50; equally clearly, the owners of the £1,000 deposits, who probably knew nothing about the loan, would assume they could still lay their hands on £1,000 if they wished, though in fact this would not now be the case. In short, the money stock did not rise, but the amount of money people between them thought they had did rise.

Prudent early bankers would always maintain a high cash-to-loan ratio and this explains why they undertook little lending. There were two reasons why they wanted a high ratio. First, if the bank's depositors heard it had done much lending, then they might be afraid that it could no longer pay them all in full, and hence they might all try to beat each other to its premises to withdraw their own deposits, so causing a run on the bank. Secondly, at a time when coins alone were acceptable as a medium of exchange, bankers might well find themselves called on at times to meet a substantial demand for coin withdrawals. On market days, for instance, they might find large proportions of their coin stocks being withdrawn early in the morning as people pre-pared for a spending spree, albeit to be replenished in the evening when those who had been busy selling deposited their day's takings.

## Seventeenth-century developments in England

Depositors at English banks or goldsmiths in the early 1660s, like depositors at all earlier banks, would always want some acknowledgement of their deposit, and this was generally given in the form of a piece of paper, termed here a named IOU, on which the banker wrote the depositor's name and the sum deposited. An interesting development took place by 1670 in that some IOUs, issued in a limited number of fairly standard values or denominations, had the words 'or bearer' added after the depositor's name, and shortly afterwards many IOUs omitted his name altogether. Such IOUs can be termed unnamed IOUs or bank-notes. Banks would print their own bank-notes, and these, of course, had the bank's own name on the top. The criti-cal point about the bank-notes is that, being unnamed, they soon became as good as coins for making purchases. After all, a man who sold an item for £100 would often be just as happy to accept an unnamed IOU entitling him to withdraw £100 in coins from a given bank as he would be to accept coins themselves, especially if he found he could easily pass the note on in payment to someone else in due course. In short, these bank-notes in time became generally acceptable as a medium of exchange and so themselves became money. Unlike the coins of the day, they had no intrinsic value at all, but they were accepted because they entitled their holders to withdraw coins if they so wished.

These bank-notes gave rise to some interesting consequences, for they meant banks really could increase the stock of money, or as economists would put it, create money by their lending activities. To see this, suppose for a moment that all the banks have issued bank-notes to depositors but that no bank has lent. At noon one day, a bank might have the situation shown in Table 1.4. This shows it has received deposits totalling £1,000 and has accordingly issued £1,000 worth of IOUs. Some of these may

**Table 1.4** Balance sheet (1) for note-issuing bank

£

| Liabilities | | Assets | |
|---|---|---|---|
| IOUs | 1,000 | Coins | 1,000 |
| Total | 1,000 | Total | 1,000 |

be named IOUs, but for simplicity it will be supposed that all the IOUs issued are unnamed bank-notes, circulating as money. Despite this, the money stock at this point still equals the total value of the country's coins (other than those not yet issued by the mint), though here it also equals the value of the issued unnamed IOUs plus the value of issued coins not deposited in banks. This can be seen by considering an individual citizen and asking how much money he has. He could say he had a sum equal to the coins in his home plus the number he could obtain by taking his bank-notes to the appropriate banks and demanding coins in return; so could all citizens, and adding up their answers would give a money stock equal to the total value of issued coins. Alternatively, he could say he had a sum equal to the coins in his home plus the value of his bank-notes; so could all citizens, and adding up their answers would give a money stock equal to the value of all issued coins outside the bank plus the value of all issued bank-notes. Note that the two estimates are the same, in the special circumstances under consideration, because it is assumed that the value of issued bank-notes precisely equals the value of coins in banks. Note, too, that it would be tempting but absurd for a citizen to believe that the value of his money equalled the value of coins in his home, plus the value of his bank-notes plus the value of the coins he could exchange them for; this would be tempting as it would be a larger sum than before, but it would be absurd because he can either have the bank-notes or exchange them for coins, but he can't have both!

Now Table 1.4 bears a striking resemblance to Table 1.1, but a different situation arises if these note-issuing banks decide to lend money. Suppose lending starts soon after noon on the day concerned in Table 1.4, and the bank there is asked for a £50 loan by a merchant. The bank may agree to the loan, but insist in the first instance on lending him bank-notes which, of course, it can print. In this situation, its balance sheet would be as shown in Table 1.5. At this point, the money stock has increased by £50, for the borrower now has £50 more which he can spend while no one else has any less. However, the value of issued coins has not changed. Accordingly, the money stock cannot now be valued with reference to the value of issued coins, which has not risen; it must now be viewed as the value of IOUs in circulation plus the value of coins outside the banks, and this has risen as a result of the extra IOUs.

**Table 1.5** Balance sheet (2) for note-issuing bank

£

| Liabilities | | Assets | |
|---|---|---|---|
| IOUs | 1,050 | Coins | 1,000 |
| | | Loans | 50 |
| Total | 1,050 | Total | 1,050 |

**Table 1.6** Balance sheet (3) for note-issuing bank

£

| Liabilities | | Assets | |
|---|---|---|---|
| IOUs | 1,000 | Coins | 950 |
| | | Loans | 50 |
| Total | 1,000 | Total | 1,000 |

Notice that the borrower could at once seek to swap his IOUs for coins. In this case, the bank would end up with the balance sheet shown in Table 1.6. The number of IOUs in circulation would fall by £50 but the number of coins outside the banks would rise by £50. Accordingly, the money stock would be the same as in the Table 1.5 situation and so would still be £50 higher than the Table 1.4 situation. In short, the money stock here has still risen by the amount of bank lending. Despite an apparent similarity, the situation is very different from that in Table 1.3. There, although depositors thought they could acquire £1,000 worth of coins to spend, in fact they could acquire only £950 to spend as the banker only had that number to hand. Here, the depositors can still spend £1,000 as they can spend their IOUs. In other words, there the loan of £50 gave the borrower that sum but reduced the money available for spending by others by the same amount, but here it does not.

Naturally the early bankers charged interest on their loans, so naturally they too were tempted to lend on a large scale, but this temptation had to be tempered by a need to maintain a prudent coin-to-loan ratio. What constitutes prudence is considered further in Chapter 3, but it deserves to be said that they could operate with much lower ratios than earlier bankers, for the constraints on lending which applied earlier were now less acute. On the one hand, depositors were a little less alarmed if they heard their banker was lending, and so they were less likely to have a stampede run on the bank demanding coins, for it mattered less if the bank was unable to swap all its issued IOUs for coins since now the IOUs could themselves be used for purchases. Secondly, the fact that the IOUs could be spent meant that the demands for coins were less substantial. On market days, for instance, people could go shopping with their IOUs and need not draw out coins.

The reader may have followed all this reasoning, and yet have asked a question which is often overlooked, namely why anyone would take coins to a bank for safe-keeping in exchange for unnamed IOUs or bank-notes as these were lighter than the coins and so seemingly even easier to steal! There are really three answers to this question. First, depositors may often have asked for a mixture of named and unnamed IOUs, and the former, at least, would have been useless to a thief, unlike the coins for which they had been exchanged. Secondly, unnamed notes were originally offered only for high denominations, £20 being the smallest until 1759, and this at a time when £20 would be worth over £1,000 today. Of course, the high value in itself would tempt thieves, but it would also attract attention if they sought to use stolen notes, and this attention would deter them. Thirdly, each bank would number its notes, and its notes would generally be used only in the smallish area where the bank was known, so a potential thief knew he would have to use the note in that small area and he would fear detection from people keeping an eye open for stolen notes.

In any case, the issue of individual bank-notes by individual English banks was a practice which was neither long-lived nor very widespread. Its short time-span is indicated by the fact that the Bank of England, which was founded in 1694, became in 1742 the only English bank allowed to issue bank-notes other than small banks owned by less than six partners, and most of these small banks had ceased to issue notes by 1750 (though there were still a few notes issued by other banks up until 1921). Its modest geographical coverage is indicated by the fact there were hardly any banks outside London in the period up to 1742, when even large banks could issue notes. Thus the general issue of bank-notes is closely associated with the Bank of England itself. This bank has evolved into a particular type of bank, known as a central bank, whose functions are considered more fully in later chapters. Its bank-notes soon became as acceptable as coins as a medium of exchange, and for the rest of this book the term cash will be used to cover both coins and Bank of England notes (as well as notes issued by Scottish and Northern Irish banks).

This widespread acceptance of Bank of England notes was encouraged by the fact noted earlier that, for many years, these notes could be converted at the Bank into gold coins at a rate which was equivalent to one ounce of gold being priced at £3 17s 10½d (about £3.89). As noted earlier, this price was first established by Sir Isaac Newton in 1719, and convertibility at the same price continued until 1931 with breaks from 1797 till 1821 (on account of the wars with France which caused a 'run' on the Bank's gold) and from 1914 to 1925. Throughout the periods of convertibility Britain was said to be on the gold standard. During these periods, the Bank of England would not only sell gold for £3 17s 10½d an ounce, but was also always prepared to buy gold for £3 17s 9d an ounce. In its early days, almost all the Bank's notes were backed by gold (and some silver) in its vaults; but now, as explained in Chapter 7, this is not the case.

The other banks had no difficulty surviving without issuing IOUs. Named and unnamed IOUs merely served to show that deposits had been made, although unnamed ones had the attraction of being a safer medium of exchange than cash for large transactions. However, almost as soon as they started issuing IOUs, banks also started operating accounts very much like those operating today. Consider an account-handling bank starting up. It might initially attract total cash deposits for safe-keeping of £1,000, as shown in Table 1.7. Depositors here would not be given IOUs as such, but merely a statement showing how much they had deposited. They would also be given cheque books. They would be issued with updated statements at regular intervals, each statement showing how much had been added to or taken from their deposits since the last one. These statements shared one property with IOUs in that depositors could at any time demand cash from the bank to the value of their deposits, as shown on their statements (subject, of course, to an allowance for withdrawals and deposits made since the date of that statement).

Unlike bank-notes, though, statements were of no use as a medium of exchange. However, depositors were able to spend sums equal to the amounts they had deposited for safe-keeping merely by completing cheques. Cheques are simply

**Table 1.7**   Balance sheet (1) for account-handling bank

| | | | £ |
|---|---|---|---|
| Liabilities | | Assets | |
| Deposits | 1,000 | Cash | 1,000 |
| Total | 1,000 | Total | 1,000 |

instructions to a banker to reduce the amount of money in the deposit of the person making out the cheque, who is spending money, and to increase the amount in the deposit of the person receiving the cheque, who thereby ends up with a larger deposit at the bank. As far as depositors are concerned, a cheque system has great advantages over one comprising bank-notes; for cheques can be used for any amount, small or great, and they are safe inasmuch as they are no use to a thief unless filled in in his favour and signed!

Replacing bank-notes with a system of accounts and cheques in no way hindered banks' ability to lend or create money. To follow the explanation of this, it is necessary to say at the outset that the money stock will now be measured with reference to the value of cash (coins plus Bank of England, Scottish and Northern Irish bank-notes) held outside the banks together with the value of money held in bank deposits and so available to be spent by cheque. Cash held inside the banks is excluded, for this can be obtained for spending only by depositors withdrawing it in return for equal reductions in their deposits and hence in the amounts available for spending by cheque. The money stock cannot be defined simply as the total amount of cash issued, for, as will become clear shortly, this is likely to be way below the value of bank deposits plus cash held outside banks.

Now, suppose the bank balance sheet in Table 1.7 represents the situation for the bank concerned at noon one day shortly after it sets up in business, and suppose that a little later someone, say a stranger to the bank, asks to borrow £50. If it agrees, the bank could open an account for him and 'create' £50 for this account simply by writing that number against his name in their books and on his opening statement. At this point, the bank would have the balance sheet shown in Table 1.8. It may seem strange that banks can, indeed, create money merely by writing numbers against borrowers' names, but it is little stranger than creating it merely by printing and issuing IOUs. Once the borrower has been given some money in his deposit, he can then be given a cheque book and use it to spend his deposit. Note that the borrower now has £50 to spend, while no one else has less to spend, so the money stock really has risen by £50.

**Table 1.8**  Balance sheet (2) for account-handling bank

|  |  |  | £ |
|---|---|---|---|
| Liabilities |  | Assets |  |
| Deposits | 1,050 | Cash | 1,000 |
|  |  | Loan | 50 |
| Total | 1,050 | Total | 1,050 |

Of course, the bank will have to maintain a prudent ratio of cash to loans, for depositors are always at liberty to come and demand cash in return for a cut in the amount shown in their deposits, and as soon as the level of deposits exceeds the level of cash the bank risks bankruptcy in the event of a stampede or run for cash. Notice that as soon as banks have deposit levels exceeding their cash levels, it becomes important to add the value of the former rather than the value of the latter to the value of cash held by the public in order to estimate the stock of money which the public can spend.

Incidentally, the borrower of the £50 in Table 1.8 could at once ask to have £50 in cash and thus extinguish his account. In this case, the bank would move to the

**Table 1.9**   Balance sheet (3) for account-handling bank

£

| Liabilities | | Assets | |
|---|---|---|---|
| Deposits | 1,000 | Cash | 950 |
| | | Loans | 50 |
| Total | 1,000 | Total | 1,000 |

position shown in Table 1.9, since it would lose £50 cash and its (new) depositor's account would fall by the same amount. The cash withdrawal would not affect the new level of the money stock, though, for the only citizen involved would be replacing £50 money in one form (a bank deposit) by £50 in another form (cash held outside the bank).

Despite the similarities, there is an important difference for banks between a bank-note system and an account plus cheque system. With bank-notes, a bank's depositors can go around spending their notes with negligible implications for the bank. The spending will not initially alter its balance sheet or records at all, though it could do so eventually if the notes ended up with people who decided to come along and swap them for cash. On the other hand, with accounts and cheques, each payment with a cheque involves some work for the bank. The effects of any one cheque differ according to whether or nor it is payable to someone who has an account at the same bank.

Suppose, for instance, that the bank in Table 1.9 has fifty depositors each with an account standing at £20, and then suppose one of these depositors makes out a cheque for £10 in favour of another depositor, perhaps the one being a housewife and the other a shopkeeper. The shopkeeper will take (or send) the cheque to his bank, and they will then make a note in their records that the housewife's account has fallen to £10 and the shopkeeper's has risen to £30. These changes will also be noted on the two depositors' next statements. However, total deposits at the bank will be unchanged, and so too will be the bank's balance sheet as shown in Table 1.9.

The effects would be different if the shopkeeper had his deposit at another bank. He would take the cheque to his bank and ask for his deposit to be raised by £10. Before agreeing to this, his bank would send the cheque to the housewife's bank and demand £10 in cash from them. Then the shopkeeper's bank would add £10 to its liabilities, in the form of a higher deposit for the shopkeeper, and £10 to its assets, in the form of £10 more cash. Conversely, the housewife's bank would take £10 off the housewife's deposit, so reducing its total liabilities to £990, and it would have £10 less cash, so reducing its total assets to £990. In principle, all payments by cheque between people in different banks imply cash transfers between the banks, although Chapter 3 shows that the physical movement of cash can be avoided by the use of what is termed a bankers' bank. It may be noted that an individual bank will hope that any losses of cash in this way will be broadly offset by gains when its depositors bring along cheques made out in their favour by people who bank elsewhere.

This discussion can be concluded with some comments about prudent cash ratios and the risks of a bank going bankrupt. It will be seen that the bank in Table 1.7–1.9 ended up in Table 1.9 with a cash ratio, that is a ratio of cash to total deposits, of 95 per cent. In practice, as later chapters will show, banks generally have very small cash ratios, perhaps being little over 1 per cent. There are various ways in which banks can have such low ratios in reasonable safely, but an important factor in many countries is that the central bank acts as what is known as the lender of last resort whereby it will lend, probably at high interest rates, to banks in trouble. The reason for such behaviour is to promote confidence in the country's financial institutions. In return, the central bank may exercise some control over the activities of the other banks in the country.

# 2

# Financial claims

## Introduction

Chapter 1 showed how banks can create money. Chapters 3 and 4 build on that analysis to indicate how a modern banking system works, and further details of the system in the United Kingdom are contained in Chapters 7 and 8. It will be found that financial claims play an important part in this system, and it is appropriate to devote this chapter to a consideration of them. The discussion in this chapter relates most closely to the financial claims found in the United Kingdom though very similar claims can be found in many other countries.

## Financial claims and real wealth

Table 1.1 presented a balance sheet for a company. In principle, it is possible to produce a balance sheet for all the economic units in a country, that is to say for each household, each productive enterprise and each government department. On the basis of normal accounting practice, the assets side of Table 1.1 split the assets of the company concerned into two groups, fixed assets and current assets, fixed assets being items which the company would generally expect to keep for a year or more and current assets being those which it would generally expect to keep for less than a year. Of course, it will no doubt expect to have some stocks and some loans to debtors in a year's time, but probably the stocks would be different items and the debtors different people from those now involved. Likewise, it will expect to have some cash in hand and some money in a bank deposit in a year's time, but its present cash and its present deposit will probably have been spent and replaced by then.

For the moment, though, it is convenient to split the assets up differently into physical assets and financial assets. The physical assets of the company would comprise its land and buildings, plant, machinery and vehicles, fixtures and fittings, and stocks and work in progress. Its financial assets would comprise its investments, loans to trade debtors, bank deposits and cash in hand. The distinction between physical and financial assets is of limited interest to the company, which is why it is not shown on its balance sheet, but it is of considerable importance to the country, for physical assets comprise stocks of finished goods and other assets which can be used to produce finished goods and services in the future, whereas financial assets do not.

Another characteristic of any economic unit's financial assets is that they relate to items termed financial claims which occur as liabilities in the balance sheets of other economic units. Consider again the financial assets of the company involved in Table 1.1. Its investments, say in shares in another company, will show up as liabilities in that company's balance sheet, just as the shares issued by the present company show up as liabilities in Table 1.1. Its loans to trade debtors will show up as liabilities in the balance sheets of the firms concerned, just as the present company's loans from trade creditors show up as liabilities in Table 1.1. Its bank deposit will show up as a liability to the bank where it is held, just as deposits held at the account-handling bank in Table 1.9 show up as liabilities there. And its cash in hand, if held in note form, will be included in the liabilities of the Bank of England, or perhaps of Scottish or Northern Irish banks if their notes are held, just as issued IOUs showed up as liabilities for the note-issuing bank in Table 1.6. Cash held in coin form, usually a trivial amount, is also matched by liabilities for the Bank of England (or, more precisely, its Banking Department) as explained in Chapter 7.

The fact that all financial assets represent financial claims which are matched by financial liabilities elsewhere is of use when it comes to estimating a country's wealth. Suppose, for simplicity, that the country is financially self-contained inasmuch as all financial assets held by its citizens reflect financial liabilities of other home citizens (not foreign ones) and that all its citizens' financial liabilities reflect financial assets of other home citizens (not foreign ones). An estimate of the nation's wealth could be made by adding up estimates of the wealth of each economic unit within it. In estimating the wealth of, say, a household, the first step would be to estimate the value of its physical assets, which would cover any possessions of land and buildings, consumer durables and furniture (all of which help to provide goods and services for the household such as shelter, food and comfort) along with stocks of, for instance, food and fuel; and the second step would be to estimate the value of its financial assets, which would cover, for instance, cash in hand, deposits at the bank and the financial value of any shares owned. However, an estimate of the household's true wealth would then have to deduct the value of any financial liabilities, such as a mortgage (that is a loan, usually from a building society) or a loan from a credit card company, for a household with assets of £50,000 and debts of £10,000 can really claim in its own name a wealth of only £40,000.

In a similar way, each other unit would find its wealth, or net worth as it is often called for companies, by deducting the value of its financial liabilities from the figure for its total assets. In the case of the company in Table 1.1, this would actually mean deducting all its liabilities, except those labelled profit and loss account and revaluation reserve. In short, the wealth or net worth of any unit is the value of its physical assets, plus the value of its financial assets, minus the value of its financial liabilities. Similarly, the value of the wealth for the country as a whole is the total value of its physical assets, plus the total value of its financial assets, minus the total value of its financial liabilities. Now for any household or firm, the value of its financial assets would not equal the value of its financial liabilities except, perhaps, by chance, in a few cases; but for a financially self-contained country, the total values of its financial assets and liabilities must be the same because each financial asset of each unit is also a financial liability of another unit, so such a country's total wealth precisely equals the value of its physical capital. This result emphasizes the fact that though financial claims represent wealth to some people, they do not generally reflect wealth to the country as a whole. In practice, of course, nations are not financially self-contained. Accordingly, a nation's wealth is augmented by financial claims against foreigners, but against these must be offset financial liabilities to foreigners.

This discussion of wealth and financial claims may be concluded by making a few further points about each. As far as wealth is concerned, the first point to note is that the emphasis has been on valuing a nation's physical or tangible wealth. This wealth generally serves to provide goods and services. However, such production is aided by the skills and abilities possessed by the country's people, and these skills are often termed human capital. Secondly, both physical and human capital can be enhanced only by sacrificing current consumption, as would occur in a country which decided to produce less beer in order to release resources either to build more factories or to enable more people to increase their human capital through training. Thirdly, it may appear from balance sheets, such as those in Tables 1.6 and 1.9, that banks have no physical assets and therefore have no direct share in the nation's wealth; but it was stressed in the last chapter that banks do have other assets which were ignored in those tables, for simplicity, because they typically constitute a relatively small proportion of banks' assets. These other assets would include buildings and fittings.

As for financial claims, it should be noted that ultimately most of these arise when units whose incomes exceed their expenditures lend money, or transfer money in other ways, to units whose expenditures exceed their incomes. Thus a business needing to finance a new factory may issue and sell new shares bought by households who are otherwise spending less than their present incomes. While the transfers typically pass from households to businesses, they often pass indirectly through banks or other financial companies, such as life-insurance companies, who collect premiums from households and buy shares in companies. For this reason, financial companies are generally known as financial intermediaries. As explained in Chapter 3, a distinction is often made between banks and other financial companies, such as building societies, known as non-bank financial intermediaries (NBFIs).

## Types of financial claim

There are many different types of financial claim, but it is possible to regard most of them as falling into seven different groups. First there is cash; as noted before, this consists of notes and coins which represent assets to their holders that are matched by liabilities for the banks concerned with their issue. Secondly there are deposits at banks and at NBFIs, which represent liabilities to the intermediaries and assets to the depositors. Thirdly there are loans made by these financial companies which are assets to them and liabilities to their borrowers. More is said in later chapters about all these first three groups of financial claims.

The fourth group comprises claims held against life-insurance companies. There are two main types of claims held against them. First there are claims held by people who have taken out life-insurance policies, in which case they will usually be paying premiums over a period of years in return for a lump sum to be paid either on a specified date in the future or on death; and secondly there are claims held by people who have contributed towards pension schemes, in which case they will be paying – or will have paid – regular contributions when in work in return for regular income receipts for the duration of their retirement. As with deposits at financial intermediaries, these claims represent liabilities to the companies and assets to their holders. However, these claims differ from deposits in that there may be many years between the day when a claim is established with a life-insurance company and the day when it may be redeemed (or at least redeemed without some financial penalty). This fourth group of financial claims is of little relevance to the rest of the book and is not discussed in detail elsewhere.

The fifth group comprises what are generally termed securities. There are frequent references to securities in the following chapters so it is useful to have some understanding of the main types. These types are explored in the following sections, but it is helpful here to make a few points applicable to all securities. A key common feature is that they are created when money is passed to a company or to central or local government (perhaps in the form of a loan) in return for a piece of paper which gives its holder the right to be paid a specified lump sum at some specified date in the future and/or the right to some form of annual income so long as he holds the paper. Moreover, the piece of paper may be sold by the holder to a third party, perhaps privately in the case of securities issued by small companies, but usually on the stock exchange in London, or, indeed, on any of the twenty other much smaller stock exchanges which are located in other United Kingdom towns. Indeed, until the development in the 1960s of certain special types of marketable deposits discussed in Chapter 7, securities were the only marketable financial claims. Securities are assets for their holders and liabilities for their issuers.

There seems to be some confusion in the literature about precisely how the name security arose. Sometimes it is said that it came about because the borrower, by giving a piece of paper to the lender, has made the loan (more) secure since his obligation to the lender has been put in writing above his signature. At other times it is said that it came about because the holder of a security may find it helps him to obtain a loan, especially from a bank. The point is that a bank will usually be quite willing to lend to a person who gives them custody over his securities, for the bank knows that if the borrower is slow to repay his loan then they can hold on to his securities (and hence prevent him selling them to help finance, say, a holiday or new car) by way of encouragement. According to the Oxford English Dictionary the first meaning has the longer usage, dating back to 1576, but the second meaning has been recorded as early as 1690.

The final two groups of financial claim comprise loans which are not made by financial intermediaries (and so differ from loans in the third group of claims) and where the borrower does not issue the lender with a marketable security. The distinction between these two final groups is that the sixth comprises loans on which some form of return (generally interest) is paid and the seventh comprises loans on which it is not. The former group is in practice dominated by loans made by and to the central government, but this group also contains any interest-bearing loans made by private sector businesses and households. The chief loans made by the central government are those to local authorities and public corporations (or nationalized industries); the chief loans in this group made to the central government concern purchases of National Savings Certificates, which are redeemed when the purchasers choose and attract interest payments only at redemption, save-as-you-earn schemes (SAYE), where savers lend certain amounts on a regular basis and get interest only when they seek repayment, and premium bonds, where lenders opt for the chance of a prize instead of a guaranteed payment of interest.

Turning now to the seventh group, it might seem surprising that there are any loans made free from interest to fall into it. In fact there are many such loans, but it should be stressed that they are very short term loans that are made for convenience rather than because borrowers are short of funds. The group consists chiefly of those items which show up as creditors and debtors on balance sheets, and they arise, for instance, when an employer pays his staff at the end of the week or the month, and so owes them money most of the time, or when producers supply items such as gas, electricity or milk in return for periodic payments and so are owed money most of the time by buyers. These two final groups of financial claim are of considerable importance to the economy but generally of little importance to the rest of this book.

# Bills

The main types of security are indicated in Table 2.1. It will be seen that there are four groups: bills, fixed-interest securities, equities and unit trust units. These will be examined in turn, and then there will be a discussion of the factors affecting the likely return on any particular security. The present section is concerned with bills.

There are three main sorts of bills, namely commercial bills, Treasury bills and local authority bills. Commercial bills evolved in the Middle Ages, became more important with the extension of trade in the industrial revolution, and reached their hey-day by the mid-nineteenth century. After that they declined, especially in relation to transactions between buyers and sellers in the same country, as deposit-banking with loan (and overdraft) facilities expanded. However, bills have never died out, and they enjoyed a brief rise in popularity in the period 1978–80.

The use of these bills stemmed chiefly from the understandable desire of commercial enterprises not to have to pay for the inputs they were using until those inputs had been used up in the production of outputs and subsequently sold. The inputs and outputs might be physically similar, as with the coal purchased and sold by a coal merchant, or very different, as with the planks bought by a cabinet-maker and the chairs eventually sold. For the last century or so, such enterprises have most usually solved their problems by arranging for loans (or overdrafts) with their banks, for in this way the purchasers of the inputs borrow money which they will repay when their outputs are sold, and the sellers of the inputs are paid at the time when they are sold.

Commercial bills offer input purchasers an alternative solution to their problems. In essence, these bills are pieces of paper on which they write a promise to pay their suppliers on a specified date in the future. This 'maturity' date tends to vary from one to six months after the date on which the bill is first made out, but the great majority of bills are three-month (strictly 91-day) bills. The purchaser would be said to accept the bill, for by signing it he accepts an obligation to pay the debt at a specified date in the future. The input seller would be said to draw the bill, for he regards it as an obligation to pay him money just as he regards a cheque made out by him, or drawn by him on his bank, as an obligation for the bank to give some money to him (and then, in turn, to whoever he has indicated on the cheque). Because they are issued when commodities change hands, commercial bills are often termed bills of exchange.

On the face of it, a major disadvantage for the seller in dealing with a purchaser who issues a bill rather than borrowing from his bank is that the seller is not paid at once. However, this will be taken into account in deciding on the amount the buyer must pay. Thus a buyer may be offered his goods for £985 if he pays on the spot, or asked for a £1,000 bill if he wishes to pay in three months. In this way, the buyer is paying

£15 for the privilege of deferring his payment for the goods, just as he would have to pay interest on a bank loan if he had used that system instead. In effect, the buyer is borrowing from the seller rather than from the bank. However, this situation might seem unsatisfactory because sellers of inputs, unlike banks, are not necessarily willing to make loans, and they may not be able to wait for payment anyway. The solution to this problem for the seller has always been the option of at once selling the bill to a third party who is able and willing to make a loan; for bills are made out in words which oblige their issuer, who accepted them, to pay whoever is the bearer of them – that is to say whoever holds them – on the maturity date.

Of course, the third party will not offer to pay the input seller £1,000 for a piece of paper whose only attraction is that its holder will be paid £1,000 three months hence. The third party will offer a smaller amount, and is said to buy the bill at a discount. Indeed, the third party gets a return only by buying at a discount, and if interest rates available elsewhere are high then the buyer will agree to buy the bill only if he can obtain it for a large discount. If the buyer offered £985, offering a £15 return in three months, that is about 1.5 per cent in a quarter of a year – or the equivalent of some 6 per cent in a full year – then the discount rate would be said to be 6 per cent.

It is clear that the drawer of a bill will find that its resale value is affected by general interest rate levels. If these levels rise, then maybe people will buy his next bill for only £980 reflecting a discount rate of 8 per cent – as the buyer would get £20, or some 2 per cent, in three months. The drawer will also find that the resale value depends on the age of the bill. If people buying the bill wanted a discount rate of 6 per cent, then they would pay around £985 for it when new, but £990 after one month and £995 after three months, as shown by the continuous line in Figure 2.1. This is because a payment of £990 for a one-month-old bill promises £10 return in two months, whereas £995 for a two-month-old bill promises £5 return in one month, and each of these returns is equivalent to about 6 per cent per annum; they are not exactly equivalent, and hence these prices – and those shown on the line in the figure – are slight approximations to those which such a discount rate would create. The dashed line in the figure shows the approximate values at different dates which would apply to a bill being discounted at 8 per cent. An important point to note is that the value of bills will alter on any day when interest rates change. If interest rates are such that one particular new £1,000 bill would today be bought at a discount rate of 6 per cent, then its value with three months to run will be £985; but if interest rates rose tomorrow so that it would now only be bought at a rate of 8 per cent, then its value would fall to just over £980 (just over because it has just under three months to maturity).

A further factor affecting a bill's resale value is the credit-worthiness of whoever accepted it. In the example considered above, the drawer was prepared to take a £1,000 three-month bill in return for £985 worth of goods. Maybe he reckoned the bill from the accepter could be sold for £985 as people would buy it at a 6 per cent rate. However, another less well-known customer might be offered only £980 worth of goods for a £1,000 three-month bill if the drawer felt this bill would generally be regarded as more risky and so could be sold to a third party only if it promised the higher 8 per cent rate of return that its purchaser would get if he paid £980. In effect, the first accepter would be getting credit for 6 per cent and the second would be getting it for 8 per cent. It is clearly desirable for accepters to be well known and trusted, for then their bills command lower discount rates. Equally, it is clearly difficult for thousands of traders to become generally well known as credit-worthy.

It was to help enterprises wishing to make purchases with bills that the traditional

**Table 2.1**   Types of security

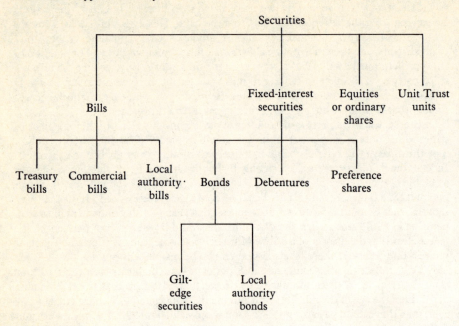

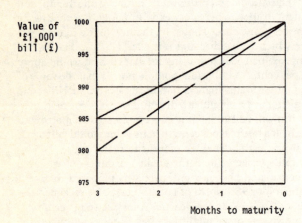

Months to maturity

**Figure 2.1**

business of accepting houses came into being. In effect, a trader who wishes to make purchases with bills can have his affairs examined by an accepting house, that is a firm specializing in this business. If he satisfies them with his credit-worthiness, then they will themselves accept (or endorse) his bills, that is to say they will undertake themselves to pay the bearer at the maturity date. With this backing, the bill will be less risky, for there are a limited number of accepting houses each of good repute. With such bills, the less well-known purchaser in the last paragraph might at once find that his three-month £1,000 bill will entitle him to £985 worth of goods instead of £980. At the date of maturity, he will have to give £1,000 to the accepting house to enable them in turn to pay off the holder of his bill. He will also have to pay the house a fee for the service of accepting his bill. This fee is really a return to them for examining his business and for taking the risk of accepting his bill. In the present example, the purchaser might be willing to pay any fee under £5 to have a bill accepted by an accepting house since the process enables him to buy £5 more goods with it. In practice, competition can keep fees at a rather lower level than this. Indeed, competition for accepting comes not only from specialist accepting houses but also from banks, bills accepted by banks being known as bank-bills.

As implied in Table 2.1, there are two other types of bills besides commercial ones. The most important of these are Treasury bills, first issued in 1877. New Treasury bills are issued with a life of 91 days, except when adjustments are needed on account of public holidays. They are issued each week by the Treasury, and essentially reflect short-term borrowing by the central government to finance its expenditure. Now certain government departments have their bank accounts, known as public deposits, at the Bank of England. These departments include the tax-collecting departments and the Treasury. Broadly speaking, taxes are paid into the accounts of the tax-collecting departments which then pay the money over to the Treasury which in turn pays it to the government's spending departments. Taken together, the public sector deposits generally have a very low total compared with the total level of government spending. There is limited need for large balances because money is flowing in – chiefly from taxes – and flowing out tolerably steadily throughout the year. Occasionally, there is a good week for tax receipts and the public sector deposits tend to become larger than needed for the moment, but generally tax receipts are incapable of sustaining the government's expenditure commitments which is why the government regularly tops up its tax receipts with substantial long-term borrowing. In practice, any occasional tendency for large balances to accumulate, even temporarily, is generally offset very quickly by the government paying off past long-term loans, thereby minimizing the amount of outstanding loans on which money has to be raised in taxes to pay the interest. This strategy is pursued so assiduously that there tends, every week, to be rather less money available in public sector deposits than the government departments wish to spend. A major purpose of the weekly issue of Treasury bills is to enable the Treasury to borrow enough money to enable it to transfer enough funds to other departments to finance their expenditure.

It may seem odd that this need for short-term loans is at times made greater by enthusiastically paying off long-term ones. However, it is actually a prudent policy because, for reasons considered later, interest rates on short-term loans are typically lower than those on long-term ones. It may be wondered why the government makes use of long-term loans at all if short-term ones have lower interest rates. This is done partly to avoid the inconvenience and uncertainty which would arise if the government had to borrow vast sums every few weeks..A further advantage of borrowing long-term is that the government can seek to borrow much when interest rates are generally low and little when they are generally high.

As with commercial bills, Treasury bills are bought at a discount off the face value that they will achieve on maturity, and their resale value rises as maturity approaches, but there are two significant differences between commercial bills and Treasury bills. First, Treasury bills are effectively accepted by the Treasury, and as the Treasury always has access to tax receipts its acceptance needs no endorsement by anyone else. Secondly, Treasury bills are not drawn by people selling goods to the Treasury, and hence they are not bills of exchange since no goods change hands when Treasury bills are issued.

The initial purchasers of Treasury bills fall into three groups. The new bills they buy comprise the tap issue and the tender issue. Tap issue bills are bought only by government departments with a temporary surplus of funds. The price at which these bills are initially bought is fixed by the Treasury but is not publicized. All other new Treasury bills are sold on behalf of the Treasury by the Bank of England in what is known as the tender issue. By convention they are sold only to discount houses and banks, who may buy them on their own behalf or on behalf of their customers. More is said about discount houses in later chapters, but two points should be made here. First, these institutions make some of their profits by borrowing from the banks money which is repayable at 24-hours notice and using these loans to buy Treasury bills. Naturally they seek to get a return on the bills which exceeds the interest they have to pay to the banks. Secondly, they have a special arrangement with the Bank of England whereby the Bank will always lend money to them if they need it, which they might if the banks demanded almost instant repayment of some of their loans. In return, the discount houses accept an obligation to buy any new Treasury bills for which the Bank of England can find no other buyers.

Tender issue bills are allocated by the Bank of England to the banks and discount houses every Friday. The mechanism of each allocation is fairly simple. On the previous Friday, the Bank will have announced the total face value of the new bills which will be available. It may revise the amount slightly downwards before the allocation but will not revise it upwards. Of course, no one buys new bills at their face value, so the prospective purchasers make offers, or tenders, in which they indicate how many bills they would like and the prices they are prepared to pay. The Bank examines the tenders on the Friday concerned and allocates the bills available to the purchasers who have made the highest offers. Purchases actually take place in the following week, on whatever day purchasers choose; large purchasers often spread out their allocation and buy some bills on each day.

Sometimes the offers that are made for the new bills are more than sufficient to cover the bills made available, in which case prospective purchasers making low offers get none. At other times, the tenders may be insufficient to cover the bills available, in which case the Bank would seem to be in danger of being unable to sell as many as the Treasury wishes. However, the discount houses always get together as a syndicate to fix an agreed price at which they are prepared to buy any bills which the Treasury is unable to sell at a higher price. This syndicate price is, of course, lower than the varying prices offered by the discount houses in their main tender. When the Treasury is obliged to dispose of some bills to the discount houses at this syndicate price, it allocates them between the houses in numbers which result in the total number of bills bought by each house – both from its main bid and as a result of its participation in the syndicate bid – being roughly proportional to its size. A point to note is that no bank making tenders at prices below the price of this syndicate dis-count house bid will be allocated any new bills.

The final type of bill is the local authority bill. These bills are issued by some local authorities, generally for three months but sometimes for as little as two months and sometimes for up to six months. Like Treasury bills, they are not bills of exchange. They are frequently purchased by the discount houses. As local authorities can raise tax receipts through the property tax known as rates, they should never be in default in redeeming their bills, so there is no need for these bills to be accepted. However, the recent introduction of rate-capping, which in effect means that the central govern-ment can limit the taxes imposed by certain high-spending authorities, could conceiv-ably lead to their claiming to be unable to set the tax rates needed to redeem their bills, though this has not happened.

## Fixed-interest securities

It was explained in the last section that bills are issued by borrowers who want to borrow money for a short time, that they are initially sold by borrowers for less than their face value, and that each lender gets a return either by waiting for maturity – when the holder of a bill will be paid its full face value, which will be higher than the amount he paid for the bill – or by selling it to a third party before maturity – for an amount greater than the amount he paid for it. In contrast, fixed-interest securities are generally issued by borrowers who want to borrow money for a long period, they are initially sold by borrowers for their full face value, and each lender is given a return in the form of interest payments made to him by the borrower. The rate of interest which will be paid will be printed on the security and cannot be altered once it has been issued. This rate of interest is known as the coupon. Thus the holder of a £100 fixed-interest security, that is a security sold initially for £100, which bears an interest rate of 10 per cent per annum, will be entitled to receive £10 in interest every year; interest payments are usually made in two equal instalments at six-monthly intervals so that the holder in this example might receive £5 each 17th May and £5 each 17th November. Should he sell his security on the stock exchange to someone else, then the new owner will be entitled to the six-monthly receipts of £5 irrespective of the price he paid for this second-hand purchase.

An interesting aspect of fixed interest securities concerns their final repayment. Some have a specific date, known as the redemption date, printed on them; with these, the issuer is obliged to pay to the holders on the redemption date a sum equal to the face value of the securities they hold. Others have two dates on them indicating a period of time within which redemption may be made; the borrower can effect redemption on any date he chooses provided it is not before the first date or after the last date. There are two further possibilities, though both are rare. One is for the security to have a date showing the earliest day on which redemption may be made, but to have no date showing the last day, and the other is to have no dates at all, thereby giving the borrower no constraints at all. With securities such as these, the borrower is effectively under no obligation ever to make a redemption, though he is, of course, under a corresponding obligation to make interest payments in perpetuity. It might seem odd for lenders to buy new securities of this last sort since they will never be entitled to repayment from the borrower; but they can always sell their securities to a third party if they want to cease being lenders (as, of course, can holders of any other securities if they do not want to keep their money tied up in securities all the time until redemption). Similarly, if the borrower wishes to reduce his annual payments of interest, then he can purchase his own securities on the stock exchange as and when they come up for sale.

Table 2.1 shows that fixed-interest securities can be subdivided into bonds, debentures and preference shares. The term bonds is usually retained in the UK for securities issued by the central government or local authorities whereas debentures and preference shares are securities issued by companies, and this definition will be used throughout this book. However, in the United States the term bonds is also taken to include debentures, and it is sometimes so used in the United Kingdom.

Bonds issued by the UK central government are often termed gilt-edged securities or gilts. This name is used because it is reckoned that there is no risk of the central government being unable to pay interest or to effect redemption since it can always levy taxes to honour its obligations. In principle, of course, there is a risk that a government might decide not to honour its obligations, particularly if it is a new government which refuses to acknowledge obligations incurred by its predecessor. This has never occurred in the UK and is most unusual elsewhere. Perhaps governments which have come to power through a democratic process are generally deterred by the fear that the bond-holders would not vote for them at the next election, while governments which have come to power through a revolution may generally be deterred by the fear that the bond-holders will plan a counter-revolution! However, upheavals do sometimes occur, and there are, for instance, a large number of people who hold bonds issued by the Chinese Government before 1949 which have not been honoured by later communist governments there.

The UK central government has never issued undated bonds. However, some bonds, known as consols, were issued in the eighteenth and nineteenth centuries, and also until the First World War in the present century, which had only a 'first possible' date on. As they have not yet been redeemed, there are still some held privately, though not often by the original purchasers! Of course, these consols still earn interest for their holders. As it happens, there are a few British local authority bonds with no dates on. Most gilts are now issued with a final redemption date of 20 years or less from the date of issue. The term shorts (or short-dated stock) refers to gilts with less than five years to run before their final redemption date; medium-date gilts have from 5 to 15 years to run, and long-dated gilts have over 15 years to run before redemption must occur.

When bonds are redeemed, the holders at the time of redemption are generally paid a sum equal to the face value of the bonds they hold which is, of course, the value they had when originally purchased. Since 1981, however, a number of index-linked bonds have been issued whose redemption value will equal the initial purchase value adjusted for any subsequent increase in retail prices. Thus if prices double during the life of these bonds, then their redemption value will be double their initial purchase value. Inflation is also taken into account in working out the annual interest payments. Suppose a lender bought a £100 index-linked gilt in 1981, and suppose this gilt has a 2½ per cent coupon. In 1985 the lender would ordinarily expect to receive interest of £2.50 (or, more precisely, two payments of £1.25 at six-monthly intervals); but with index-linked gilts the payments would take inflation into account, so that if prices had risen by 20 per cent since the date of issue, then the holder would receive 20 per cent more than £1.25, that is £1.50.

Debentures and preference shares are both issued by companies and are in many respects very similar. Debentures are almost always dated and are usually redeemed between 10 and 40 years from the date of issue. In contrast, it is quite common for preference shares to be undated. However, the main differences between these two forms of security stem from the fact that a company's debenture holders are regarded as creditors, just as a bank would be if it had lent the company money, whereas its preference shareholders are regarded more as owners of the company. As a result, interest paid to debenture holders can be deducted from a company's profits before calculating the taxable profits on which corporation tax is due, just as interest to a bank can be so deducted, but interest to preference shareholders is not deducted, just as payments to holders of ordinary shares (discussed in the next section) are not. Also, in a year when profits are low, a company is obliged to pay interest in full to debenture holders and other creditors before paying a penny to preference shareholders; however, preference shareholders must then be paid in full before any money is paid to ordinary shareholders, which explains the use of the word preference. Being a bit like owners, preference shareholders have some voting rights at shareholders' meetings, though they always have fewer rights than ordinary shareholders. In their role as creditors, debenture holders generally have no voting rights, though they can force the company to go into liquidation if their interest is not paid in full. Liquidation means the company would cease trading and would sell all its assets. The proceeds from such sales would have to be used to meet in full all outstanding interest obligations to creditors, and to redeem all loans including debentures, before any money could be given to preference shareholders, though obligations to them would in turn have to be met in full before anything could be given to the holders of ordinary shares.

An important point to appreciate with all fixed interest securities is that although annual interest payments are fixed by the coupon as a percentage of the security's face value, they are likely to fluctuate as a percentage of its second-hand value on the stock exchange. This point can be illustrated in the case of undated debentures. Suppose a company wishes to issue some undated debentures and finds that with interest rates at their present levels on various other securities available, it needs to offer a 10 per cent rate of interest to attract enough buyers. It will therefore print 10 per cent on the debentures and the buyer of a £100 debenture will acquire a certificate recording this purchase and entitling him to a fixed £10 interest per annum indefinitely. Any subsequent buyer of this debenture would also be entitled to £10 interest per annum indefinitely. Should the original owner wish to sell his debenture a week or two later, perhaps to raise money for some unexpected expenditure, he would hope to be able to sell it for £100 with no difficulty.

Suppose, however, that shortly after the issue, interest rates generally rise sharply. For the sake of simplicity, suppose that interest rates double. In that case, the buyer could not hope to sell his debenture for £100. The reason is straightforward. People now have opportunities to make loans for around 20 per cent and will not pay £100 for a debenture which offers only 10 per cent. Even so, the debenture will not be unsaleable, and its owner should find a buyer if he offered it for sale at £50, for the buyer would pay £50 for debenture with a face value of £100 and entitlement to £10 interest each year. In effect, the second-hand buyer will be spending £50 on a debenture which yields £10 per annum and so secures each year a return equal to 20 per cent of the second-hand price he has paid, which means the purchase of the debenture at this price makes its return comparable with returns available elsewhere.

Suppose, instead, that interest rates fall shortly after the debenture is issued. For simplicity, suppose interest rates halve. In this case, the initial purchaser will be able to sell his security for twice what he paid for it, that is for £200. This is because buyers will be willing to pay £200 for a debenture with a face value of £100 and entitlement to £10 interest each year. In effect, a second-hand buyer will be spending £200 on a debenture which yields £10 per annum and so secures each year a return equal to 5 per cent of the second-hand price he has paid, which means the purchase of the debenture at this price makes its return comparable with returns available elsewhere. It follows that the second-hand prices of undated or perpetual securities move in opposite directions to changes in interest rate levels, but to the same extent; that is, a halving of interest rates doubles the price and vice versa.

The second-hand prices of redeemable securities also react to changes in interest rates, though the reaction is less marked the nearer they are to redemption. Consider, for instance, a £100 debenture issued with a redemption date 20 years hence, and suppose it bears an interest rate of 10 per cent and that its annual £10 interest is paid in a single instalment at the end of each year. Suppose, too, that after exactly 19 years of its life interest rate levels are such that its second-hand value is exactly £100, and so equals its face value. The implication is that borrowers wishing to lend for one year could get returns of 10 per cent on other comparable securities. Next, imagine that interest rates double. Clearly the second-hand value of the debenture would fall, for no one would pay a full £100 for a debenture which offered interest of £10 over the next year if their £100 could get them £20 on a one-year loan elsewhere; but the price would not halve to £50 because buyers would be willing to pay far more for a debenture which will be redeemed for £100 in a year's time. In fact, its price would be about £91.67, for the buyer would then get a return of about £18.33, that is £100 from redemption plus £10 in interest less the amount paid, and £18.33 represents a return of around 20 per cent of his purchase price. The return of 20 per cent in this example is termed the security's gross redemption yield. It is derived from the return of £18.33 which comprised £10 interest and £8.33 capital gain, so that some 11 per cent of the yield was accounted for by interest and 9 per cent by the capital gain.

Conversely, imagine instead that interest rates had halved. Clearly the second-hand value of the debenture would rise, for people would willingly pay over £100 for a debenture which offered interest of £10 in the next year if their £100 could get them only £5 on a one-year loan elsewhere; but the price would not double to £200 because buyers would not pay nearly as much for a debenture which will be redeemed for only £100 in a year's time. In fact, its price would rise to £104.76, for the buyer would then get a return of £5.24, that is £100 from redemption plus £10 as interest less the amount paid, and this represents a return of around 5 per cent of his purchase price. This return of 5 per cent represents the gross redemption yield in this example. It is derived from the return of £5.24 which comprised interest of £10 and a capital loss of £4.76, so that the interest amounted to just under 10 per cent and the loss to just under 5 per cent.

These two examples show that if a debenture has, say, one year to run, then buyers would probably pay less than its face value if interest rates at the time were much higher than they had been when the debenture was first issued, and they would probably pay more than its face value if they were much lower than they had been when it was first issued. Suppose two £100 debentures, perhaps issued by the same company, have one year to run, but suppose one was issued 19 years ago with a 20-year life, and that the other was issued nine years ago with a 10-year life; and suppose interest rates today are much higher than they were 19 years ago but are much lower than they were nine years ago. In that case, the older bond will have a second-hand value of under

**Table 2.2** Prices and yields on 19 January 1987 of four bonds with similar maturities

| Bond | Coupon (%) | Redemption date | Price (£) | Interest yield (%) | Gross redemption yield (%) |
|------|-----------|-----------------|-----------|--------------------|-----------------------------|
| A | $2\frac{1}{2}$ | 1990 | $81\frac{13}{16}$ | 3.06 | 8.12 |
| B | 3 | 1990 | $85\frac{1}{8}$ | 3.53 | 8.27 |
| C | $8\frac{1}{4}$ | 1987–90 | $94\frac{15}{16}$ | 8.71 | 10.11 |
| D | $12\frac{1}{3}$ | 1990 | $105\frac{1}{16}$ | 11.90 | 10.57 |

Source: *Financial Times*, 20 January 1987, p. 34.

£100 and the newer one a second-hand value of over £100. The former was issued when interest rates were low and hence has a low coupon, so buyers offer a low price in order to get a compensating capital gain, while the latter was issued when interest rates were high and hence has a high coupon, so buyers are willing to pay a high price and so incur an offsetting capital loss. In short, the returns from interest will be very different, but the gross redemption yields should be similar for each will be comparable to the returns lenders today could get on one-year loans made elsewhere. An important implication of this point is that as the yields on different fixed interest securities tend to be similar, so they tend to move up and down together.

In practice, the gross redemption yields for two securities issued by the same borrower and having the same maturity date may differ rather more than the last paragraph suggests. This can be seen from the figures in Table 2.2 which relates to four £100 bonds maturing in 1990 (or possibly before in one case). The coupon figures make it clear that bonds A and B were issued at times when interest rates were much lower than they were when bonds C and D were issued. The prices shown for these bonds relate to 19 January 1987, and from the prices it is possible to work out the interest yields and the gross redemption yields. The interest yields are low on bonds A and B whose low prices of around £82 and £85 imply that there will be substantial capital gains; the interest yield is higher on C whose price of some £95 offers a smaller capital gain, and it is much higher on D, whose price of some £105 promises a capital loss.

However, the prices shown in Table 2.2 actually result also in different gross redemption yields. Indeed, the last column shows that these yields are lowest on A and B. Why is this? In other words, why don't holders of bonds A and B sell them and use the proceeds to buy C or D which have higher gross redemption yields? The answer is that the returns from C and D come largely in interest while the returns on A and B come largely from capital gains. Since the majority of investors pay less tax on capital gains than they pay on income, they might well find that the benefits from the switch in the form of a higher (before tax) income would be offset by extra tax payments. If this tax consideration means there are no widespread sales of A and B and no widespread purchases of C and D, then the relative prices of the bonds are likely to be stable and their gross redemption yields will continue to differ.

# Equities and unit trust units

Equities or ordinary shares are issued by companies to their ordinary shareholders who are in fact their owners. Unlike bills and most fixed interest securities, equities have no date for maturity or redemption, and the reason is simple. The ordinary shareholders in a company can be regarded as having pooled some of their savings to get the company going. Of course, their company may borrow further money from non-owners such as the bank or trade creditors, or from the holders of commercial bills, debentures and preference shares, and hence the company and its owners, or ordinary shareholders, can be regarded as having an obligation to pay interest to these creditors and (in most cases) obligations to repay these loans at various dates in the future. However, the ordinary shareholders have not borrowed money from themselves, for no one can be considered to borrow money from himself, and hence they cannot be regarded as having an obligation to repay themselves in the future or as having an obligation to pay themselves income meanwhile. Of course, owners who so wish can seek to sell some or all of their shares to someone else; such sales would be done on the stock exchange in the case of large companies but may be done privately in the case of small ones with few shareholders.

Another distinction between equities and fixed interest securities is that the income paid to the holders of equities is not fixed in the sense of being constant. As the owners of a company, the (ordinary) shareholders are entitled to a share of any profits it makes, once all payments of interest to creditors and all payments of corporation tax have been made. In general, a substantial proportion of all these residual profits is distributed to shareholders in the form of dividends. However, some of the residual profits are usually kept undistributed, partly to help finance expansion and partly, perhaps, to enable comparable dividends to be paid in future years when the residual profits may be lower; for most companies try to keep dividends fairly stable, or perhaps rising steadily, even though profits inevitably tend to fluctuate appreciably over time. In principle, the amount of dividend paid each year is determined by shareholders at their annual general meeting; in practice the few who bother to attend, plus the few who exercise their right to a postal ballot on the issue, almost invariably accept the recommendation of the directors. Incidentally, new directors to help run the company are also in principle chosen from time to time by shareholders at their annual meetings, but in practice the nominations made by existing directors are almost always adopted.

As with bills and fixed-interest securities, the second-hand prices of equities tend to react in response to changes in the general level of interest rates, the prices falling when interest rates rise and vice versa. In other words, the return on an equity – that is the dividend as a percentage of the second-hand price – tends to rise when interest rates rise and vice versa. Why is this? Consider the shares in company X which may have a face value of £1, that is to say they were originally sold to shareholders for £1 and have this value printed on them. Now suppose there is a good prospect of a 10p dividend each year for the indefinite future. The result is that this share might fetch £2 at times when interest rates are low and the expected annual return of 10p or 5 per cent of the second-hand price looks reasonable, but it might fetch a mere 50p at times when interest rates are high and buyers could be tempted only if the second-hand price resulted in the 10p annual dividend giving them a return of 20 per cent. Of course, the prices of shares in individual companies also fluctuate in response to changes in expectations about their own future profit and dividend levels.

In general, the money put up by the shareholders in a company may be supposed to be used by the company to help it purchase physical assets needed for the production of goods and services. However, some companies, known as investment trusts, act differently and use the money put up by their shareholders to purchase shares in other companies, and perhaps to purchase other types of securities too. These companies pay dividends which are financed from the income derived in dividends on the shares bought by the company, plus the returns on any other securities it may have purchased.

The price of an investment trust's own shares fluctuates in line with the prices of the shares it itself has bought, though the trust's share prices also reflect the perceived competence of its managers. Thus two investment trusts might by chance own similar amounts of shares in the same lists of companies and they might be paying similar dividends at present, but the price of one trust's own shares could be higher than the price of the other's if it was felt that the managers of the former would make more shrewd decisions about what shares to buy and sell in the future, and when to buy and sell them, and hence be likely to be able to pay higher dividends in the future.

Shares in investment trusts tend to have prices which reflect a lower total resale value than the total resale value of the securities they own; in part, at least, this is because the dividends they pay out fall short of the income they earn, by perhaps up to 15 per cent, to cover their operating costs, chiefly their managers' salaries and office accommodation. It might be wondered why private citizens would buy shares in these companies if, as happens, some of the return on their money is used to cover their operating costs. Why wouldn't their shareholders instead buy shares directly in the companies in which investment companies buy shares and acquire the whole return on their money?

The answer to this question is that investment companies offer two main benefits for small investors. First, they reduce the risks their investors face. The point is that a few companies do really badly each year and hence their shares plummet in value. Now a small saver may have shares in only a handful of companies, and could lose a large slice of his savings if one of these turns out to be one of the duds; but if he instead uses all his money to buy investment trust shares then it will be spread over the many companies in which the trust has shares, and may be little affected even if one or two of those do badly. Secondly, the small investor may feel the managers of an investment trust will do a much better job of deciding what shares to buy and sell and when, and hence he may feel his savings will in the long run give him a better return if handled by them, despite their taking a slice of the returns, than if he handles them himself.

Small investors can get very similar benefits by putting their money into unit trust units rather than investment trust shares. The principal difference between unit trust units and investment trust shares is that the former are bought and sold directly from the company, so that the total number of issued units can fluctuate daily as new purchasers come along or old ones decide to opt out, whereas investment trust shares can be bought and sold only on the stock exchange, and the total number issued will change only on the rare occasions when the trust decides to issue some new ones or buy (second-hand) some existing ones. The issuers of unit trust units are obliged by law to buy and sell their units at prices which relate closely to the value of the securities they own and hence these prices tend to relate more closely to that value than is the case with investment trust shares. It may be noted that there are other technical differences between investment trusts and unit trusts; for instance, only the former are allowed to borrow funds on a long-term basis.

# The reasons for returns on financial claims

The previous sections have outlined a number of different types of financial claim. Most of these attract a return to the holder of the claim, generally in the form of interest payments. To understand the reasons why the issuers of these claims have to offer a return to the holders, it is important to realize what the holders might do with their money if they did not use it to buy claims which entitled them to a return. The chief options would be to spend it on goods and services, or to hoard it in the form of notes and coins, or to use it to acquire a claim which attracted no return, that is to say to place it in a bank deposit on which no interest was paid. The attraction of purchasing goods and services is, of course, the benefits which can be derived from consuming them, while the attraction of a hoard of cash or a large bank deposit is that the money is available for future use. Many people like to set some money aside, either to save enough for a future large purchase (a car perhaps) or to meet a foreseen need (such as retirement on a low income) or to have for use if some unforeseen contingency arises (such as redundancy or ill health). Given a choice between keeping their money in cash or in a bank deposit, many people would prefer the latter for the protection it offers from theft.

Now when people issue financial claims on which a return is offered, they are generally borrowing money to make some purchases, perhaps of raw materials or machinery if they are firms or of items such as new hospitals or submarines if they are the government. As a group, these issuers can be seen as offering a return partly to tempt savers who want to set money aside to lend it to them instead of keeping it as cash or in a bank deposit. There are a number of reasons why savers might be unwilling to make such loans and so would do so only if tempted by interest payments.

One important reason is that savers might feel that their money would be put at risk if lent to the claim-issuers. There are actually two different types of risk to consider. One is a risk of default which can arise if the issuer is a business, for a business might start making a loss and cease operation before the loan was repaid; of course its assets would then be sold and the proceeds divided among its creditors, but the proceeds might well be too small to pay each creditor in full. The risk of default is generally felt to be absent in the case of loans to the central government, and virtually absent in the case of loans to local authorities, for these borrowers can raise taxes to finance the repayment of their loans. Many claims have a different type of risk, namely that of a capital loss. It was explained in an earlier section that the second-hand value of fixed-interest securities would fall if interest rates rose, so someone buying bonds with 10 years to maturity and intending to sell them in one year's time could lose money if interest rates rose meanwhile. It was also explained earlier that the prices of bonds react less to changes in interest rates the nearer the bonds are to maturity, so shorts are less risky than longs.

Now there are actually some claims which carry no risk of either sort. These are non-marketable claims issued by the government, notably National Savings Certificates, for holders of these can always insist on having the full value of their loans repaid, along with interest earned to·date. Why is any interest at all paid on these claims? There are two reasons, and they apply also to other claims where risk merely constitutes a third reason for interest. The first reason is that a saver's money is fully liquid when held in cash, meaning that it can be spent at any time, and virtually fully liquid when held in a bank. It is true that banks are often shut, though cash dispensers mitigate this problem, but bank deposits can be used for purchases at all times simply by giving a cheque to the seller. The only liquidity problem with a bank deposit arises if a seller insists on cash and the purchaser is some distance from the bank or if the bank and its cash dispensers are closed. In contrast, the holder of a financial claim other than a bank deposit may find that it is much less liquid, and that it can take days or weeks before he can exchange the claim for money. For example, the time lag between instructing a stockbroker to sell a marketable security on the stock exchange and actually receiving a cheque can vary from about 10 days to 25. Of course, savers may not want instant access to all their savings, but the widespread existence of interest payments encourages them to keep their liquid funds lower than they otherwise would and so encourages them to buy more of the claims concerned than they otherwise would.

To see the second reason, suppose it was felt that financial claims carried no risk of default and no risk of a capital loss, and suppose they could be instantly exchanged for cash. The point is that circumstances like these would merely make people as happy to purchase claims as they are to hold cash or bank deposits. The claim issuers would still have the problem that, between them, their demands for borrowed funds are so vast that if they paid no interest then those demands would not be met. In short, one reason for returns such as interest payments is to tempt people to spend less money on goods and services and so to save more money which will be used to acquire financial claims. This means that interest payments persuade some people to forgo some goods and services today and so save and earn interest which will enable them to buy even. more goods and services in the future. Of course, this reason for interest payments might not be present in a period of time when households wanted to save large sums, perhaps for retirement, while businesses and governments had little need to borrow.

Notice that, other things being equal, the general level of interest rates will be higher in a period of inflation than in a period of stable prices. This arises chiefly as a result of the facts mentioned in the last paragraph. For instance, in a period of stable prices borrowers may be paying an interest rate around 5 per cent to persuade people to defer consumption. If prices started to rise by 5 per cent annum, then lending at that interest rate means savers would not eventually be able to buy more by saving, for the value of their savings will grow no faster than prices. In this situation, interest rates might have to rise to around 10 per cent to produce as much saving as there was before.

However, although nominal interest rates, that is the ones agreed between borrowers and lenders, will be higher in periods of inflation, the real rates of interest, that is the difference between the nominal rates and the inflation rate, may be lower. To see this, consider first a period of stable prices when there is little demand for borrowing and a high willingness to save. Businesses and governments will still have to offer some interest, say around 4 per cent, to meet their modest demands, for they must persuade savers to accept the illiquidity and any risks incurred in holding their claims; thus interest rates will be positive and so exceed the rate of inflation which is zero if prices are stable.

Now suppose prices start to rise at a rate of 10 per cent per year. Interest rates will rise, but they could settle at nominal rates of around, say, 13 per cent thus giving real rates around 3 per cent. Indeed, they could even settle with nominal rates below 10 per cent, say around 7 per cent, thus causing real rates to be negative. The point is that claims will now be much more attractive than cash or bank deposits whose real value will be falling as a result of inflation, and enough people may be willing to save at a negative real rate (but positive nominal rate) to meet business and government needs. Why would people save at all at a negative real rate rather than buy goods and services? To give just one reason, people will save for retirement. It is true that, in the circumstances, their savings plus interest may buy fewer loaves of bread when they retire than they could buy now if they did not save; but people retiring in one year's time might well prefer 100 fresh loaves bought then to the 103 they could have bought and stored today!

This section has indicated that financial claims generally offer returns to offset the risks and illiquidity entailed in holding them and to encourage people to consume less and save more. Now the returns vary substantially between different claims because different claims give rise to different degrees of risk and illiquidity. On the whole, governments are reckoned safer than businesses, so government claims have lower returns; likewise, large and well-known businesses are often thought to be safer than small unknown ones, so the large and well-known ones may be able to offer lower returns.

Again, the returns on different equities depend greatly on anticipated future returns. Companies X and Y may at present pay dividends of 10p a year on each of their shares, but if X's profits are expected to rise and Y's to fall, then X's shares may sell for £2 and Y's for 50p so that buyers of Y shares would, at present, get four times the return obtained by buyers of X shares; but purchasers of X shares expect to be compensated by higher dividends in future and, in turn, by perhaps an even higher price for their shares when they eventually sell them again. Incidentally, it should be noticed that because the price of an equity depends so much on present and future dividend levels, so equity prices are likely to be high when the economy is flourishing and expected to continue to flourish, and they are likely to be low when the economy is depressed and expected to stay that way. In contrast, because the returns on long-term fixed-interest securities are fixed, so their prices fluctuate much less over time than equity prices.

# The time structure of interest rates

As far as fixed-interest securities are concerned, returns are generally higher on those with a long period to maturity than on those with a short period to maturity. This tendency is reflected in the first two lines of Table 2.3. These lines show the gross redemption yields of bonds with 5, 10 and 20 years to maturity on 27 October 1971 and also on 27 October 1976. On each date, it can be seen that the yields on longs were several per cent higher than the yields on shorts, though the difference was more pronounced on the earlier date. However, the yields on shorts do occasionally exceed the yields on longs, and did so, for example, on 26 October 1981 and 27 October 1986, as shown by the bottom two lines of the table, though the tendency was more pronounced on the earlier date. It is necessary to explain why loans of different lengths tend to have different returns. In other words it is necessary to explain what is known as the term structure of interest rates. This section begins by considering why longer term loans tend to attract higher returns and then shows why they sometimes have lower returns.

In part, the tendency for longs to have higher returns than shorts can be explained by the desire of many households, and indeed business, to have funds quickly available for spending when they wish to make purchases. As explained in Chapter 4, this

**Table 2.3** Gross redemption yields on bonds with 5, 10 and 20 year maturities on four selected dates

| Year | Date (%) | Short-dated (5 years) | Medium-dated (10 years) | Long-dated (20 years) |
|------|----------|----------------------|-------------------------|----------------------|
| 1971 | October 27 | 6.25 | 7.23 | 8.28 |
| 1976 | October 27 | 15.77 | 16.13 | 16.40 |
| 1981 | October 26 | 17.88 | 16.74 | 16.24 |
| 1986 | October 27 | 11.09 | 11.00 | 10.66 |

Source: *Bank of England Quarterly Bulletin*, December 1971 Table 30, December 1976 Table 26, December 1981 Table 9 and December 1986 Table 9.1.

desire explains why household and business units keep funds in bank accounts, even when no interest is available, because these funds are highly liquid in the sense that they can be withdrawn – or spent by means of cheques – whenever they wish, and they know precisely how much can be so withdrawn or spent. By extension, units may be willing to hold some funds in those bank or NBFI deposits which earn interest but where a few days' notice of withdrawal is required, for the amount of such funds is also known with certainty, even though they may be less liquid in the sense of not being instantly accessible. By further extension, units may be willing to hold some funds in short-dated fixed interest securities, perhaps for use if some unexpected spending need arises or when some large purchase expected some time hence is actually made; shorts may be held in preference to longs, even though at the time of eventual sale on the stock exchange the receipts will be received no quicker, simply because the prices of securities near to maturity are less volatile and so their values are known with more certainty. In other words, shorts tend to be regarded as less risky than longs, and thus they are likely to have lower returns.

There is, however, a further reason why short-term securities tend to have lower interest rates than long-term ones. To explain this, suppose for a moment that all securities carried equal returns of, say, 10 per cent, and assume for simplicity that there is no inflation. Next, consider a lender who might be prepared to lend £1,000 for, perhaps, 10 years until he retires when he will want his money back, and suppose for simplicity that he always buys newly-issued securities. If he buys fixed-interest securities, then it might seem that he will be indifferent between buying, say, a series of five short-dated two-year securities or buying one 10-year security, or even buying a 20-year security which can be sold later with 10 years still to run. However, the first option carries the risk that interest rates might fall over the 10 years, so that after two years he could find he was able to lend the money repaid to him at only 8 per cent; this risk would be avoided by the second and third options since he would have a security giving him a return of 10 per cent of its purchase price for the whole 10 years. On the other hand, the third option carries the risk that if interest rates are higher in 10 years' time than now, then his security will be worth less than £1,000 and he will make a capital loss. This risk is avoided on the first and second options since, with them, he always holds securities until they mature at face value. It follows that the lender can avoid both risks by buying securities which mature at the time when he wants his money back to spend.

Now consider a business which wants to borrow £1m to finance a new factory with a 20 year life. Suppose for simplicity that it intends to accumulate funds over this period in order to repay its loan at the end. If it issues one million £1 fixed interest securities, then it might seem it will be indifferent between issuing, say, a series of four 5-year debentures, or issuing a single issue of 20-year debentures, or even issuing a single issue of 40-year debentures with a view to buying them back on the stock exchange, as they become available, when the 20 years are complete. However, the first option carries the risk that interest rates will rise over the next few years so that the second and later issues may have to offer higher returns than need be offered now; this risk would be avoided by the second and third options since with them the firm would have only to pay interest each year at the level set initially no matter how much interest rates rose in the meantime. On the other hand, the third option carries the risk that interest rates may be much lower in 20 years' time, so that the firms' securities will be fetching prices higher than their face value and it would cost the firm more than £1 each time it buys one back. This risk would be avoided by the first and second options as the firm would then never have to do more than redeem its debentures at face value. It follows that the borrower can avoid both risks by issuing securities which mature when it wants to repay its loans.

At any moment in time, there will be many lenders who want their money back at different future dates and many borrowers who want to repay on different future dates. Conceivably, their preferences for loans of differing maturities could be met with a common interest rate on all loans. However, suppose that lenders generally prefer shorter-term loans than borrowers. It would be expected that borrowers would offer slightly higher interest rates on longer-term loans to encourage lenders to take the risks they prefer to avoid; and it would be expected that lenders would accept slightly lower interest rates on short term loans to encourage borrowers to take the risks they prefer to avoid. More generally, it can be seen that a divergence of preference between borrowers and lenders over loan lengths offers an explanation of why short-term loans tend to have lower returns than long-term ones.

It should be noted that this tendency gives the opportunity to NBFIs, such as building societies, the chance to make profits for, as Chapter 3 explains, they borrow on a short-term basis and lend long term. Indeed, much the same applies also to banks who, by offering depositors the ability to withdraw on demand, effectively 'borrow' on a very short-term basis, often offering no interest at all – and attracting funds purely because of the safety and convenience they offer depositors – and then use their funds to make loans which are not so readily redeemed. These financial institutions tend to reduce the gap between short and long-term interest rates because they increase the demand for borrowing short and increase the supply of lending long.

It remains to explain why short-term interest rates may sometimes exceed long-term ones. To see this, suppose for the moment that there is no mismatch between the average terms preferred by borrowers and lenders and so, on the basis of the arguments considered in the last few paragraphs, no tendency for long-term claims to offer higher rates than short term. Next, suppose for simplicity that there are just two terms of security available, one-year and two-year, and consider an individual who wishes to lend funds for just two years and who thus has a choice of buying a one-year security now and another in 12 months' time, when the first one matures, or of buying a two-year security now. The individual will prefer the option that offers the higher return over the two-year period. Finally, suppose the interest rate on one-year securities is at present 10 per cent.

Now if the individual expects the rate on one-year securities offered in one year's time to be also 10 per cent, then he would be indifferent between holding two one-year securities in turn or a single two-year security for the whole time if that too had a rate of 10 per cent. If all lenders had similar expectations, then it follows that the rate on two-year securities must be 10 per cent, for if it were higher then no one would buy one-year ones now, and if it were lower than no one would buy two-year ones. If, instead, the individual expects the rate on one-year securities offered in one year's time to be 12 per cent, then he would consider a two-year security as comparable to a succession of two one-year securities only if it had a rate of some 11 per cent. So, if all lenders had similar expectations, then the rate on two-year securities must be some 11 per cent, for if it were lower then no one would buy two-year securities now, and if it were higher then no one would buy one-year ones. Finally, if the individual expects the rate on one-year securities offered in one year's time to be 8 per cent, then he would consider a two-year security as comparable to a succession of two one-year securities only if it had a rate of some 9 per cent. If all lenders had similar expectations, then it follows that the rate on two-year securities must be some 9 per cent, for if it were higher then no one would buy one-year securities now, and if it were lower than no one would buy two-year ones.

Now suppose short-term rates tend to fluctuate between, say, 5 per cent and 15 per cent. Then, when they are 5 per cent, there is likely to be a widespread expectation that they will rise, and such expectations tend to result in long-term rates being higher than short-term ones; conversely, when they are 5 per cent, there is likely to be a widespread expectation that they will fall, and such expectations tend to result in long-term rates being lower than short-term rates. In other words, long-term rates will tend to fluctuate less widely than short-term ones. It follows that if there were no mismatch between the average terms preferred by borrowers and lenders, then short-term rates might exceed long-term ones just as frequently as long-term rates exceed short-term ones. In practice, there is a mismatch and it has been seen that this creates a pressure for long-term rates to exceed short-term ones. However, at points in time when sharp falls in interest rates are thought likely, the forces just outlined can result in this pressure being overcome and short-term rates exceeding long-term ones. The figures in the bottom two lines of Table 2.3 suggest that such thoughts were widespread in October 1981 and October 1986. Why might this have been so? The answer is no doubt that nominal interest rates in October 1981 and real interest rates in 1986 were close to their all-time highs!

# 3

# The elements of a banking system

## Introduction

Chapter 1 noted that various items have been used as money, and looked particularly at precious metals, coins, bank-notes and bank deposits. It will be recalled that when the first three of these types of money are used, then a physical object is transferred from the buyer to the seller, but when the fourth type is used, then bankers are instructed to reduce the buyer's deposit and increase the seller's. Chapter 1 explained, too, that in England there is now only one bank – the Bank of England – which is permitted to issue bank-notes. A similar arrangement applies in many countries, though in some, such as Scotland, several banks are allowed to issue notes. It was seen, also, that banks could actually create money by creating deposits, simply by writing larger numbers in the accounts of borrowers. Chapter 2 looked at many of the main types of financial claims that can be found in a modern economy.

The purpose of the present chapter is to build on the material in the previous two chapters to give a general idea of how a banking system works in a modern economy. The description given here corresponds broadly to what happens in present-day England, though the arrangements are much the same in many other countries. In the interests of clarity, however, the description presents a simplified view of the real world. Later chapters, especially Chapter 7, give more details of the arrangements in the United Kingdom.

The two essential features of any modern banking system are a central bank and clearing banks, and most of this chapter focuses on the relationships between the two. However, the final section looks at non-bank financial intermediaries, or NBFIs. As their name implies, these are not banks, and they are not able to create money, but they have some features in common with banks.

## A bankers' bank

It was explained at the end of Chapter 1 that when one customer of a bank makes out a cheque in favour of another customer of the same bank, then the banker merely reduces the payer's account and raises the payee's. There is no change in the total level of deposits and so no change in the bank's total liabilities; moreover, there is no change in the composition or the level of the bank's assets. However, if a customer of one bank, A, makes out a cheque in favour of a customer of another bank, B, then A will reduce the account of its customer, thus cutting total deposits and so liabilities at bank A, while B will raise the account of its customer, thus raising total deposits and so liabilities at bank B. At the same time, Chapter 1 argued that bank B will demand an equivalent amount of cash from bank A, a reasonable request as one of A's customers is transferring money to one of B's, so that A's cash, and hence its assets, will fall by the amount of the cheque concerned while B's will rise by the same amount.

This simple system suggests that all cheque payments by the customers of one bank to the customers of another will involve movements of cash between the two banks concerned. It is easy to see, though, that if cash did in practice move in response to each such payment, then it could be moving between banks A and B many times each day, even though the total amounts moving in each direction might be very similar. It is clearly sensible for each bank merely to note how much it should pay to the other and receive from the other during the course of the day, and to settle matters up at the end of the day with a single movement. The amount moved may be very small compared to the amounts of the cheques concerned. For instance, if A's customers pay cheques for £1,000 to B's and B's customers pay cheques for £950 to A's, then a single movement of £50 from A to B at the end of the day will be all that is required. This periodic settlement of net amounts owed is termed clearing.

In eighteenth-century England, clearing took place more frequently in London than elsewhere, and Kindleberger (1984, 78) noted that in northern England clearing occurred only once or twice each week. The banks at that time cleared their debts to each other with Bank of England notes. It will be recalled that no other big bank could issue notes after 1742, so these were clearly the best notes to use. Now the banks soon realized that the physical movement of these notes, which led to transport costs and security risks, would be avoided if all the banks agreed to open accounts for themselves at one bank, for then bank B, if it owed money to bank A, could simply make out a cheque which reduced its deposit at this 'bankers' bank' and raise A's deposit there. As debts were initially settled in Bank of England notes, it is not surprising that when banks decided to open up accounts at one chosen bank then it was the Bank of England which was chosen. The banks which belong to this clearing system are known as clearing banks and their deposits at the Bank of England are included on the assets side of their balance sheets. The English banks who operate the system have set up an institution known as the London Bankers' Clearing House which works out the amounts owed to and by each bank. The Bank of England clears the debts of the clearing banks banking there at daily intervals.

The last paragraph showed what happened if bank A's customers receive more money from bank B's customers than they pay to them: bank A will want to be given money by bank B, and the Bank of England handles the situation by raising bank A's deposit with it and cutting bank B's deposit. But what happens if bank A's customers receive more money from the Bank of England's own depositors than they receive from them? This is perfectly possible as the Bank of England has depositors of its own quite apart from the clearing banks. In this situation, bank A will want to be given money by the Bank of England, and the Bank of England obliges by simply raising the amount recorded in bank A's deposit with it. Conversely, the Bank of England reduces the size of bank A's deposits on days when A's customers pay more to the Bank of England's own depositors then they receive from them.

Even before it assumed the role of bankers' bank, the Bank of England was distinct from other banks on account of it being the main issuer of bank-notes. As it happens, the issuing of these notes has been handled since 1844 by a separate department known as the Issue Department; the activities of this department are considered further in Chapter 7 and need not be explored here.

The Bank of England's banking activities are handled by its Banking Department. This department is much like any other bank with liabilities consisting of deposits from its customers, among whom of course are the clearing banks, while its assets comprise a prudent amount of cash plus loans. A key difference from other banks is that the prudent amount of cash is very small. Most banks must keep cash equal to a few per cent of their total deposits or liabilities so that they can quickly meet any sudden widespread desire for cash by their depositors. The Bank of England could quickly meet such a desire by its depositors without actually keeping a large stock of bank-notes for the simple reason that it can print new bank-notes as and when required! Of course, the fact that the Bank of England can print as many notes as it likes and have a negligible cash ratio means that in principle there is little constraint on the amount of money it could create in either cash form or deposits. In practice, though, there is a very effective constraint which is that the Bank, which is owned by the government, has the responsibility of trying to keep the total stock of money in the country at the level desired by the government. More generally one function of the Bank of England – as indeed is the case with all central banks – is to promote financial stability, and this objective would not be helped if the Bank was tempted to generate frequent increases in the money stock by creating more money itself.

## The government's bank

Although the Banking Department does not need much cash, it would have had an influx of cash when the other banks decided to open up deposits there. However, it would not have kept most of this cash for long, and it could carry on as the bankers' bank perfectly well without. These points can be illustrated with the help of the purely hypothetical figures in Table 3.1. As with the tables in Chapter 1, it is supposed that the total value of a bank's main liabilities equals the total of its main assets. This assumption is purely for simplicity and does not affect the implications of the analysis in any way. The top part of Table 3.1 relates to the Banking Department of the Bank of England and the bottom part to the clearing banks; the figures at the bottoms are combined figures for all the clearing banks. For convenience, the details of assets in each part are shown below those for liabilities rather than to the right of them as was done in the tables in Chapter 1.

Stage 1 indicates the situation just before the Bank of England becomes adopted as the bankers' bank. The Bank of England is supposed here to have total deposits of £100m, while the combined deposits of the other banks are £1,000m. It follows, incidentally, that the total money stock in the country will equal the total value of all bank deposits (that is £1,100m in all) plus the amount of cash held outside banks. It is supposed that the assets of all banks initially comprise cash (that is notes and coins) and loans, just like the assets of the bank shown in Table 1.9. The Bank of England is assumed to want a cash ratio, that is the ratio of cash to total liabilities, of just 1 per cent whereas the other banks want a ratio of at least 10 per cent (though in practice cash ratios are much lower than these). The only further feature to notice is that the

**Table 3.1**   Basic central and clearing bank relationships

| Bank of England | Stage 1 | Stage 2 | Stage 3 | Stage 4 |
|---|---|---|---|---|
| | | | | £m |
| **Liabilities** | | | | |
| Public deposits | 20 | 20 | 70 | 20 |
| Bankers' deposits | 0 | 50 | 50 | 90 |
| Other deposits | 80 | 80 | 80 | 80 |
| Total | 100 | 150 | 200 | 190 |
| **Assets** | | | | |
| Notes and coin | 1 | 51 | 51 | 41 |
| Securities | 0 | 0 | 50 | 50 |
| Loans | 99 | 99 | 99 | 99 |
| Total | 100 | 150 | 200 | 190 |

| Clearing banks (combined balance sheet) | Stage 1 | Stage 2 | Stage 3 | Stage 4 |
|---|---|---|---|---|
| | | | | £m |
| **Liabilities** | | | | |
| Deposits | 1000 | 1000 | 1000 | 1050 |
| Total | 1000 | 1000 | 1000 | 1050 |
| **Assets** | | | | |
| Notes and coin | 100 | 50 | 50 | 60 |
| Balance at Bank of England | 0 | 50 | 50 | 90 |
| Loans | 900 | 900 | 900 | 900 |
| Total | 1000 | 1000 | 1000 | 1050 |

upper part of the table splits the Bank of England's deposits into two parts, public deposits and other deposits.

The public deposits are effectively the government's deposits. They are separated from other deposits in order to clarify what happens in the later stage 3, but for the moment the important point to grasp is that the government holds deposits at the Bank of England, that is to say the Bank of England is the government's bank. In principle, bankers need not choose to use the government's bank as the bankers' bank, but in practice the same bank does fulfil both functions in most countries for various historical and institutional reasons. In England, for instance, the Bank of England has had a special relationship with the government from the time it was founded in 1694. It was this relationship which led to it becoming the government's bank and led also to it becoming the main issuer of notes; and, as explained above, it was because banks initially cleared their business with these notes that the Bank of England seemed the logical choice for a bankers' bank.

In stage 1, the other banks have no deposits at the Bank of England, a point confirmed by the zeros for the relevant entries in their assets and its liabilities. Now suppose they decide to open accounts there in order that clearing can in future be done by directing the Bank of England to transfer money from one bank's account to another's rather than with the physical movement of cash between the banks concerned. Suppose, too, that the other banks deposit half their holdings of notes and coin at the Bank of England for this purpose. Accordingly, the entry for their assets of notes and coin (which refers to cash held on their own premises) falls from £100m to £50m, but their assets remain at the same total level as before because they now have a new asset, namely deposits at the bank of England totalling £50m. This information is shown in the lower part of the table for stage 2. Notice that the clearing banks can still be held to have a cash ratio of 10 per cent, for if there was a sudden widespread desire by their depositors for cash, then they could meet it with the £50m in notes and coin held on their premises and the £50m they could withdraw in cash from the Bank of England. The upper part of the table shows that the Bank of England has acquired £50m extra assets of cash deposited by the other banks, matched by £50m of extra liabilities as a result of the accounts opened up in the process by the bankers. From now on, clearing between the other banks can be done each day by reducing the bankers' deposits of banks whose customers pay more to customers of other banks than they receive and vice versa, a process which will not in fact alter the total amount of bankers' deposits at the Bank of England or indeed any other numbers under stage 2. Individual banks will find their total assets and liabilities falling and rising as they lose or gain at the expense of other banks, but their combined assets and liabilities may well be constant at the figures shown.

It can be seen that the total level of bank deposits in the country has risen from £1,100m in stage 1 to £1,150m in stage 2, so it might be assumed that statistics for the country's money stock would also show a rise of £50m. The statistics certainly would show this rise if they were based on the simple money stock definition so far used, that is total bank deposits plus cash held outside banks, for the former have risen while the latter has stayed constant. However, measures of the money stock are ultimately meant to show how much money the people in a country can use as a medium of exchange and this has not risen between stages 1 and 2. The people had £1,100m between them in deposits in stage 1, and there is nothing more for them to spend in stage 2. Accordingly, the money stock definition must now be modified to cover bank deposits *other than those held by bankers* plus cash held outside the banks, and this is £1,100m plus any cash held outside the banks in both stages 1 and 2. Another way of seeing why bankers' deposits are excluded is to recall that the money stock does not rise when a private citizen places some cash in a bank, for the rise in the level of deposits will be offset by a fall in the cash held outside banks; and there is no reason to regard it as rising if some banks in turn decide to deposit some of the cash they hold with other banks.

As a result of the changes between stages 1 and 2, the Bank of England has now acquired a new ratio of 51/150, or just about a third, which is much higher than it needs, but this could soon fall. To see how, suppose, for instance, that the government decides to purchase some military equipment for £50m from private firms all of which bank at the clearing banks. The government may wish to have a deposit still worth £20m even after the purchase and so it may not want to use the money already in its deposit. It could decide to finance the purchase by raising taxes of £50m, but suppose instead it decides to borrow £50m from the Bank of England. The Bank could simply increase the government's deposit by £50m, raising its own liabilities by the same amount, and it could regard this as just another loan, so that it would raise the figure for loans in its assets by £50m and hence raise its total assets by £50m. A more conventional arrangement is actually for the Bank to buy £50m worth of bonds from the government. These might be new bonds with maturity in, say, fifteen years when the government would be obliged to buy them back for £50m; meanwhile the government would have to pay interest to the Bank each year. On this approach, the Bank's balance sheet would become as shown in stage 3, with both assets and liabilities £50m more than in stage 2, for it has acquired securities worth £50m as assets (just as the investments of the firm concerned in Table 1.1 were assets to it) and the £50m it has paid to the government have been put into the public deposits. The word 'put' is perhaps a little strong, for all that has happened is that a higher number will have been recorded for the government's account.

The government can now purchase its equipment. It will make out cheques totalling £50m to the suppliers and these cheques instruct its bank, the Bank of England, to pay £50m to the suppliers. The suppliers will take the cheques to their banks which will raise the suppliers' deposits by £50m, so that the combined clearing bank deposits rise to £1,050m. These banks will then demand £50m from the government's bank. They might well ask the Bank of England to place the £50m in their deposits there, so raising both their balances there and their total assets by £50m; but they could instead decide to take £50m cash from the bank of England, in which case the figures for their assets of notes and coin, and also their total assets, would rise by this amount. Suppose they decide to do a bit of both, taking £10m cash out to raise their assets of notes and coin and having £40m added to their balances at the Bank of England. In that case, their assets will have the composition shown at the bottom of stage 4 with a total of £1,050m.

Now consider what will happen to the Bank of England's balance sheet. As far as its liabilities are concerned, it will take £50m from the public deposits when the government's money is spent, so these return to £20m. Had the other banks decided to keep all the £50m they acquire in their Bank of England deposits, then these would have risen by that amount to £100m, so that the Bank's total liabilities would have stayed at £200m. Its assets would also have been unaffected, though its cash ratio would have fallen to 51/200, or just about a quarter. As it is, the banks take £10m cash out, so that their deposits rise only to £90m, and this leaves the Bank's total liabilities at £190m. At the same time, its holding of cash falls from £51m to £41m, leaving its assets also at £190m.

A number of points need to be made about the new situation. First, the Bank of England's cash ratio has fallen from the one-third it was in stage 2 to little over a quarter (51:190). Its cash ratio could fall further in time, when the government borrowed from it again and spent the money thus acquired. In practice, this happens so often that the Bank would have no difficulty in soon securing the negligible cash ratio it likes. Secondly, the clearing banks have deposits of £90m at the Bank of England and could demand this amount in cash, even though the Banking Department at present has only £41m worth of notes and coins. If the Banking Department ever found itself faced with a demand for cash withdrawals by the clearing banks that exceeded its current holding of notes and coins, then (as explained in Chapter 7) it could always replenish those stocks by suitable dealings with the Issue Department. Thirdly, notice that the total assets and liabilities of the clearing banks have risen by £50m because their customers have received £50m from a customer of the central bank. The clearing banks' total assets will rise whenever their customers receive more from the central bank's customers than they pay to them, and they will fall whenever the converse happens.

Finally, notice that the money stock is now £1,150m plus any cash held outside banks. It is true that total bank deposits are now £1,050m plus £190m, which is £1,240m, but of course the £90m of bankers' deposits at the Bank of England must be deducted from this to leave just £1,150m deposits to be included in the money stock figure. It is not surprising that the stock has risen by £50m for the Bank of England created an extra £50m in stage 3 when it increased the size of the government's deposit, just as the bank in Table 1.8 created money by giving a £50m deposit to a borrower. It follows that the money stock will rise whenever the government borrows money from the Bank of England.

The money stock may also rise if the government borrows from the clearing banks. To see this, return to stage 2 and suppose that the government sought to open accounts with these banks and asked them for a loan totalling £50m. The initial effect would be to raise these banks' assets by £50m (in the form of extra loans) and also to raise their liabilities (in the form of extra deposits) and so, in turn, to raise the money stock. The only effects of the government then spending its new deposits would be that clearing bank deposits would change hands while the total remained at £1,050m. Notice, though, that the banks' cash ratio would now be £100m to £1,050m or under 10 per cent. If they sought to restore this ratio to 10 per cent by calling in other loans, then the money stock would fall again.

Interestingly, there would be no expansionary effect on the money stock if the government borrowed from ordinary members of the public, known as the non-bank public. Any potential changes to the stage 2 figure caused by £50m passing in loans from the non-bank public to the government would be precisely offset by the government expenditure of £50m to its suppliers, so the stage 2 figures would also show the final position. Thus the money stock would be unaltered at £1,100m plus cash held outside banks.

## Money creation and the credit multiplier with one clearing bank

It will have been noticed from the discussion of stage 4 in Table 3.1 that once the government starts borrowing from the Bank of England so the Bank of England's assets end up including some securities as well as cash and loans. In practice all banks have assets in the form of securities as well as in the form of loans. In Chapter 1, it was explained in connection with Table 1.9 that a deposit-taking bank which so desired could expand both its assets and its liabilities by giving a loan to someone simply by writing a larger number in that person's account. It could instead expand both its assets and liabilities by buying a security off a depositor and writing a larger number in that person's account, just as the Bank of England expanded both its assets and liabilities between stages 2 and 3 of Table 3.1 by writing a larger number in the government's account and acquiring some securities from the government in return.

The advantages to banks of expanding their assets and liabilities are obvious, for they will charge interest on any loans they make and hope to get a return from any securities they hold; they hope such returns will come as capital gains on bills, which gain in value as they approach maturity, as interest and, perhaps, capital gains, on fixed-interest securities, and as dividends and capital gains on equities. (They would also hope to earn dividends and capital gains on any unit trust units they held, but on the whole they do not have such units as they are of most appeal to small investors.)

However, such expansion also carries disadvantages for banks. First, there can be risks from the new assets themselves, particularly the risk that loans made by banks will not be repaid, and that companies in which banks hold securities may not earn sufficient profits to pay the expected dividends and interest or to redeem fixed-interest securities. Secondly, the expansion reduces the ratio of cash to deposits and so raises the chances of the bank being unable to meet its obligations to its depositors if there is a sudden widespread demand by them for cash. Of course, this second problem is really only applicable to clearing banks as the Bank of England can always print more notes to meet the demands of its depositors.

It is to keep this second risk at an acceptable level that all banks seek to keep the ratio of their cash to their deposits at or above some minimum prudent level. Indeed, in many countries a minimum ratio is laid down which the banks must adhere to. In calculating a bank's cash ratio, of course, its cash can be taken to comprise both stocks of notes and coin held on its premises and its deposit at the Bank of England which it could always demand to withdraw in cash. Now if the clearing banks maintain a minimum ratio of cash to total deposits, and if the amount of cash held by them is fixed at a particular point of time, then there must also be some upper limit on their total levels of liabilities and assets. Equally, if the amount of cash held by them rises (and it rose, for example, from £100m to £150m between stages 3 and 4 of Table 3.1) then the total level of their assets and liabilities can also rise. This section considers how far this level can rise in a simplified case where there is only one clearing bank. The next section considers the slightly more complex real world situation where there is more than one clearing bank.

To consider the situation with one bank, return to Table 3.1 and assume that all the clearing banks merged to form a single bank. At stage 3 this bank would have had assets of £1,000m with £100m in cash; it would then have acquired a further £50m in cash in stage 4. A similar situation applies to the single clearing bank shown in Table 3.2 which starts in stage 1 there with total assets and liabilities of £1,000m of which £100m are in cash, and then moves in stage 2 to a situation where an injection of an extra £50m cash has raised its cash holdings to £150m and its total assets and liabilities to £1,050m. The extra cash might have arrived as a result of government purchases from the bank's customers. These purchases could relate to military or any other equipment desired by the government, or to purchases of labour from government employees, or even to purchases by the government of securities held by the general public. It will be noticed that the bank in Table 3.2 is reckoned to have both securities and loans for its non-cash assets, and it will be seen that no distinction is made between cash held as notes and coin and cash held as a deposit at the Bank of England, for the way in which the clearing bank divides its cash holdings has no bearing on the present discussion.

Two further points should be made about the starting position of stage 1 in Table 3.2. First, the total money stock will be the £1,000m of deposits held at the clearing bank, plus any deposits held at the central bank (other than bankers' deposits) plus any cash held by the public. Secondly, the bank in Table 3.2 has a cash ratio of 10 per cent (that is the ratio of its cash to its total liabilities). Suppose that 10 per cent is the lowest ratio the bank considers prudent (or is allowed to have). In that case, it would at this stage be unwilling to lend money to any new prospective borrowers seeking loans.

**Table 3.2**   Deposit creation with a single clearing bank

| Clearing bank | Stage 1 | Stage 2 | Stage 3 | Stage 4 |
|---|---|---|---|---|
| | | | | £m |
| **Liabilities** | | | | |
| Deposits | 1000 | 1050 | 1500 | 1200 |
| Total | 1000 | 1050 | 1500 | 1200 |
| **Assets** | | | | |
| Cash | 100 | 150 | 150 | 120 |
| Securities | 400 | 400 | 600 | 480 |
| Loans | 500 | 500 | 750 | 600 |
| Total | 1000 | 1050 | 1500 | 1200 |

If, for instance, a large company sought a loan for £1m, then the bank knows that granting it the loan by writing an extra £1m in its deposit will raise the bank's total liabilities to £101m, matched by a £1m rise in the loan component of its assets; but its cash holding would stay put at £100m, as the bank would have acquired no more cash, so its cash ratio would become £100m to £1,001m which is below 10 per cent. Thus the bank will not give any new loans, at least not until some current ones are repaid, and it is regarded as being 'fully lent'.

Now as soon as the clearing bank acquires its extra £50m cash as a result of government purchases, its total liabilities and assets rise by £50 as shown in stage 2 (which corresponds closely to stage 4 in Table 3.1). There is an extra £50m in the accounts of those depositors who have received cheques from the government, and an extra £50m in cash which the bank receives from the government's bank, that is the central bank. As a consequence, the bank's cash ratio has risen to £150m : £1,050m which is nearly 15 per cent. In this situation, the bank will be willing to make more loans and to acquire more securities, and it might well have its eyes on a situation like the one shown by stage 3. For if the bank can persuade enough people to take out more loans and to sell it securities, in return for more money in their deposits, then it will itself get more income from interest and so on during the year; and it may well hope to raise the total level of loans and securities up to £1,350m, as shown for stage 3, for it will then have total liabilities of £1,500m which is the highest level it can sustain with its cash of £150m if it wants a cash ratio no less than 10 per cent. Of course, the people who borrow from the bank or sell it securities may well spend the deposits they acquire in the process, perhaps using them to buy items such as new cars, but so long as they make these payments by cheque and withdraw no cash, then the bank will find its total level of liabilities (and assets) staying at £1,500m, though the deposits of the borrowers or security sellers will fall while the deposits of the sellers of cars and so on will rise.

As shown by stage 1 and 3 in Table 3.2, the initial rise in cash of £50m could lead to a subsequent rise in liabilities of £500m. With a cash ratio of 10 per cent, or 1/10, an initial rise in the clearing bank's cash could lead to a tenfold rise in its liabilities because each £1 extra cash permits liabilities to rise by £10 without the target cash ratio being overstepped. If the bank wanted a ratio of, say, 1/8, or 1/12, then it would find an extra £1 cash enabling it to raise its total liabilities by £8 or £12. Indeed, it can be seen that if the ratio is expressed simply as r, then a rise in cash of £1 could enable total liabilities to rise by £(1/r); thus if r = 1/10, say, then the expansion allowed by an extra £2 in cash will be £(1/(1/10)) which is in fact £10. More generally, an initial rise in cash of $\Delta C$ will lead to a maximum rise in liabilities of $\Delta L$ with $\Delta L$ given by $\Delta L$ = $\Delta C/r$ where r is the target cash ratio. This tendency for bank deposits, that is to say money, to expand by far more than the expansion in the amount of cash held by the clearing bank is known as the credit multiplier.

In practice, though, it might well be the case that purchases of £50m by the government would not lead to the clearing bank's liabilities rising by £50m/r, that is £500m in the present example, despite the analysis of the last two paragraphs. There are four reasons why the increase might be a little less dramatic. First, the clearing bank might not find it easy to persuade enough credit-worthy people to take out new loans or enough people to sell it securities for it to be able to expand by £500m, even though it is willing to lend and buy. Of course, it can tempt people to borrow by reducing the interest rates it charges on loans, but there is a minimum level it must charge to feel it worthwhile to take the risk of lending, and if there is not much demand for loans then it might find insufficient new loans being taken out, even at this minimum level. Equally it can tempt people to sell securities by offering very high prices, but many security holders may hang on to them, pleased to see their wealth increasing as security prices start rising but still anxious to acquire the income their securities give them. However, the bank will probably find that these problems disappear eventually. In particular, those businesses which do borrow money may expand and pay more wages, and some workers whose incomes rise will then decide to take out new (or larger) loans for, perhaps, new cars; this will increase car sales which may tempt car manufacturers to borrow to expand, and it may increase their workers' wages and tempt them to borrow for, say, house improvements and so on.

Secondly, if the bank is generally successful in raising the level of its liabilities and deposits, then the public will end up holding higher deposits and so have more money. Now people can hold money in two forms, namely cash and bank deposits, and they may feel there is an optimum ratio between the two. So if the bank's strategy of lending and buying securities initially succeeds in raising the stock of money, then it is also likely to stimulate a cash drain from the bank as people seek to restore their preferred cash to deposit ratio. To see the effect of this cash drain, return to the example in Table 3.2 and assume that the public like a cash to bank deposit ratio of 15 per cent.

Now suppose that everything was in equilibrium in stage 1. If so, then the public would have had cash of £150m, this being equal to 15 per cent of their deposits of £1,000m. The bank, of course, had cash of £100m, this being equal to 10 per cent of total deposits. So the banks and public had £250m cash between them, and in an equilibrium position like this 2/5 of the cash is held by the banks and 3/5 by the public. When the government pays out its £50m in cheques in stage 2, £50m is initially added to the accounts of the recipients and the bank's cash holdings also rise by £50m. However, the system is no longer in equilibrium, partly because the banks now have a cash ratio of nearly 15 per cent, as discussed earlier, and partly because the public now have a ratio of under 15 per cent, for their cash in stage 2 is still £150m, yet their deposits have now risen from stage 1. The public will now start to withdraw some cash, and in fact a new equilibrium cannot be reached until the extra £50m cash in the system is split in the equilibrium ratio of 2/5 (or £20m) to the banks and 3/5 (or £30m) to the public.

Thus the final position is not as shown in stage 3, which ignored the cash drain, but as in stage 4 which shows that this drain eventually leaves the bank with only £20m extra cash. Its total cash is thus £120m which supports total assets and liabilities of £1,200m, and indeed all the figures on its balance sheet are just 20 per cent higher than they were originally in stage 1. The public end up with cash of £180m which is £30 more than before and is 15 per cent of their new level of bank deposits, that is £1,200m. The effect of the cash drain is to make the impact of the initial cash injection on the bank's liabilities much less dramatic. Indeed, $\Delta L$ is given now not by $\Delta C/r$ but by $\Delta C/(r + d)$ where d is the percentage of L which the public likes to hold in cash. In this example $(r + d) = (0.10 + 0.15)$ which is 0.25, so $\Delta L = \Delta C/0.25$. As $\Delta C = 50$, so $\Delta L = 50/0.25$, that is 200, as shown by the rise in liabilities between the initial stage 1 and the final equilibrium in stage 4. It should be noticed that the initial increase in cash of £50m led to an increase in bank deposits, $\Delta L$, of £200m, and it led to a rise in cash held by the public of £30m, which is $d\Delta L$. Thus the rise in the money stock, $\Delta M$, can be found as $\Delta L(1 + d)$ which is $\Delta C(1 + d)/(r + d)$ since $\Delta L$ is $\Delta C/(r + d)$.

A third reason why the rise in deposits may be less dramatic than suggested by stage 3 is that as the bank's customers collectively acquire more money, partly through their initial receipts of £50m and partly through borrowing from the bank and selling securities to it, so they will doubtless spend more money. So long as they confine their cheque purchases to one another, the process taking the bank from stage 2 to stage 4 will not be affected. However, some cheque purchases may be from the central bank's customers, perhaps in the form of putting more money into National Savings Certificates sold by its chief customer, the government. This will cause a further cash drain as the clearing bank then loses cash, just as it gained cash in stage 2 when its customers sold items to the government.

Fourthly, it is possible that the clearing bank will want a higher cash ratio after the cash injection than it wanted before. The point is that in reality a bank may well not adopt a fixed ratio and decide, say, that 10.001 per cent is always safe and acceptable while 9.999 per cent is always dangerous and imprudent. Rather, it will simply feel that any ratio below 100 per cent carries some risk, and that lower ratios are more risky than higher ones. Of course, the bank makes a profit by making loans and buying securities, actions which cause it to take risks by having a ratio below 100 per cent. It is not difficult to imagine that the bank would be willing to take more risks, by operating with a lower ratio, at a time when the returns (or interest rates) on loans and securities were high than at a time when they were low. It follows that if interest rates fall, then the bank will seek a higher cash ratio.

Now in the example considered in Table 3.2, interest rates would be expected to fall after stage 2 as the bank sought to lend more money and to buy more securities. So instead of ending up in stage 4 with the same ratio that it had to begin with, it might end up with a slightly higher one and so have total liabilities rather less than shown there. It should be stressed, though, that this point is relevant only when banks can choose the ratios at which they operate. In many countries, they probably operate much of the time with a ratio higher than they would choose, the ratio probably being laid down for them by the central bank. In such cases, the ratios they actually use may change very little when expansion or contraction take place. They might change very slightly, though, for banks will typically operate with a ratio slightly above the one required in order to have a safety margin, that is to ensure they can sustain a small cash loss without breaching the rules, and they may risk lower safety margins when interest rates are high.

# Money creation and the credit multiplier with several banks

The previous section showed how deposits, and so money, would be created when there is an injection of cash into the only clearing bank in an economy. Ignoring the possibility of cash drains to the public and to the central bank, and assuming the bank adopts a constant cash ratio, r, then an injection of cash equal to $\Delta C$ could cause a rise in its liabilities of $\Delta L$ where $\Delta L = \Delta C/r$. Strictly speaking, this shows the increase in liabilities if the bank starts off being fully lent and ends up being fully lent.

In the real world, however, there is more than one clearing bank. Suppose they each adopted the same ratio r. Would their combined liabilities be liable to rise by $\Delta C/r$ if they enjoyed between them a cash injection of $\Delta C$? The answer is that they would, so that the same formula $\Delta L = \Delta C/r$ applies. Nevertheless, there is an important difference from the one-bank case. In a one-bank situation, the bank can seek to expand its loans and securities rapidly when it receives new cash. In contrast, a bank in a many-bank case must expand more cautiously, even though the banks between them can eventually expand by the same total amount. The need for caution can be illustrated with the help of Table 3.3. The figures here relate to one bank, bank A, in an economy with several clearing banks. It is assumed that bank A seeks a 25 per cash ratio and that it also seeks to have securities forming a further 25 per cent of total assets so that loans make up the remaining 50 per cent. Thus A is happy with the starting position shown in stage 1. Two final assumptions in this example are that just one-fifth of the country's depositors bank at A, and that A has just one-fifth of total deposits (which must therefore be £10,000m).

Now suppose the government makes a major purchase for £255m and that it makes it from one of A's depositors. The immediate effects, shown in stage 2, will be to raise total deposits at A by £255m and to raise A's cash by £255m as A can claim this amount from the government's bank, that is the central bank. Bank A now has a much

**Table 3.3** Deposit creation with several clearing banks – the results of imprudence

| Clearing bank A | Stage 1 | Stage 2 | Stage 3A | Stage 3B | Stage 4 £m |
|---|---|---|---|---|---|
| **Liabilities** | | | | | |
| Deposits | 2000 | 2255 | 3020 | 2816 | 2408 |
| Total | 2000 | 2255 | 3020 | 2816 | 2408 |
| **Assets** | | | | | |
| Cash | 500 | 755 | 755 | 551 | 143 |
| Securities | 500 | 500 | 755 | 755 | 755 |
| Loans | 1000 | 1000 | 1510 | 1510 | 1510 |
| Total | 2000 | 2255 | 3020 | 2816 | 2408 |

higher cash ratio than its target of 25 per cent, for its ratio is over 33 per cent (£755m to £2,255m). Inspired by the analysis of the last section, A's directors might reckon that with £255m extra cash they could afford to buy £255m extra securities and to make £510m new loans, and so try to take the bank to the position shown in stage 3A, where they would again have a cash ratio of 25 per cent (£755m to £3,020m). As it happens, the bank certainly could buy securities and make new loans to these amounts, but it would be very imprudent. The reason is that, with such action, A would be much more likely to move straight from stage 2 to the position shown in 3B, not the one in 3A, and it would then soon move to the one shown in stage 4. In stage 3B its cash ratio is just under 20 per cent (£51m to £2,816m) and in stage 4 it is under 6 per cent (£143m to £2,408m)!

Why would A move straight to position 3B? The reason for this relates to its purchases of £255m worth of securities. It would instruct a stockbroker to buy these securities on the stock exchange. The stockbroker would have no idea which banks the sellers held their deposits at, so he could not ensure that all the sellers banked at A. Indeed, given that only one-fifth of the country's depositors bank at A, the odds are that only one-fifth of the securities, or £51m, would be sold by A's depositors and that the rest, £204m, would be bought by depositors at other banks. The other banks would raise their combined deposits by £204m and would balance this by raising their assets by £204m in cash which they would demand from A, which means A's cash would fall by that amount from £755m to £551m. As for A's deposits, these would actually rise by £561m from £2,255 to £2,816m; £510m of this increase would go to those depositors taking out the new loans for this amount, for they would have larger numbers written in their accounts, and the remaining £51m would go to those of A's depositors who did sell securities to A on the stock exchange.

It can be seen that the imprudent purchase of £255m securities plus the making of £510m new loans has taken A to stage 3B with a cash ratio of £51m to £2,816m, which is under 20 per cent and well below A's target of 25 per cent. Worse will follow. The people who have borrowed the £510m will have borrowed with a view to spending. Business borrowers may buy new machinery while domestic borrowers may buy new cars or extend their homes. So the new loans of £510m will soon be spent, and it is likely that some four-fifths, or around £408m, will be spent in favour of depositors at other banks. This means total deposits at A will fall by that amount to the £2,408m shown in stage 4, while cash will also fall by that amount to £143m. The upshot is a cash ratio of £14.3m to £2,408m, which is under 6 per cent when A seeks a ratio of 25 per cent! A may be able to redeem the situation a little by borrowing from other banks. Also – as explained in a later section – some bank deposits attract interest and A may raise the rate it pays on these interest-earning deposits in the hope of attracting funds presently held at other banks. However, both these options are costly.

It is clear that A should have considered a more cautious approach. Table 3.4 shows what this would entail. The starting position is illustrated in stage 1, and the immediate effects of the new cash are illustrated in stage 2, the figures in each stage being identical to the corresponding columns in Table 3.3. To ensure that its cash ratio does not fall below the target 25 per cent, A must actually expand its securities and loans by just £225m, and to keep these two assets in the desired proportion it should buy securities worth £75m and make new loans for £150m. If, by chance, all the securities were bought from its own depositors, then it would end up as shown in stage 3A with the increases in securities and loans raising total deposits by £225m to £2,480m. In fact, it is likely that four-fifths of the securities, that is £60m, will be bought from depositors elsewhere, and only one-fifth, or £15m, from A's own depositors, so that the immediate effects of the expansion will be as shown in stage 3B. A's deposits rise by just £165m, from £2,255m to £2,420m, £150m of the increase going to those of its depositors who have taken out the new loans and £15m to those of its depositors who sold it securities. A's cash falls by £60m, from £755m to £695m, as it is obliged to give cash to the other banks whose depositors have sold it securities for £60m. Of course, the depositors who have borrowed the new £150m will want to spend it, and are likely to spend four-fifths, or £120m, in favour of depositors at other banks. The upshot, shown in stage 4, is for deposits at A to fall by £120m, from £2,420m to £2,300m, and for cash also to fall by £120m, from £695m to £575m. This leaves A with a cash ratio of just 25 per cent (£575m to £2,300m).

It must be stressed that stage 4 is not an end to the story. Bank A initially acquires £255m extra cash, but it now has only £75m more than it started with, that is £575m less £500m. The remaining £180m of the new cash in the system has passed to the other banks. This means that they can each expand, and hence that some of the cash will return to A, just as A's expansion caused cash to flow elsewhere. Thus A can expand again, and so on and so on. Where will it all stop? The answer is that if cash drains are ignored, then the banks between them – but not A alone – will keep the whole £255m extra cash, and if they all seek a 25 per cent cash ratio then the system will not settle down until the banks' combined deposits are £1,020m more than they were to start with – this assumes they start off fully lent and end up fully lent – for until there has been this much expansion there will be one or more banks with cash ratios above target and these banks will embark on more expansion. Thus the multi-plier formula $\Delta L = \Delta C/r$ still applies, $\Delta L$ being £1,020m which equals $\Delta C/r$, that is £255m/0.25, but it could be some time before the full $\Delta L$ is realised.

It is perfectly appropriate to consider the effects of the initial cash increase on the banking system as a whole by using balance sheets relating to all banks combined, as shown in Table 3.5. Stage 1 shows the initial position, and the figures reflect the corresponding ones in Table 3.4 by showing that the assets and liabilities of all banks combined were, initially, five times as large as those for bank A alone. Stage 2 shows the immediate effect of £255m paid to a depositor at bank A, for this raises total

**Table 3.4**  Deposit creation with several clearing banks – the effects of caution

| Clearing bank A | Stage 1 | Stage 2 | Stage 3A | Stage 3B | Stage 4 |
|---|---|---|---|---|---|
| | | | | | £m |
| **Liabilities** | | | | | |
| Deposits | 2000 | 2255 | 2480 | 2420 | 2300 |
| Total | 2000 | 2255 | 2480 | 2420 | 2300 |
| **Assets** | | | | | |
| Cash | 500 | 755 | 755 | 695 | 575 |
| Securities | 500 | 500 | 575 | 575 | 575 |
| Loans | 1000 | 1000 | 1150 | 1150 | 1150 |
| Total | 2000 | 2255 | 2480 | 2420 | 2300 |

**Table 3.5**    Deposit creation with several clearing banks

| All clearing banks combined | Stage 1 | Stage 2 | Stage 3 |
|---|---|---|---|
| | | | £m |
| **Liabilities** | | | |
| Deposits | 10000 | 10255 | 11020 |
| Total | 10000 | 10255 | 11020 |
| **Assets** | | | |
| Cash | 2500 | 2755 | 2755 |
| Securities | 2500 | 2500 | 2755 |
| Loans | 5000 | 5000 | 5510 |
| Total | 10000 | 10255 | 11020 |

clearing bank deposits by £255m, from £10,000m to £10,255m, and it raises the total cash held by the banks by £255m, from £2,500m to £2,755m. Stage 3 shows the final outcome, which will not emerge until long after stage 4 in Table 3.4 was reached. By ignoring cash drains, the banks are shown in stage 3 as still having £2,755m cash, and as using this to support total deposits of £11,020m, since they would thus have a cash ratio of 25 per cent. Securities have risen from 25 per cent of the initial level of total assets to 25 per cent of the final level, and loans have risen from 50 per cent of the initial level to 50 per cent of the final level.

The figures in Table 3.5 are perfectly legitimate for they show the initial equilibrium (stage 1) and the final equilibrium (stage 3) and they show that $\Delta L$ (of £1,020m) does equal $\Delta C/r$, that is £255m/0.25, provided of course that all banks expand whenever their cash ratio exceeds r. But three things must be clearly understood. First, the numerical outcome shown assumes no cash drains. Secondly, the expansion cannot be as rapid as was possible in the one clearing bank situation shown in Table 3.2. Thirdly, the suggestion in Table 3.2 that an individual bank in receipt of an initial cash injection can undertake an instant expansion in deposits equal to several times the cash injection is false; it was seen in Table 3.4, that, in the present example, the bank received an initial injection of £255m, but could only initially expand securities and loans by £225m. The system as a whole can, in turn, react to the extra injection of £255m by eventually raising securities and loans by the much higher figure of £765m (so creating a total rise in assets – including cash – of £1,020m). However, at a particular point in time, any bank receiving extra cash must usually expand its securities and loans by a smaller amount; a larger amount would only be possible if it had a very large share of total deposits – and especially if it were the only bank – so that the cash outflow to other banks reflected in stages 2 to 4 of Table 3.4 was small, or if it wanted a very low cash ratio, so that it would be happy to have a large cash outflow. In general, though, individual banks cannot instantly use an extra £1 cash to create more than £1 extra deposits, though in time the banking system as a whole can.

It has been seen that the formula $\Delta L = \Delta C/r$ is applicable as far as a banking system is concerned (ignoring cash drains) no matter how many banks there are. However, it should be noted that banks are likely to use a higher cash ratio (r) the more banks there are, and so the numerical value of the multiplier (l/r) is likely in practice to be lower in a many-bank case than in a few-bank case. The reason is best explained with the help of extreme examples. Consider, first, the extreme 'few-bank' case where there is just one clearing bank. Such a bank needs cash only in case the public as a whole want to withdraw more cash than they deposit or in case they pay more to central bank customers than they receive. In such circumstances, the bank's cash needs will be modest and can be met by a very small cash ratio. Consider, next, the extreme 'many-bank' case where each bank handles just one depositor. Each bank would be afraid its depositor would one day pay out most (perhaps all) of his deposit, so the bank would want a cash ratio approaching 100 per cent. More generally, the smaller a bank is, the less stable its total deposit level will be and the higher will be the cash ratio it desires.

Finally, it should be noted that just as the formula $\Delta L = \Delta C/r$ is applicable in a many-bank case where there is no cash drain, the formula for the increase in liabilities would be $\Delta L = \Delta C/(r + d)$ if the public sought always to hold cash to the amount of Ld. Thus the eventual increase in the money stock, $\Delta M$, caused by an increase in cash of $\Delta C$, would be given by $\Delta M = \Delta C(1 + d)/(r + d)$ since deposits would rise by $\Delta C/(r + d)$ and publicly held cash by $\Delta C.d/(r + d)$. At least this result for M holds, as before, if there is no cash drain to the government caused, perhaps, by extra purchases of National Savings Certificates, and if the fall in interest rates which is likely to accompany the rise in bank lending and security purchases does not lead to banks deciding to opt for higher cash ratios (in other words, the formula assumes r is constant).

# A closer look at a clearing bank's balance sheet

The tables in previous sections have mentioned just four items on a clearing bank's balance sheet: deposits on the liabilities side and cash, securities and loans on the assets side. These are, indeed, the principal liabilities and assets which banks hold, but it is necessary to look at them in more detail in order to understand the next chapter which considers how a country's money stock can be controlled. Accordingly, further details are given in Table 3.6 which gives some figures for an imaginary bank, but it should be stressed that even this is still a somewhat simplified balance sheet. Further details of clearing bank balance sheets are given in Chapter 7.

The first refinement shown in Table 3.6 concerns deposits which are now divided into sight deposits and other deposits. It will be appreciated from earlier discussion that banks seeking to maintain a prudent cash ratio must always be alert to any tendency for their depositors to spend their deposits in favour of depositors at other banks or to withdraw their deposits in order to have larger personal cash holdings. One way of reducing such tendencies is for a bank to offer to pay interest on its deposits, thereby making it more attractive for depositors to maintain them. In principle, a bank could decide to pay interest on all its deposits, but the normal practice has been for banks to ask depositors to split their deposits into two groups. One group would consist of sight deposits – often termed current accounts or demand deposits – on which, traditionally, no interest was paid but from which money could be withdrawn in cash or spent by cheque at any time. The other group would comprise a variety of accounts – such as savings accounts and deposit accounts – which attract interest but where, strictly speaking, some notice (often a week) is required for withdrawals; deposits where notice of withdrawal is required are often termed time deposits. The reason that banks have operated like this is to encourage people to put funds in deposits where notice is required, for the more money depositors have tied up in such deposits, the less the risk for the bank of a sudden loss of deposits and so the less its need for cash reserves.

In practice, banks have generally allowed depositors to transfer money from time deposits into sight deposits without delay, but have then deducted some interest (perhaps that attributable to the last week) which would otherwise have been payable. Given this arrangement, it might be wondered why depositors have not tended to keep all their funds in interest-bearing time deposits. The reason is that banks generally make charges for handling cheques and cash withdrawals but reduce these charges, perhaps to zero, for people who keep their sight deposits above some specified level. So it is usually prudent for a depositor to keep some money in a sight deposit and thereby reduce his bank changes, even though this deposit may earn no interest. Recently banks have been more inclined than they used to be to offer some interest on sight deposits, though naturally the interest offered on these tends to be lower than the interest offered on time deposits.

It should be stressed that although some sight deposits now attract interest while other sight deposits do not, the definition of such a deposit is that, whether interest-bearing or not, money can be withdrawn at any time without penalty. It is clear that sight deposits count as money, but it is sometimes argued that other deposits do not count as money. Indeed, these other deposits have at times been regarded as a form of near-money or quasi-money, rather than money itself, because they are not, strictly speaking, available for instant spending. However, the fact that in practice banks do now usually allow instant transfers to sight deposits means that this argument is rather stretched, so this chapter will include all deposits as part of a country's stock of money. The issue will be considered further in Chapter 8.

Turning now to the assets side, Table 3.6 has more categories than earlier tables,

**Table 3.6**    Balance sheet for a hypothetical English bank

| Liabilities | | £000s |
|---|---|---|
| Sight deposits | | 400 |
| Other deposits | | 600 |
| Total | | 1000 |

| Assets | | | £000s |
|---|---|---|---|
| C | Notes and coin | | 19 |
| C | Balances with Bank of England | | 6 |
| L | Market loans: | | |
| | Secured loans to LDMA[1] | 40 | |
| | Other | 160 | |
| | | | 200 |
| S | Bills | | 50 |
| S | Investments | | 75 |
| L | Advances | | 650 |
| | Total | | 1000 |

[1]London Discount Market Association

but the various items can still be divided into cash, securities and loans, as indicated by the letters C, S and L. In discussing the various items shown, it will be emphasized that they are listed in an order which corresponds roughly to what is known as their degree of liquidity, the most liquid assets coming first and the least liquid last. What does liquidity mean? Its meaning has changed a little with the passage of time. Originally, assets were split into just two groups, liquid assets and illiquid assets; those assets which could be converted immediately into money without loss, that is for the full value shown on a balance sheet, were regarded as liquid, while all other asseets were regarded as illiquid. Now, however, it is more usual to think in terms of a spectrum of liquidity. Money is by definition completely liquid and assets which their owners think can be converted quickly into money without significant loss are regarded as highly liquid, but assets which can be converted into money only after some time has elapsed, or more quickly but without the certainty of reaching the full value shown, are held to be less liquid.

To understand the relevance of liquidity, it should be recalled that, in general, a bank likes to have access to cash for reasons of prudence, but is tempted to have high levels of securities and loans because these earn income. As explained earlier, any attempt by a bank to expand its assets of securities and loans will lead to a lower cash ratio, so prudence will dictate some limits to such expansion. The bank in Table 3.6 has total liabilities of £1,000 and total cash holdings of just £25m, £19m being held by the bank's branches and £6m being held at the Bank of England. This gives it a cash ratio of just 2.5 per cent, a fairly typical ratio in the UK today.

This low cash ratio might seem a little rash, but a banker would defend it on two scores. First, his experience teaches him that the amount of cash he has to pay out each day when depositors withdraw cash or make out cheques in favour of depositors at other banks is very closely matched by the amount of cash he receives each day from depositors who take cash to him or receive cheques from depositors elsewhere. Secondly, he has other non-cash assets which can be converted into cash very quickly should the need arise.

The most useful assets for this purpose come in the next group called market loans. Broadly speaking, market loans are like any other loans made by banks in that they are made by writing larger numbers on the accounts of the depositors to whom they are made with the expectation that the depositors will then quickly spend their new deposits. The only distinctive feature of market loans is that they are made to participants in the money market, that is to say financial businesses who use their new deposits by lending the money in them to someone else at a slightly higher rate of interest. In contrast, most of a bank's loans, which come under the heading advances, are made directly to households or businesses who use their new deposits to purchase goods and services. Market loans are divided into two groups, secured loans to the London Discount Market Association and other market loans.

The London Discount Market Association (LDMA) comprises nine particular discount houses. Discount houses are discussed further in Chapter 7, but it has already been noted in Chapter 2 that these companies borrow much of their money from clearing banks and then lend it, using roughly half their funds to lend by means of buying commercial and Treasury bills. The banks' loans to the LDMA are generally secured loans in that the discount houses place items such as bills with the banks for security. The loans are made by the clearing banks for very short periods. They are usually repayable by noon on the following day, in which case they count as call-money or money-at-call. They may be made for longer periods, in which case they count as money at short notice, but they are at most repayable after about 14 days. As it happens, secured loans to the LDMA cover only about two-thirds of the clearing banks' assets of money-at-call and short notice, for some other market loans are made on a similar basis to other concerns, notably to concerns called discount brokers and to the 'money-trading' departments of certain banks – both of which tend to use the funds for buying bills – and to certain members of the stock exchange. Now the important thing from a clearing bank's point of view about all this money-at-call and short notice is that is highly liquid, or it can be rapidly converted into money (indeed money in the form of cash) for the full value shown on the bank's balance sheet.

The reader might wonder if all the money-at-call really could be rapidly converted into extra cash for a bank. After all, it seems possible that if the bank in Table 3.6 demanded repayment from a discount house, then the house might seek rapidly to build up enough money its own deposit by borrowing money from one of the bank's own depositors, or perhaps it could sell bills to one of the bank's own depositors; this would initially involve a switch of funds from one depositor to another, with no effect on the figures in Table 3.6, and it would then mean that the bank could call in the loan to the discount house by writing a smaller number in its account, thus reducing secured market loans and deposits by matching amounts, and yet not actually acquire any cash! In practice, a discount house would not have time for the negotiations involved. It can obtain the money needed for repayment in the short time available only by borrowing from the Bank of England (or by selling bills to it) or by borrowing from another bank and by transferring the funds it thus acquires elsewhere to the bank in Table 3.6 thereby raising that bank's cash by raising its deposit at the Bank of England. (See the discussion of Table 5.1 for further details.)

As it happens, the Bank of England has an agreement with the discount houses that it will *always* buy bills from them (or, perhaps, lend to them on the strength of bills deposited by the houses at the Bank for security). In this way, the Bank acts as what is termed the lender of last resort to the banking system, for when the banks are short of cash they turn to the discount houses knowing that they, in turn, can turn to the Bank of England. It is in return for this agreement that the discount houses undertake to buy all new Treasury bills not bought by other buyers, an arrangement discussed in the last chapter. Of course, the Bank of England can set the rate of discount it will use when deciding the price at which it will buy bills from the discount houses when they approach it as lender of last resort, and it can set the rate of interest charged on loans made to them for the same purpose. Changes in this rate can actually affect the money stock, as explained in Chapter 5.

It has been noted that the banks have some money-at-call and short notice to non-LDMA institutions, and that these loans are included in the item 'other market loans'. This item contains further loans to money market institutions that are generally made for periods between two weeks and two years. Of course, at any point in time some of these loans will have been freshly made, but others will be close to repayment and will count as highly liquid. It might seem odd to regard loans coming up for repayment as liquid, for when these loans are repaid the bank will simply reduce the deposits of the institutions concerned by the appropriate amount. Thus the bank's liabilities (in the form of deposits) and its assets (in the form of market loans) will fall by corresponding amounts, yet seemingly the bank acquires no money as such. However, the fact is that money which the banker has created and lent has now been repaid to him.

The next group of assets, bills, are also generally regarded as reasonably liquid. It will be recalled from the last chapter that bills are generally drawn for 91 days. So a bank will typically have some bills maturing within a few days, and hence highly liquid, and others maturing in a few weeks and so a little less liquid. Of course, bills some way from maturity can be sold on the stock exchange, but daily (indeed hourly) fluctuations in interest rates make their second-hand value a little uncertain and hence cause such bills to score less well in terms of liquidity. Note that when a Treasury bill matures, the bank will find its deposit at the Bank of England increasing as the government will be paying off the bank.

The next item on the assets side is termed 'investments'. This item covers all securities except bills. These other securities are also tolerably liquid, for they can be sold on the stock exchange at any time, though it would be some days before the purchasers were obliged to pay. Note that if, say, one fifth of the country's depositors bank at the bank concerned, then sales of all £75,000 securities would probably bring in just £60,000 cash from other banks, for only some four-fifths would be sold to other banks' customers. The £60,000 sold to them would have no effect on the value of the bank's total deposits or its total assets, but would raise its holdings of money (in the form of Bank of England balances) by £60,000 and would reduce its investments by £60,000. The £15,000 sold to the bank's own depositors would reduce its total deposits by £15,000 and match this by the £15,000 fall in investments.

The least liquid assets are advances, the name used to cover all loans made directly to businesses, households and other depositors who want to borrow money in order to make purchases rather than in order to lend again. It was seen in connection with Table 3.3 that when such a loan is made, the initial effect is to raise assets, under the heading of loans, and also to raise liabilities, as deposits have risen. Subsequently, the loan will be spent, mostly to customers of other banks, so that deposits fall, and this is matched by a fall in the bank's holding of cash. When a loan is due for repayment the reverse occurs. The borrower must first acquire some money, mostly it may be assumed from depositors elsewhere, thereby raising his own deposit and the bank's holdings of cash; then he can repay the loan by having his deposit reduced, an event matched by a fall in advances on the assets side of the balance sheet. Now if the bank suddenly wanted extra cash and demanded repayment from a number of people who had been given advances, then it would find that it would take those people some time to build up their deposits in order to effect repayment, and it is this delay which is the principal cause of illiquidity. Even so, the illiquidity should not be over-stressed, for some advances will be being repaid every day, so the total level could be reduced fairly quickly if the need arose.

As explained earlier, the assets in Table 3.6 are listed in roughly their order of liquidity, the one perfectly liquid asset, notes and coin, coming first, and the least liquid asset, advances to non-money market borrowers last. However, there is an important qualification to the liquidity of certain assets shown on the table which must now be mentioned. This results from the fact that UK clearing banks are broadly required (1) to hold a deposit at the Bank of England not less than 0.5% of their total assets, (2) to have secured loans to the LDMA not less than 2.5% of total assets (this figure was reduced from 4% in 1983) and (3) to have money-at-call and short notice not less than 5% of their total assets (this figure was reduced from 6% in 1983). More precise details of these requirements are given in Chapter 7. Requirement (1) means that with total liabilities of £1,000,000, the bank must have a Bank of England deposit of at least £5,000. It actually has a deposit of £6,000, but clearly it could not withdraw or spend more than £1,000 without breaching requirement (1).

In other words, £5,000 is effectively unusable and illiquid, so that only £1,000 is really liquid. Likewise, requirement (2) means that secured loans to the LDMA must be at least £25,000; the actual figure is £40,000, but only £15,000 could actually be recalled without breaching requirement (2), and so only £15,000 is really liquid. Requirement (3) means that money-at-call and short notice must be at least £50,000; thus the bank cannot regard the first £50,000 of such money (whose total is not given in Table 3.6) as at all liquid.

The purpose of these three requirements, which are imposed on clearing banks by the Bank of England, is to limit the total level of bank deposits the banks can create. However, it might be thought that these three requirements do *not* in fact limit the total level of bank deposits. After all, it seems the banks could create any amount of money-at-call simply by giving larger advances, perhaps at temptingly low interest rates, to the concerns involved; accordingly, it seems the banks could always meet requirements (2) and (3), no matter how large their total deposits were. Likewise, it seems the banks could always demand any amount of money-at-call to be repaid in cash, relying on the discount houses' access to the Bank of England as a lender of last resort; accordingly, it seems the banks could always go on to top up their balances at the Bank and hence always meet requirement (1). In practice, the banks can indulge in these activities, but the Bank of England is able to control the use made of them in two main ways.

First, the Bank can use the arrangement whereby the discount houses must buy any new Treasury bills not bought by other buyers. Suppose the banks have total liabilities of 10,000 (all figures in £m), deposits at the Bank of England of 50 (the minimum of 0.5 per cent allowed) and loans to the LDMA of 250 (the minimum 2.5 per cent allowed). To expand their lending and hence their deposits, the banks must raise these last two figures. They might seek to advance 30 more to the LDMA, raising loans to them to 280, and then demand repayment of 5 in cash which they will then deposit at the Bank of England. This would raise their deposits there to 55 and leave 275 with the LDMA. Seemingly, it would permit expansion of total liabilities to 11,000 without falling foul of the rules. However, when the extra advances were made, the Bank of England could raise the issue of new Treasury bills with the result that the discount houses had to buy some to a value of 30. The LDMA would do this by means of cheques drawn on the clearing banks. Thus the banks would find deposits at the Bank falling by 30. The banks would then have to recall loans of 30 from the LDMA to restore their deposits at the Bank. Accordingly, they would end up in their original position unable to expand their lending activities. The Bank's second control over the situation stems from the fact that it imposes limits (considered further in Chapter 7) on the total asset levels of the discount houses. Once the houses reach these levels, they are not able to borrow any more money, no matter how much the banks might try to tempt them!

# Non-bank financial intermediaries

Aside from the central bank, the discount houses and the clearing banks, a key part in the money market is made up by the non-bank financial intermediaries or NBFIs. As their name implies, these are businesses other than banks which engage in financial intermediation, that is in taking deposits or loans from people who wish to lend and then lending at slightly higher interest rates to businesses or householders who wish to borrow. There are a number of different types of NBFI, and it is useful to divide them into two groups. The first group comprises building societies, savings banks and finance houses which are regarded as deposit-taking institutions. Essentially, this means that funds placed with them by lenders can always be withdrawn in full, generally at short notice. The second group comprises companies where this is not the case, perhaps because the funds placed may rise or fall in value, as with unit trust institutions, or because the funds are not expected to be withdrawn for some time unless some particular event occurs, as with pension funds and insurance companies, or because those who have placed funds have bought shares and so cannot ever withdraw, as with investment trusts. Insofar as they take deposits, institutions in the first group are closer to banks than ones in the second group.

To see the implications of NBFIs it is useful to take a single example, and building societies will be considered here. These come closer to banks than any other NBFIs, and, as will be seen, the distinction between them and the banks is becoming very blurred. However, a key feature of building societies is their principal objective which is to borrow money from the public with the intention of making loans known as mortgages to people who wish to borrow in order either to purchase new or second-hand dwellings, or to improve the dwellings in which they currently live.

This role can be seen from the balance sheet of a hypothetical society as shown in Table 3.7. As with the balance sheets given earlier for banks, this one lists only the main assets and liabilities and assumes that they exactly balance. The liabilities side shows the money placed with the society by savers or lenders. In view of the discussion in the last paragraph, it is a little curious to find that most of these funds are defined as shares rather than deposits! The difference in this context is purely a technical one in that a saver at a building society can choose whether to place his funds in what is strictly termed a deposit or in what are strictly termed shares. Note that building society shares are not at all like the shares discussed in the last chapter; they cannot be sold on the stock exchange, they do not fluctuate in value, and the money involved can be withdrawn from the society issuing them at fairly short notice. Building society shares are essentially very similar to building society deposits, but are more attractive to savers because they earn more interest. The only difference between these shares and deposits is that should a building society ever have to stop

**Table 3.7** Balance sheet for a hypothetical building society

| Liabilities | £000s |
| --- | --- |
| Shares | 480 |
| Deposits | 20 |
| Total | 500 |

| Assets | £000s |
| --- | --- |
| Cash and bank balance | 25 |
| Investments | 50 |
| Mortgages | 425 |
| Total | 500 |

trading, then deposit holders would be paid in full before any funds were allocated to shareholders.

On the assets side, most of the funds placed with the society are used to finance the loans known as mortgages. These loans are generally secured as borrowers place the title documents for their dwellings with the society. However, mortgages are long term loans while holders of deposits and shares may demand payment at short notice. To reduce the risk of sudden widespread withdrawals, a building society generally has a variety of share funds between which savers can choose, some offering slightly higher interest in return for a longish notice being required, perhaps some months, and others offering even higher interest if funds are left alone for some years. Nevertheless, funds are withdrawn from time to time so the society in Table 3.7 keeps some cash on its premises and some money in an account with a clearing bank. It also keeps some assets in the form of investments, probably mostly in bonds, and these could be sold quickly in case of need. These investments and cash form the society's liquid assets, and they must form a stipulated minimum percentage of total assets. The stipulation is determined by the Chief Registrar of Friendly Societies under powers given by the 1962 Building Societies Act. The requirement in 1986 was for a minimum liquid assets figure of 7.5 per cent, but the society in Table 3.7, as with most societies, opted for a higher figure of 15 per cent (that is 25 + 50 as a percentage of 500).

It is now possible to see how NBFIs interact with the banking system. Suppose, for a moment, that there are no NBFIs and that the total level of bank deposits (ignoring, for reasons explained earlier, clearing bank deposits at the central bank) is £10m. Suppose, also, that the banks are fully lent. Next, suppose that the level of cash held outside banks is £1m so that the money stock is £11m. Finally, suppose that various NBFIs, say deposit-taking building societies, are established. They will doubtless seek to tempt people who hold deposits at banks to switch some of their funds to the NBFIs. No doubt they will offer interest rates slightly higher than those offered on interest-bearing bank deposits, though NBFI deposits will probably be less liquid in the sense of having a longer notice of withdrawal period.

The NBFIs can now go and compete with banks as lenders, and they can do so even though they are paying higher rates to depositors. Two factors enable NBFIs to compete with banks despite having to pay these higher rates. One factor is the relative illiquidity of their deposits, for this means that they need have fewer liquid assets and so can have more longer term loans than the banks, and these longer term loans should bring in slightly higher returns. The other factor is that NBFIs tend to specialize in one branch of lending, such as loans for house purchase, and such specialization may help them to have lower costs in terms of checking the credit-worthiness of borrowers and the likelihood of their defaulting than the banks can have, given that the banks lend to a wide variety of people for many purposes. Despite these two factors, the reader may wonder why the banks didn't expand their lending if the NFBIs can find people willing to borrow; a major reason can be taken to be the fact that the banks were fully lent to begin with!

Now suppose the NBFIs attract deposits of £2m. This means that bank depositors instruct their banks to pay £2m to the NFBIs. However, the NBFIs will have opened bank accounts of their own, so the £2m will initially be paid into these. Accordingly, there is no change to the total level of bank deposits, and indeed no effect on the banks except that the NBFIs, by increasing the availability of loans to borrowers, are likely to put downward pressure on interest rates. The impact of NBFIs on interest rates is considered further at the end of the next chapter. There is still no change in total bank deposits when the NBFIs lend some, or indeed most, of their newly acquired funds by making out cheques to the borrowers, for this merely causes the banks to switch funds from the NBFI deposits to those of the borrowers. Moreover, there is no change in total bank deposits when the borrowers use cheques to spend their loans, for this just results in the funds going from the deposits of the borrowers to the deposits of those from whom they make their purchases.

Despite the analysis of the last paragraph, it should be noted that NBFI lending could actually lead to a slight change in the money stock. Surprisingly, perhaps, any effect such lending might have on the money stock is likely to be in a downward direction. The point is that the increased amount of borrowing in the economy could raise the level of spending on newly finished products. In turn, it could raise the level of incomes in the economy, and this could cause the public to want to hold more cash. In that case, the public would withdraw some cash from the banks, or, perhaps, from NBFIs who would probably then withdraw some cash from their own bank deposits. With less cash, banks would have to start a multiple contraction of bank deposits and the money stock would fall; at least the banks would have to do so if they were initially fully lent, as is assumed here. However, the introduction of NBFIs, and, indeed, any expansion of NBFIs, is unlikely to have much effect on the level of deposits or, in turn, on the money stock.

While the money stock defined as cash plus bank deposits should be very little affected by the introduction of NBFIs, it may be wondered if the £2m of funds placed with NBFIs should really be counted as money. On the basis that money is anything generally acceptable as a medium of exchange, the answer is that they should not. While a citizen can directly transfer cash or bank deposits, he is usually not able to transfer directly funds held by him at an NBFI, so these are not generally acceptable – indeed not acceptable at all – as a medium of exchange. Someone who wishes to spend funds held at an NBFI must ordinarily first get the NBFI to give him cash or a cheque transferring money from its bank deposit to his. The funds at NBFIs that come nearest to being money are the deposits (or rather shares) at certain building societies which have issued cheque books. However, these are in fact issued with the agreement of the banks where these societies hold deposits, and they should really be seen as enabling anyone using them to issue instructions to the NBFI's bank to pay money from the NBFI's account to their own for immediate onward transference to the person in whose favour the cheque is made out. So, once again, it is really bank deposits which are being used as a medium of exchange. Nevertheless, the liabilities of deposit-taking NBFIs are generally regarded as a form of near-money because they can typically be converted fairly quickly into money by their holder without loss.

The fact that the NBFIs were reckoned to settle down with funds of £2m may not alter the actual money stock, but it may well increase the amount of money people think they have. The point is that people with funds at NBFIs, knowing they can withdraw their funds by giving due notice, may reasonably assume they have £2m there. Meanwhile, there are still £10m bank deposits being held by people who assume they have £10m there. In addition, people have £1m in cash. So there may well be a feeling that the money available is £13m, even though the actual money stock is only £11m. Needless to say, it is the NBFI deposits which create the anomaly. If all the bank deposit holders wished to spend their money tomorrow, then there would be no problem; at least there would be no problem so long as they were happy to do their spending by making cheques out to each other and did not seek to withdraw cash. But if all the holders of funds at NBFIs wanted to withdraw their funds tomorrow, or even in a few weeks time, to spend, then there would be a major problem because the NBFIs would find their cash and bank balance holdings were inadequate (as shown by Table 3.7). Why, then, are people prepared to hold NBFI deposits at all? The answer is simply that they believe that the NBFIs have sufficient cash and bank balances to meet any likely level of withdrawals. It should be noted that the situation where people think they have more money than there is has been encountered before in connection with Table 1.3.

One final point to reiterate is that NBFIs cannot create money. In essence, they simply cause existing money to change hands.

# 4

# Controlling the money stock – the basic principles

## Introduction

Earlier chapters have indicated that the value of the money stock in a country should be measured as the amount of cash held by the public plus the total amount of bank deposits, apart from bankers' deposits at the central bank. In practice, the authorities in the UK use a number of different measures of the money stock, as indicated in Chapter 8. However, the measure suggested in this book is roughly equivalent to one of the authorities' best known measures, 'sterling $M_3$,' or £M3.

Now the authorities may from time to time wish to control the size of this stock. The purpose of this chapter and the next is to consider what factors determine the size of the money stock and then to see how the authorities can influence those factors to alter its size. In fact, the size is determined by the forces of demand and supply, that is by the demand for money by the public and the extent to which the banking system is willing to supply it. The first two sections of this chapter look at the demand for money, and also indicate briefly why a change in the stock may be of importance. The third section shows how the forces of supply and demand interact to determine the money stock. The fourth, fifth and sixth sections discuss how the monetary authorities can control the money stock. Before moving on to these sections, however, it is helpful to consider briefly two questions which may arise in the reader's mind.

First, who are the monetary authorities? Ultimately, decisions over the appropriate level for the money stock are taken in the UK by the Treasury which is under the direction of the Chancellor of the Exchequer who, in turn, is concerned with pursuing the economic policies approved by the Cabinet and Parliament. In principle, the Bank of England is charged with implementing the policies and decisions made by the Treasury; this relationship was formalized in 1946 when the Bank of England was nationalized, for the Treasury was then given powers to issue directions to the Bank. In practice, the Bank has always been willing to implement Treasury policy on request, rather than on direction. However, it should be emphasized that the Bank will generally be consulted about monetary affairs and its views will be given full consideration.

Secondly, what powers does the Bank of England have over other banks? By tradition, the Bank controls other banks by making recommendations or requests to them.

An individual bank might decide to ignore these recommendations or requests, but there would be no point as the Bank has long had the power to enforce compliance should the need arise. The Bank has had additional powers conferred on it under the 1979 Banking Act which stipulates that no institution can accept deposits unless it has authorization from the Bank. Authorization can be refused for any institution which fails to meet the various criteria for sound practice laid down by the Bank or which fails to provide any information that may be requested by the Bank from time to time. Today, therefore, a bank which ignored recommendations or requests from the Bank could find that the Bank reacted by revoking its authorization to take deposits rather than by enforcing compliance. Not surprisingly, perhaps, banks are inclined to abide by the Bank of England's recommendations!

Turning now to the question of controlling the money stock, it is useful to emphasize at the outset that although this stock comprises both bank deposits and publicly-held cash, the authorities seek to control directly only the level of bank deposits. It would be out of the question for them to seek to control directly the level of publicly-held cash, for one of the tasks of the Bank of England is to ensure public confidence in the clearing banks, and this confidence would vanish very rapidly if the Bank took any steps which prevented these banks from giving cash on demand to any depositors who wanted it. In any case, there is no real need to try directly to alter the level of publicly-held cash. For one thing, such cash holdings form a relatively small part of the total money stock, and for another, they tend to fall and rise when deposits fall and rise since the public tend to keep a reasonably stable relationship between cash holdings and deposit holdings.

Now there are a number of methods by which the authorities can seek to alter the level of bank deposits, but the nature of any lender of last resort arrangements that may be in force can affect the efficacy of certain methods. It is helpful to begin the analysis by considering what would happen if there were *no* lender of last resort facilities, and that is done in the fourth section of this chapter. The fifth section considers what happens if there is a lender of last resort. Inevitably, some simplifying assumptions are made in these two sections. The final section of the chapter considers what happens if some of these assumptions are released.

There are, however, two simplifying assumptions which are not released in the final section. One of these is that the central bank, in its capacity of lender of last resort, lends directly to the banks. This is, indeed, the arrangement in many countries, but not in the UK. It was explained in the last chapter that in the UK the Bank lends to the banks indirectly via the discount houses. It is the purpose of the next chapter to consider what happens when this procedure is used. It is perhaps helpful to say here that this procedure does not really alter the methods or their effects in any major way, but it does make the banking system more complicated and this, in turn, means the explanations of how the money stock can be controlled become rather longer.

The other simplifying assumption that is made throughout the analysis of this chapter and, indeed the next, is that it relates to a closed economy, that is one which has no economic relationship with other countries so that no money flows in or out. It is the purpose of Chapter 6 to explain what happens when this assumption is released. It is worth noting here that releasing this assumption *does* have important implications for controlling the money stock.

# The demand for money – the Keynesian view

At first sight, it might seem likely that the demand for money would be infinite: which of us would not like a vastly greater amount of money than we have today? However, people generally want to acquire large amounts of money in order to *spend* it. The question at issue in this section is why people want to *hold* money *instead* of spending it. There are two main theories about the demand for money, namely the one put forward by Keynes (1936) and since espoused by those economists known as Keynesians, and the one put forward by Friedman (1956) and espoused by those economists known as monetarists. In explaining these theories, attention will be focused on the extent to which the amount of money people wish to hold depends on interest rates. This enables a demand curve for money to be constructed. The importance of this curve will become clear in later sections of the chapter. It should be noted that in the exposition of the two theories of the demand for money it will be assumed that there is no inflation; inflation means that money loses value over time and this acts as a deterrent to holding money, so the demand for money is likely to be much less when inflation is high than when it is low.

Keynes argued that people held money for three reasons or motives which he termed the transactions motive, the precautionary motive and the speculative motive. In explaining these motives, it is convenient to assume initially that the only type of bank deposit is a non-interest-bearing sight deposit while the only securities available are consols, so that the rate of interest on consols can be termed 'the' rate of interest.*

The transactions motive for holding money arises because people and businesses need money for day-to-day transactions. Typically, people receive their income in weekly or monthly lump sums which they tend to spend more or less steadily over the following week or month. Thus an employee with an annual income of £12,000 (after tax) might receive a salary cheque for £1,000 on the first day of each month and might reckon to get through this sum during the month. Accordingly, she would have a transactions holding of £1,000 on the first day, £0 on the last day, and might have an average holding of £500. Of course, the average would be less than £500 if she tended to spend heavily in the first part of each month and then ease up towards the end. Her employer, on the other hand, would need to build up a transactions holding of £1,000 during each month to pay her, and might also have an average holding of £500 for this purpose. An interesting point to note is that if the employer decided in future to pay the employee £500 on the first day of each month and £500 on the sixteenth day, then the employee would find her transactions holding fluctuating between £500 and £0, with an average value of perhaps £250, while the employer would need to build up holdings of £500 each fortnight to pay her and so might also have an average holding for this purpose of £250. So the transactions demand for money will fall if people are paid more frequently, and it will rise if they are paid less frequently.

It should be stressed that this result assumes that people receive their incomes in occasional large amounts and it assumes that they spend it in frequent small amounts. The development of credit cards is making the second of these assumptions more doubtful. To see what effect credit cards can have, suppose the employee considered in the last paragraph manages to put *all* her purchases down to her credit card account, and suppose she receives a monthly invoice of £1,000 from the credit card company which she settles on the second day of each month, using the money paid to her by her employer on the day before. Her transactions holding will be £1,000 at the end of the first day of each month, £0 at the end of the second day when she pays the credit card company, and indeed it will be £0 on every remaining day. Thus it will have a very low average value. Now suppose her employer decides to pay her fortnightly instead. She may then have £0 from day 2 to day 16, £500 from day 16 to the end of the month, and £1,000 on day 1 of the following month, falling to £0 again the next day. Clearly her average holding could actually rise if she was paid more frequently.

Suppose, for the sake of simplicity, that there is no change in the frequency of payment and no extension in the use of credit cards. In these circumstances, the transactions demand for money will depend chiefly on the level of incomes. To see this, consider again the employee in the last two paragraphs and suppose she is paid monthly and makes negligible use of credit cards. If she had her pay increased from £1,000 a month to £1,200 a month, then she might tend to have an average transactions demand of £600 rather than £500, and her employer might have an average holding of £600 to meet her salary.

The transactions demand for money is unlikely to be sensitive to changes in interest rates. If interest rates were very high, then the employee considered here might contemplate spending part of her £1,000, say £500, on securities, bought on the first of the month, and then sell them later in the month for use when she has spent the other £500 of her income on goods and services; if she were to do this, then her holdings of money might average £250 instead of £500. In practice, though, the costs such as stockbrokers' fees of buying and selling the securities mean that operations like these are unlikely to be worthwhile at any feasible interest rate.

The precautionary motive for holding money arises because people like to have some money available to deal with unforeseen contingencies. These contingencies will include crises, such as the need to make an expensive journey to see a relative who is suddenly taken ill, or unexpected bargains, such as a desire to buy a camera offered half-price in a sale when one had anticipated buying the same camera for the full price at some distant date in the future. In general, the precautionary demand for money will depend chiefly on incomes; as a precaution against a bad cold, a poor man might want to hold enough money to buy some paper tissues while a rich man might want to hold enough money to spend a fortnight's convalescence in the Algarve. However, the development of credit cards – which effectively entitle their holders to instant loans when required – probably means that precautionary balances are far lower in relation to income in the country as a whole than was the case in Keynes's day. The precautionary demand is unlikely to be very sensitive to changes in interest rates; high rates on consols could tempt some people to risk having slightly lower precautionary holdings, though high rates on loans from credit card companies could cause people to have high precautionary holdings in order to reduce the chances of needing such loans.

The speculative demand for money will arise only with speculators, chiefly those who make speculative purchases and sales of securities which, for the moment, are reckoned to consist solely of consols. The holders of consols get some reward in the form of interest, and they may hope for an additional reward in the form of a capital gain if they can buy them at a low price and sell them for a higher price. As explained in Chapter 2, they will be able to make such a gain if interest rates fall between the date of purchase and the date of sale. Of course, consol holders stand to make a loss if interest rates rise between the dates of purchase and sale. In Keynes's view, each individual who is interested in holding securities forms expectations about future movements in consol prices and interest rates. If some of these people think consol prices will rise – perhaps they expect the government to buy up second-hand ones to reduce its future expenditure on interest payments to consol holders – then they will buy consols and hold on to any they already own. If other people expect consol prices to fall – perhaps they expect the government to sell off a large number of new consols to help finance government expenditure – then they might well be tempted to sell their consols now, presumably selling them to other speculators who think consol prices are likely to rise. The sellers will intend to hold on to the money thus raised for a while, and then use it to buy even more consols if and when the expected fall in consol prices takes place. In this way they will have, albeit temporarily, a speculative demand for money.

Notice that the speculative demand for money would arise only if speculators thought that the benefits derived from selling securities at high prices and buying them later at low prices more than offset the costs of buying and selling and the absence of interest income in the period when money was held instead of consols. In Keynes's view, at low interest rates, and so at high security prices, many speculators might expect prices to fall enough to make selling tempting, so the speculative demand for money could be very high. Conversely, at high interest rates, and so at low security prices, many speculators might expect prices to rise so that the speculative demand would be very low. Thus the speculative demand for money could be very sensitive to the rate of interest.

One implication of Keynes's formulation of the speculative demand for money is that it suggests that any particular individual will either have no speculative demand for money – if he thinks consol prices will rise, or at least thinks they will fall too little to make selling them seem an attractive idea – or will instead want to own no consols at all and so have a large speculative demand – if he thinks otherwise. In practice, individual speculators are likely at different times to have large, medium or small speculative demands for money and correspondingly small, medium or large holdings of securities, and they may from time to time make modest adjustments to the balance of their money and security holdings. This is because they are generally uncertain about the future level of interest rates and security prices. At high interest rates, they may think security prices will probably rise, and so they will seek small speculative money holdings, but they may not want these holdings to be zero for they may want some money available to buy a few more securities if their prices do happen to fall. At low interest rates, they may think security prices will probably fall, but they may not want to sell all their securities, for they may want to keep a few in order to enjoy some capital gains if their prices do happen to rise. Nonetheless, allowing for uncertainty does not change the key point which is that the speculative demand for money is likely to be higher at low interest rates than at high ones.

Taking these three motives together, it seems the demand for money will depend on the interest rate, so that a demand curve for money might be sloped like the one shown in Figure 4.1 where it is labelled $M_d$. Given the assumptions made so far, the vertical axis in this figure shows 'the' rate of interest, that is the rate on consols, and the horizontal axis shows the quantity of money, which can be held only in cash or non-interest-bearing sight deposits. It is now necessary to consider what happens to the analysis if allowance is made for different types of security and for interest-bearing bank deposits.

It there is more than one type of security, then speculators will determine their desire for speculative balances by considering the expected returns on all different securities, not just consols. Nevertheless, the demand for money is likely to be high

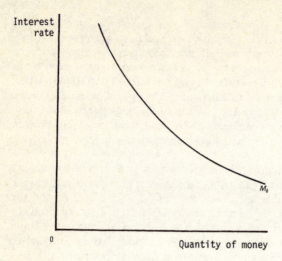

**Figure 4.1**

when the rate of interest on consols is low, and vice versa, as shown in Figure 4.1. The reason is that, as explained in Chapter 2, the rates of interest (or returns) on all securities tend to rise and fall together, if not by the same amount. Accordingly, high interest rates on consols usually occur when the returns on all other securities are also high, and this means that security prices are generally low so that price rises may be widely expected and the speculative demand for money may be low. Conversely, low interest rates on consols usually occur when the returns on all other securities are also generally low, and this means that security prices are high so that price falls may be widely expected and the speculative demand for money may be high. In essence, the rate of interest on consols shown in Figure 4.1 can be regarded simply as an indicator of the general level of returns available on securities, though most returns will be somewhat higher as most securities are riskier than consols. It would actually be possible to plot a demand curve for money against the rate on *any* security, or indeed against some sort of average rate. The rate on consols is used here purely for convenience.

If interest-bearing bank deposits are introduced, then it is necessary to decide whether to include the funds held in them as part of the demand for money covered by the curve in Figure 4.1. In fact, it seems essential to do so. The reason is that speculative demands for money are almost certain to be held largely in such deposits since they can thereby earn some interest (though the interest available on such deposits would be noticeably less than would be available on securities which are riskier and less liquid). It follows that a demand curve for money will cover the speculative demand only if it includes interest-bearing bank deposits as well as sight deposits.

One important implication of Keynes's theory should be noted. Suppose the Bank of England buys some bonds from the public. It can readily encourage bond holders to sell some of their bonds by offering high enough prices. The holders now have larger bank deposits and, indeed, the money stock has risen. In Keynes's view, some sellers will probably hold on to their new deposits in speculative balances, in anticipation of a fall in the price of bonds. Others will probably use their new deposits to buy other securities on the stock exchange, so driving up security prices and driving down their rates of return. This subsequent round of purchasing would transfer deposits from buyers to sellers but it would not affect the total level of deposits, nor would any further purchases of securities that the second-round sellers might undertake. Nevertheless, subsequent purchases would continue to push security prices up and to pull interest rates down, and would thus increase the total level of speculative balances that people want to hold. In essence, this theory suggests that the main effect of the Bank of England's purchase will be to cause people between them to hold fewer securities and more bank deposits. Indeed, the analysis given in this paragraph suggests that the whole process of second-hand security purchasing and selling would continue until it had forced interest rates down to the level where the resulting increase in the speculative demand for money 'soaked up' the whole of the increase in the money stock.

It should be observed, though, that Keynesians would not actually expect the initial rise in the money stock to lead only to increased holdings of speculative balances. The point is that interest rates will fall, for the reasons just outlined, and this will induce some rise in spending by people dependent on loans to finance their purchases. These people include businesses who borrow to finance investment, that is purchases of capital equipment, and households who borrow to finance spending on consumer durables. Extra spending by these people will lead in turn to a rise in the incomes of the people who sell to them, their suppliers, and so on. This rise in incomes will lead eventually to increases in the transactions and precautionary demands for money and, indeed, to a rightward shift in the money demand curve. Of course, these increases in transactions and precautionary balances could well be modest compared with the increased speculative balances.

It should be stressed that Keynesians tend to believe that the increase in the money stock would not lead to a big fall in interest rates. They think a small fall could be enough to lead to a significant increase in speculative balances. Also, they do not think that spending will be much affected by changes in interest rates. Since they think interest rates will change little, and think that spending is not very sensitive to any change that does occur, it can be seen that Keynesians expect rises in the money stock to have little effect on spending. In turn they predict little effect on output, unemployment or prices.

# The demand for money – the monetarists' view

The best way of approaching the monetarists' view of the demand for money is to realize that while they accept that money and securities are to some extent substitutes for one another, this is solely because they are merely two ways of holding wealth. There are several substitutes for money as there are various forms of wealth-holding, chiefly bonds and equities, physical goods and human capital (which relates to people's income-earning potential). Now each of these assets offers a return or yield, notably convenience in the case of money, interest and perhaps capital gains in the case of both bonds and equities, the services generated by physical assets (such as the comfort afforded by an armchair or the pleasure afforded by a picture), and the wages and salaries which can result from human capital.

Essentially, the monetarists' argument is that people 'invest' in each of these five broad types of wealth in such a way that the return on the last £1 invested in each type is the same. Thus the demand for any one type will rise if the return on any of the other four types falls. For this reason, the quantity of money demanded will increase if there is a fall in the return on securities. Thus this theory, too, suggests that there will be a downward sloping demand curve for money of the type shown in Figure 4.1. Now the monetarist theory goes on to imply that a fall in the return on securities would lead directly to increased investment in other assets, and so is likely to stimulate purchases of physical assets. Incidentally, the demand for money, and indeed all other types of asset, will also depend on people's total wealth, and so is likely to increase if total income rises.

On this theory, a purchase of bonds by the Bank of England which raised total bank deposits would cause some fall in interest rates and so lead directly to some increase in the total level of deposits that people wished to hold. However, the interest rate fall would also lead to a marked rise in spending on physical assets, and so to a marked rise in incomes, and, in turn, to a marked increase in the demand for deposits. This indirect increase caused by the income rise would probably be much more significant than the increase caused directly by the interest rate fall.

The different theories of the Keynesians and the monetarists have different implications about the importance of monetary policy. The Keynesians believe that an increase in the money stock will affect the demand for goods and services only because borrowing will become cheaper, and the evidence is that this effect will be small. Conversely, the monetarists believe that there will be direct effects as well, caused when holders of bonds find the return on bonds falling and decide instead to purchase more physical assets. Thus monetarists expect a rise in the money stock to have substantial effects on spending levels and so on output, unemployment and inflation.

It is not the purpose of this book to appraise the relative merits of the Keynesian and monetarist views, though it is worth remarking that in practice the demand for money is likely to be affected by the factors suggested by both schools of thought. All that is necessary here is to show that, on both views, there seems likely to be a downward sloping demand curve for money, and this result is sufficient for the purposes of the rest of this chapter, and indeed for the rest of this book. It should be mentioned that Friedman presented his theory of the demand for money on the basis that only cash and non-interest-bearing sight deposits would be regarded as money, and thus he did not imagine the demand curve as covering any other bank deposits. However, he clearly thought (1956, 5) that his theory would not be altered if interest was paid on sight deposits, and there seems little point in excluding other interest-earning bank deposits, even if some notice of withdrawal is needed. Thus there seem to be no problems in using his theory to offer an explanation of why the demand for money, taken in this chapter to include all bank deposits, increases when the interest rates on securities fall.

Despite the fact that both theories predict that the quantity of money demanded will rise if interest rates fall, it is worth drawing attention to one fundamental difference between the views of the two schools. This is that the reason for the quantity of money demanded being responsive to interest rates is different in each case. For the Keynesians it hinges on speculative behaviour, and in fact this means they see the whole demand curve for money as being very volatile. At today's interest rates, a certain amount of money is desired for speculative reasons, the amount depending on people's views about future security prices and interest rates. If, tomorrow, many people's views about future interest rates change, then the desire for holding money for speculative reasons will change even though, initially at least, interest rates may not change; the effect of the changing views will be to shift the entire demand curve. For the monetarists, the demand for money falls if interest rates rise purely because other assets then become more attractive. At a given level of interest rates, there is no reason to expect sudden significant changes in the quantity of money demanded, so the demand curve is likely to be fairly stable, at least in the short term. Of course, both schools would expect the demand curve to shift if prices or real income (or wealth) levels changed, but this possibility will be ignored until the final section of the chapter.

# How the money stock is determined

Having explained the factors which determine the demand for money, it is possible to see how the force of demand interacts with the force of supply to determine the money stock. That is the purpose of this section. The next two sections show how the stock can be altered. Four simplifying assumptions will be made in all these three sections. The first is that the demand curve for money will not shift if interest rates change, though it has been noted that falls in interest rates should increase investment and so in turn increase incomes and the transactions and precautionary demands for money, while rises in interest rates have the opposite effects. The second is that the public's demand for cash will not be affected by changes in the level of their bank deposits, though it has been noted that their cash demand could be so affected. The third is that the public will not react to falls (or rises) in their money holdings by selling (or buying) National Savings Certificates. The fourth is that there are no NBFIs. The last section of the chapter considers what happens to the analysis if these four assumptions are released.

For the purpose of the present analysis it is sufficient to suppose that the clearing banks have just three assets, namely cash (some of which may take the form of deposits at a bankers' bank), securities and advances. Also, it will be assumed for simplicity that the central bank starts with no deposits other than bankers' deposits so that public deposits are zero and the money stock equals clearing bank deposits plus cash held by the public.

Suppose, initially, that the total amount of cash available to the banks and the public is £300m, and suppose that the public want to hold cash of £200m themselves leaving £100m cash for the banks. Suppose, too, that there are no imposed rules about the cash ratio which the clearing banks must have. In these circumstances, the banks will be quite free to set their own cash ratios. For the sake of simplicity, imagine that they all seek a ratio of 10 per cent. In that case, if they were fully lent, then they might have a combined balance sheet with figures like those shown on Table 4.1 where all figures are given in £m. It will be seen that total deposits are 1,000 (half of them assumed to be sight deposits) and these are matched by assets of cash, 100, securities, 400, and advances, 500. Of course, some of the banks' cash will be held in deposits at the central bank. Now the total money stock will exceed the total level of clearing bank deposits by the amount of cash held by the public. This amount is 200 so that the money stock is 1,200.

It is, in fact, highly likely that the banks will always be fully lent, or at least nearly so. That is to say, they will always operate at, or very close to, their preferred cash ratio, the main reason for any departure being the time it takes the banks to respond to

**Table 4.1**  Combined balance sheet for all clearing banks

| Liabilities | £m |
|---|---|
| Sight deposits | 500 |
| Other deposits | 500 |
| Total | 1000 |

| Assets | £m |
|---|---|
| Cash | 100 |
| Securities | 400 |
| Advances | 500 |
| Total | 1000 |

any *changes* in their cash holdings. As this fact has an important bearing on the effects of controls by the monetary authorities, it is important to see why. Suppose, for instance, the banks were not fully lent and had cash of 100 plus securities and advances of 800, and so had total assets and liabilities of 900. The banks would feel able to support further deposits with their current cash holding, and would like to expand their holdings of securities and liabilities as this would earn them extra income. They would therefore seek to purchase more securities, so forcing prices up and interest rates down, and they would offer advances at lower interest rates. These events would cause an initial rise in deposits. However, it is possible that the security sellers and the borrowers might then spend their new deposits, perhaps making some purchases from businesses; in turn, it is possible that some of the businesses might then use their new receipts to pay back some of their bank loans! Can the banks take steps to ensure that the demand for deposits really rises permanently to the level they desire? In fact they can, though it might be a little while before they fully succeed. The reasons are contained in the analysis of the last two sections which showed that there is likely to be a downward sloping demand curve for money. The banks' actions put downward pressure on interest rates which will increase the demand for money and so bank deposits (as implied in Figure 4.1).

This analysis is often summed up in a diagram such as Figure 4.2. This shows a demand curve for money ($M_d$) and a supply curve ($M_s$). The demand curve slopes down from left to right, like the one in Figure 4.1, but is drawn as a straight line to simplify the following analysis. The supply curve is drawn as a vertical line at level of the money stock where the banks would be fully lent, that is 1,200. The implication of $M_s$ is that so long as the banks have 100 cash, then they will want total assets and total liabilities of 1,000 no matter what interest rate is necessary to persuade the public to hold that level of deposits; these deposits can be added to the level of cash held by the public, 200, to show the money stock the banks want to see at each rate of interest, namely 1,200.

This analysis is not implausible. Any bank which is not fully lent will have an incentive to lend more, because that will result in it having more income-earning securities and advances. It is true that its actions will depress interest rates, and so somewhat offset the rise in its income caused by having more income-earning assets. However, as the individual bank sees it, its own expansion will have negligible effects on the level of interest rates and yet will have a noticeable effect on the level of its

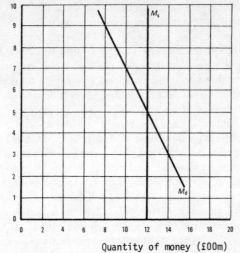

**Figure 4.2**

income-earning assets. $M_d$ suggests that the interest rate will settle at 5 per cent, for this is the level necessary to persuade the public to hold a total money stock of 1,200.

The level of interest rates where $M_d$ and $M_s$ intersect is known as the equilibrium level for, once established, there are no forces tending to make it change. This state of affairs would not apply at any other interest rate. Suppose, for instance, that the interest rate was actually 7 per cent. In that case, the demand for money would be 1,000 which, given public cash holdings of 200, means a demand to hold bank balances of just 800. At the same time, the banks want the money stock to be 1,200 which, given public cash holdings of 200, means they want deposits to be 1,000. What will happen? This depends on what the level of deposits actually is.

Suppose, first, that the level of deposits was the 1,000 that the banks want. The problem here is that the public as a whole have more deposits than they want. The most likely members of the public to have an excess are people who have built up large speculative balances but who have recently decided that security prices are likely to rise. The substantial excess supply of deposits implies that many people are in this situation. They will therefore seek to buy securities from the perhaps few people who think that security prices will fall. This process will result in bank deposits changing hands but not in any increase in the total level. It will also result in security prices rising since there has been a sudden increased demand for securities. (This rise will be gratifying to the recent purchasers of securities and distressing to the recent sellers!) The rise in security prices means that interest rates will fall. Indeed, the process will continue until they fall to 5 per cent and the demand for deposits reaches 1,000, for until that point the demand for deposits will be less than the supply and some people will still be wishing to buy securities. Suppose, instead, that with an interest rate of 7 per cent the level of deposits was the 800 that the public want. This time it is the banks who will take action, for they have cash of 100 and so a cash ratio above the 10 per cent level they desire. It has been seen that when banks are not fully lent then they will take steps which increase this lending. These steps would reduce interest rates, and they would continue until interest rates reached 5 per cent, for then the total demand for money would reach 1,200 so that deposits would reach the 1,000 desired by the banks.

What would happen if the interest rate was below the equilibrium level, say 3 per cent? At this level, people would want a total money stock of 1,400 and hence want bank deposits of 1,200. On the other hand, the banks would want the money stock to be 1,200 and so want deposits to be 1,000. Again, the likely events depend on what the level of deposits is to begin with.

Suppose, first, that the level of deposits is the 1,000 that the banks want. In that case, the problem is that the public as a whole want more deposits than they have. The most likely members of the public to be in that position are people with securities who have recently decided that security prices are likely to fall and so want to build up speculative holdings. The substantial excess demand for deposits implies that many people are in this position. They will therefore seek to sell securities to the perhaps few people who think security prices will rise. This process will result in bank deposits changing hands but not in any increase in the total level. It will also result in security prices falling since there has been a sudden drop in the demand for securities. (This drop will be gratifying to the recent sellers of securities and distressing to the recent buyers!) The fall in security prices means that interest rates rise. Indeed, the process will continue until they rise to 5 per cent and the demand reaches 1,000, for until that point the demand for deposits will be greater than the supply and some people will still be wishing to sell securities. Suppose, instead, that with an interest rate of 3 per cent the initial level of deposits was the 1,200 that the public want. This time it is the banks who will take action for they have cash of just 100 and so a cash ratio less than the desired 10 per cent. They will seek to reduce deposits by selling securities, which will force security prices down and interest rates up, and also by raising the interest on advances to persuade people to borrow less from the banks. These steps would raise interest rates and they would continue until interest rates reached 5 per cent, for then the total demand for money would be reduced to 1,200 so that deposits would be at the level of 1,000 desired by the banks.

Actually, there are a number of reasons for supposing that the vertical supply curve $M_s$ is a little unrealistic. One reason concerns the implication of $M_s$ that banks would supply deposits of 1,000 even if the interest rate were zero or a little above. Clearly there would be no point in having income-earning assets if the interest rate were zero; and banks might find that the costs of administering their holdings of securities and – more especially – advances would exceed the returns if the interest rate were positive but very low. Moreover, suppose banks find that out of every £100 used for securities and advances they 'lose' £1; for instance some firms issuing securities might go bankrupt and be unable to honour their debts, and some borrowers of advances will default in their repayments. In that case, the banks would want an interest rate in excess of 1 per cent in order to expect to make any income at all from their income-earning assets. Although all these points are valid, interest rates are never likely to fall to the levels which would make them very important, so subsequent analysis will ignore them.

There are two rather more pertinent reasons for believing that the level of bank deposits desired by the banks will depend on interest rates, and so for believing in turn that the supply curve shown in the figures should have a positive slope like the one shown as $M_s$ in Figure 4.3, as opposed to a vertical supply curve like $M_s$ in Figure 4.2. For convenience, $M_s$ in Figure 4.3 is drawn along with the same demand curve used in Figure 4.2 and it intersects $M_d$ at the same equilibrium position where interest rates are 5 per cent and the money stock is 1,200.

The first reason of these two reasons for believing that the supply curve will slope hinges on the fact that when interest rates on securities (which are indicated on the vertical axis) rise, banks will be able to increase the interest rates they pay on their interest-bearing deposits and yet still make profits. Now competition between banks for deposits is likely to mean that they actually will pay higher interest rates on these deposits when interest rates rise (though the rates on deposits will be some way below the rates at which banks lend). In turn, interest-bearing deposits in banks will become more attractive relative to cash held outside the banks as far as the public is concerned. Thus a rise in interest rates may reduce the level of cash held by the public as people deposit some cash in the banks, and so the banks will find their cash stocks rise. Now the movement of £1 from a piggy bank at home to a clearing bank does not of itself change the money stock, for the rise in deposits is offset by a fall in the public's cash-holdings. However, with a 10 per cent cash ratio, it means the banks will want deposits to increase by a further £9; the extra cash will support an extra £10 but deposits have already risen by £1. In short, higher interest rates raise banks' cash holdings and so increase the level of the money stock they desire. The sloped $M_s$ reflects this fact, for it shows that banks want a higher money stock when interest rates are high than they want when interest rates are low. In the case of the sloped $M_s$ in Figure 4.3, and in later related figures, it is supposed that the public want cash of 200 when the interest rate is 5 per cent; and it is supposed that they will want less cash if the rate rises, so that they will then deposit more cash with the banks, but want more cash if the rate falls, so that they will then withdraw some cash from the banks.

The second of these reasons for a sloping $M_s$ is that higher interest rates could encourage banks to operate with lower cash ratios. This means that higher interest rates could cause them to want a higher level of deposits and, in turn, a higher money stock. Lower cash ratios could come about in two ways when interest rates rise. First,

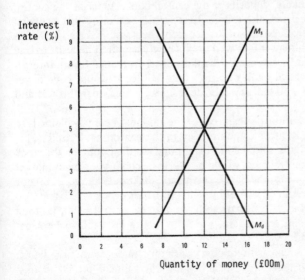

**Figure 4.3**

such rises mean that interest-bearing bank deposits become more attractive relative to non-interest-bearing ones, and so there is likely to be a shift of deposits to the former, which are generally not sight deposits, from the latter, which generally are. Such shifts may make banks feel it safe to operate with slightly lower cash ratios. The second way was noted in Chapter 3. It was explained that, as far as a bank is concerned, any cash ratio below 100 per cent carries some risk, but the higher the return they can get on lending, that is the higher interest rates are, so the more risk they are likely to take.

Although the sloping $M_s$ curve of Figure 4.3 is more realistic than the vertical one in Figure 4.2, it has no substantive effect on the analysis made so far. With the curves shown in Figure 4.3, the interest rate will settle at 5 per cent and the actual money stock will settle at 1,200 with the public holding cash of 200 and bank deposits of 1,000. If the interest rate was higher or lower, then the forces discussed earlier would operate to cause it to change until it was 5 per cent.

## Control when there is no lender of last resort

Suppose the money stock has settled at 1,200 and suppose the authorities want it to change. Perhaps they want it to fall. How could they bring the fall about? This section gives the answer in a case where there is no lender of last resort. In these circumstances, the authorities have essentially three options.

First, they could take steps to reduce the amount of cash available. One way this can be done is by arranging for clearing bank depositors to pay money to the government. Suppose, for instance, that the government sold some new bonds, or that it sold some state-owned assets, such as a water board, or that it simply raised taxes, and suppose it did not then return any money thus acquired by spending it again. The depositors purchasing the bonds or the water board or liable for the new taxes would make out cheques in favour of the government, and so their banks would pay money to the central bank out of their bankers' deposits at the central bank. As far as the central bank's balance sheet is concerned, the initial effect would be simply that bankers' deposits would fall and public deposits would rise from their assumed starting value of zero. However, the government might well use its newly-acquired deposits to buy back government bonds held by the central bank in order to reduce future interest charges. In this case, the central bank's assets would fall, as it would have fewer securities, and its liabilities would fall, as public deposits were used up in this way and fell to zero once again.

Another way in which the authorities can reduce the amount of cash available is to arrange for clearing bank depositors to pay money to the central bank itself. This would happen if the central bank sold second-hand bonds to the public on the stock exchange, in which case the central bank would be said to be conducting open-market operations. In these circumstances, the purchasers would make out cheques in favour of the central bank itself. Their banks would lose liabilities (as deposits fell) and also assets (as their deposits at the central bank fell). As for the central bank, its total liabilities and assets would fall once again, for there would be a fall in bankers' deposits matched by a fall in its security holdings.

To consider the effects of such cash-reducing operations, suppose that the banks lost cash, in the form of deposits at the central bank, to the value of 40. The banks' total cash holdings would fall from 100 to 60. What effect would this have on the stock of money? The answer is easiest to predict if the assumptions underlying the

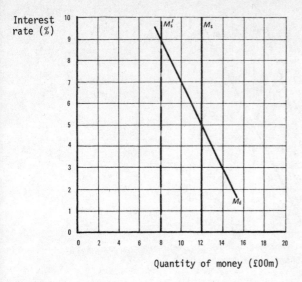

**Figure 4.4**

vertical supply curve in Figure 4.2 hold. This curve ($M_s$) and the demand curve ($M_d$) are reproduced in Figure 4.4. Now, if the banks lose cash of 40 and so have a new cash stock of 60, then their cash ratio of 10 per cent means they will in future want total deposits to be 600 instead of 1,000, so there will be a new supply curve, $M_s'$, at the level of 800 (for the total money stock would be 600 in deposits plus 200 cash held by the public). The new equilibrium interest rate can be seen to be 9 per cent, where $M_s'$ cuts $M_d$, and the money stock is 800. The money stock has fallen by 400, which is $\Delta C/r$ where $\Delta C$ is the fall in cash (of 40) and r is the banks' cash ratio of 10 per cent (or 0.1).

This situation is a shade more complex if the supply curve slopes as shown in Figure 4.3. That curve ($M_s$) is reproduced in Figure 4.5 along with the demand curve ($M_d$). Now to see what happens if the banks lose cash of 40, suppose initially that interest rates stayed at 5 per cent. In that case, the public would still want cash of 200 and there would be no incentive for the banks to change their cash ratios. Accordingly, the banks would react to the loss of cash of 40 by seeking to reduce deposits from 1,000 to 600, so reducing the money stock they desire from 1,200 to 800. This desired money stock at an interest rate of 5 per cent is indicated by the point labelled A on the new supply curve, $M_s'$, which shows a stock of 800 desired at that interest level. Not surprisingly, the stock desired at any other particular interest rate would be lower than before, and so $M_s'$ is wholly to the left of $M_s$. However, $M_s'$ is not parallel to $M_s$. This is because banks operate with lower cash ratios at higher interest rates so that a fall in cash holdings of 40 has a larger effect on desired deposit levels when interest rates are high. The upshot, though, is that the new equilibrium will be where $M_d$ is cut by $M_s'$. This gives an interest rate of 7.5 per cent and a money stock of 950. It can be seen that the effects of a fall in bank cash on both the rate of interest and the money stock are rather less marked when $M_s$ slopes (as in Figure 4.5) than when it is vertical (as in Figure 4.4).

A second method of cutting back on the money stock would be for the authorities to

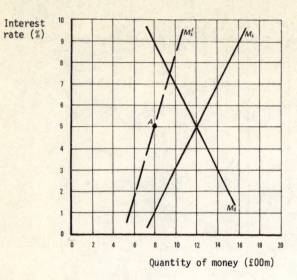

**Figure 4.5**

require the banks to hold a larger cash ratio than their present target level of 10 per cent. To see the effects of such a policy, suppose initially that the interest rate was 5 per cent and that the money stock was 1,200, as indicated by the intersection of the curves in Figures 4.6 and 4.7 which respectively reproduce the vertical and sloping $M_s$ curves of earlier figures along with the $M_d$ curves. Now suppose the authorities decided to require the banks to hold cash at a level equal to at least 12 per cent of their deposits. In that case, the banks would actually have to hold a slightly higher cash

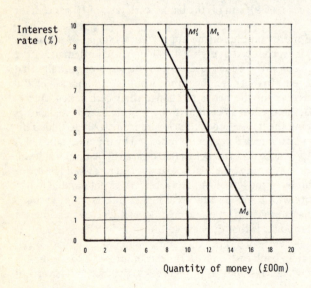

**Figure 4.6**

ratio than the one now imposed on them, so that they could handle day to day varia-tions in their cash holdings without being below the limit. Suppose they opted for a ratio of 12.5 per cent. Consider first the Figure 4.6 case where the $M_d$ curve is vertical. With bank cash at 100 and a target cash ratio of 12.5 per cent, the banks will seek a level of bank deposits of 800. Coupled with publicly-held cash of 200 this implies a new supply curve, $M'_s$, which is vertical at a desired money stock of 1,000. In this case, the interest rate would settle at 7 per cent while the money stock would indeed be 1,000.

Next consider the Figure 4.7 case. Recall that the original $M_s$ sloped partly because the banks would operate with lower cash ratios if interest rates rose and partly because the public would deposit more cash with them if interest rates rose. Broadly speaking, the first reason will cease to apply if banks feel they cannot cut their ratios below 12.5 per cent, though the next paragraph shows that it still applies at very low interest rates. However, the second reason will remain. It follows that the new mandatory cash ratio will result in a new supply curve which is steeper than the original one but not vertical. Recall, also, that at the initial equilibrium interest rate of 5 per cent, the banks had cash of 100 and a ratio of 10 per cent leading to a desired level of 1,000 for deposits and so 1,200 for the money stock when publicly-held cash was added in. If this 5 per cent interest rate happened to apply after the new mandatory ratio was introduced, with the banks holding cash of 100 and seeking a 12.5 per cent cash ratio, then the banks would want deposits of just 800 and so a total money stock of 1,000. This fact is reflected in the figure by the point labelled A on the new (steeper) supply curve, $M'_s$, for this point shows that the desired money stock would be 1,000 if interest rates happened to be 5 per cent.

Notice that $M'_s$ kinks at the interest rate of 2.75 per cent and follows the old $M_s$ at lower rates. Why is this? To see the reason, recall again that when the banks were free to choose their own cash ratio, then the ratio they would choose depended on the interest rate. It was assumed to be 10 per cent if interest rates were 5 per cent, lower than 10 per cent if interest rates were above 5 per cent, and higher than 10 per cent if interest rates were below 5 per cent. Now there was presumably some very low interest rate which would result in the banks choosing a cash ratio of 12.5 per cent. Suppose this interest rate was 2.75 per cent. Now if interest rates exceed 2.75 per cent, then the banks would like a cash ratio below 12.5 per cent and $M_s$ reflects their desired money stock at each interest rate. But if the authorities introduce a rule which imposes a ratio of 12 per cent, and if the banks respond by opting for one of 12.5 per cent, then they have to settle for lower money stocks as reflected by $M'_s$. Thus the new rule shifts the supply curve to the left if interest rates exceed 2.75 per cent. On the other hand, the new rule has *no* effect if interest rates are below that level. This is because the banks would choose to have cash ratios in excess of 12.5 per cent at such low interest rates. A rule obliging them to have ratios of at least 12 per cent will not make the slightest difference. Thus the rule will not affect the supply curve, and so $M'_s$ follows $M_s$ in this low interest rate range.

Although it has taken some time to explain why the new $M'_s$ is steeper than $M_s$ and why it has a kink, the upshot can be seen clearly on Figure 4.7. The new equilibrium interest rate and money stock can be found by looking at the intersection of $M'_s$ with $M_d$. This intersection actually shows an interest rate of 6.8 per cent and a money stock of 1,020. Again, then, the authorities would have less effect than they would have if the money supply curve were vertical as in Figure 4.6.

As an alternative, the authorities could seek to reduce the money stock by asking the

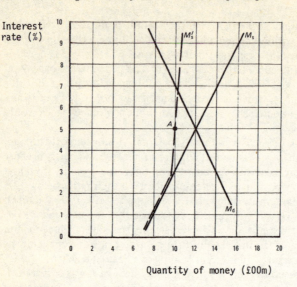

**Figure 4.7**

banks to abide by credit ceilings. It will be assumed that the banks react to such a request as though it were a requirement, perhaps out of fear that they would lose the right to take deposits if they ignored it! The banks in the country considered in the diagrams started off with figures in the balance sheet in Table 4.1. This showed them to have assets of 1,000 which comprised 100 in cash and 900 in loans in the form of both securities and of advances. The authorities could ask – but in effect require – these banks to cut back on this level of credit by, say, 200 to 700. The banks would then be unable to have deposits in excess of 800 which would be matched by cash of 100 and securities plus advances of 700. Of course, the ceiling will have this effect only if it applies to the overall level of advances plus securities. If certain types of securities or advances are exempt, then banks may expand the level of these and contract the level of the others so that their overall credit is little altered.

Assuming that the ceiling of 700 does apply to all credit, then it will affect the supply curves in the diagrams. To see this, consider Figures 4.8 and 4.9 which respectively reproduce the vertical and sloping $M_s$ curves of earlier figures along with the $M_d$ curves. Consider, first, the Figure 4.8 case where the supply curve is vertical. If the public continued to hold cash of 200 then there would be a new vertical supply curve, $M_s'$, at the level of 1,000, for the bank deposits cannot exceed 800 and publicly-held cash is 200. Here, the interest rate will settle at 7 per cent and the money stock at 1,000.

Consider, next, the Figure 4.9 case where the original money supply curve slopes. Suppose, for a moment, that the public persisted in holding cash of 200. In that case, there would be a new money supply curve, $M_s'$. Now $M_s'$ has a kink at a money stock of 1,000, below which it follows $M_s$. The point is that the money stock cannot now exceed 1,000 – 800 in bank deposits and 200 in publicly-held cash – which explains the vertical part of $M_s'$. However, the money stock could be below 1,000, and it would be below 1,000 if interest rates were so low that the banks wanted it to be below 1,000. With $M_s'$, the interest rate settles at 7 per cent and the money stock at 1,000.

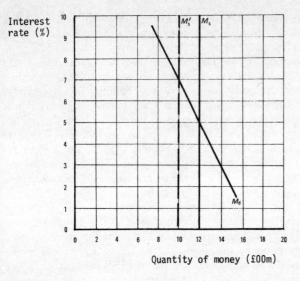

**Figure 4.8**

By creating a mostly vertical money supply curve, the policy of credit ceilings can be seen to have as much effect here as it did in Figure 4.8.

Notice that the new $M_s'$ supply curve in Figure 4.9 would actually be the same, even if the public then reacted to higher interest rates by depositing some of their cash holdings in their banks. Such action means that bank deposits would rise by as much as public cash holdings fell so that there would be no immediate effect on the money stock. More importantly, the credit ceiling means that the banks could not react to their extra cash holdings by creating extra deposits. Furthermore, even though the

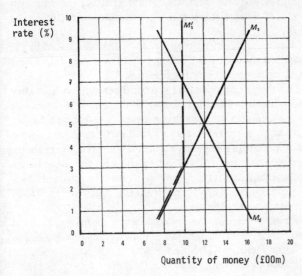

**Figure 4.9**

extra cash deposits will have raised the banks' total assets and liabilities, the fact that their extra cash can have no effect on the money stock means that the credit ceiling regulations will not have to be tightened up further.

This section may be concluded by noting that the monetary authorities could clearly set about expanding the money stock by taking actions opposite to those just described. Thus the government could raise the banks' holdings of cash by, for example, making purchases from the public, though it would have to ensure that it did not simultaneously remove cash by raising taxes or borrowing from the public. Note that despite these constraints it could finance its purchases by borrowing from the central bank, as discussed in connection with Table 3.1. Likewise, the central bank could raise the banks' holdings of cash by buying securities in open-market operations on the stock exchange. Alternatively, the authorities could seek to expand the money stock by reducing any mandatory cash ratio they had previously laid down for the banks, though this would have no further effect once the ratio had been reduced to the level that the banks would regard as prudent. Finally, they could relax any credit ceilings previously imposed, though this would have no further effect once the permitted level of credit equalled the level that the banks would seek in the absence of regulations. It should be noted, though, that the effects of expansionary measures *permit* banks to expand the money stock whereas contractionary measures *require* them to reduce the money stock, or at least they do so if the banks were initially fully lent.

## Control when the lender of last resort lends directly to the clearing banks

The previous section has discussed the situation when there is no lender of last resort. It is necessary to see how the analysis given here must be modified when there is one. This section will consider what happens if the lender of last resort, taken to be the central bank, is prepared to lend directly to banks which have a cash crisis. The next chapter will consider what happens when last resort lending is done indirectly via the discount houses, as in the UK.

To see the implications of last resort lending, consider the banks discussed in the last section in the starting position shown by the balance sheet in Table 4.1. These banks operated in a system with no last resort lending facilities. They were allowed to choose their own cash ratio, and they desired a cash ratio of 10 per cent; at least they did so if the interest rate was 5 per cent. Now the objective of these cash reserves was to enable each bank to meet any demand for cash that it considered likely, whether from depositors actually wanting to withdraw cash to spend or from them making substantially more payments to depositors elsewhere than they received from them.

Essentially, the effect of introducing last resort lending facilities for these banks would be to encourage each bank to operate with a lower cash ratio, for it would know that – in an emergency – it could always borrow cash from the central bank. However, the extent of this encouragement would depend on the interest rate imposed by the central bank on the loans concerned. The point is that when a bank expands its securities and advances and so cuts its cash ratio, it knows it may occasionally need to make use of the last resort lending facilities. The higher the interest rate charged on these facilities, the less it will want to risk using them so the higher will be its target cash ratio.

Suppose, for instance, that the facilities were initially offered at a rate of 3.5 per cent. Such facilities would doubtless tempt the banks to have a lower cash ratio at any general level of interest rates than before, and so would encourage them to expand their loans and advances. The effect of this would be to shift the money supply curve shown on the figures to the right. It will be assumed in this section that the money supply curve is positively sloped, and it will be assumed that before last resort lending facilities were introduced it was as shown by the curve labelled $M_s$ on the earlier Figures 4.3, 4.5, 4.7 and 4.9. This curve is reproduced in Figure 4.10 along with the same $M_d$ given on earlier figures. These curves intersect at the position (E) which is the equilibrium before the new facilities are introduced. This is the same position, with the interest rate at 5 per cent and the money stock of 1,200, as shown for the initial equilibriums in Figures 4.3, 4.5, 4.7 and 4.9. With the interest rate settling at 5 per cent, the banks want a cash ratio of 10 per cent, and they will have cash of 100. This enables them to have deposits of 1,000 which combine with publicly-held cash of 200 to give a total money stock of 1,200.

Now when the new last resort lending facilities are introduced, the banks might seek a cash ratio of, say, only 6.25 per cent if interest rates on securities happened to be 5 per cent. This lower ratio would lead to their wanting a total money stock of 1,800 at that interest rate, and this desire is shown by point A on the new supply curve $M'_s$. Why should they seek a figure of 1,800? It is because with cash of 100 and a target cash ratio of 6.25 per cent, the banks want deposits to total 1,600 (as 100 is 6.25 per cent of 1,600); and 1,600 deposits plus 200 for publicly-held cash means a desired money stock of 1,800.

Notice that $M'_s$ has not been drawn parallel to $M_s$. The last resort lending facilities are likely to make the banks want an increased money stock at each possible interest rate, but there is no reason to suppose that the increase will be exactly the same at each interest rate. Now point A is, of course, just one point on the new supply curve. It is not, in fact, the equilibrium point. This is at E' where $M'_s$ cuts $M_d$. The equilibrium

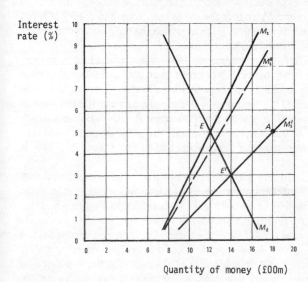

Quantity of money (£00m)

**Figure 4.10**

interest rate is shown to be 3 per cent. At this interest rate, banks would want a less risky situation than they would be prepared to take at 5 per cent and so they would want a higher cash ratio, say 8.33 per cent. This means they want deposits at 1,200 (for their cash of 100 would then be 8.33 per cent of total deposits) and hence a total money stock of 1,400 as shown at $E'$.

In this example, the final equilibrium was such that the equilibrium interest rate level, 3 per cent, was *below* the rate of 3.5 per cent for last resort lending facilities. This was because of the supposed response on banks' target cash ratios and hence the supposed new supply curve $M_s'$. In principle, the banks might have been less responsive, so that the supply curve might have moved less far to the right, say to $M_s''$, and so have given an equilibrium interest rate of 4.5 per cent which would be *above* the last resort lending rate. This might seem an implausible outcome. If the banks can always borrow at 3.5 per cent, then why would they restrict their lending at a level which produces interest rates of 4.5 per cent? Why not extend lending at least until interest rates get only just a little above 3.5 per cent? After all, lending at, say, 3.6 per cent should yield a profit if the banks can always borrow at 3.5 per cent.

One answer is that if the banks were to regard last resort lending facilities as a regular source of funds for their own lending rather than an emergency source, then they would actually want the interest rates on their own lending to be somewhat higher than the rate they paid for those facilities. They would want a higher rate in order to cover the risks and administration costs of their own lending and also to cover the risk of a sudden rise in the interest rate on last resort lending. Another answer is that the authorities are unlikely to want last resort lending to be regarded as a regular source of funds by the banks. Accordingly, they will generally keep the rate charged on it above the levels attainable on bank lending. If it happened to be below those levels, then they would keep it sufficiently close that the differential would be too small for banks to find it profitable to borrow these facilities on a continuous basis to finance their own lending.

Suppose that the introduction of last resort lending facilities at 3.5 per cent does in fact produce the new supply curve $M_s'$ so that the money stock rises to 1,400. It is not difficult to see that there would now be four ways in which the authorities could seek to reduce the stock of money below 1,400.

First, the rate of interest on last resort lending could be raised. If the rate of interest on last resort lending facilities rose to, say, 5.5 per cent, then the banks would want to reduce the chances of needing to make use of the facilities, and so they would seek to operate with higher cash ratios. This would shift the supply curve to the left, just as the introduction of the facilities shifted it to the right when it caused bankers to use lower ratios. Perhaps the rise to 5.5 per cent would shift the curve from $M_s'$ to $M_s''$, so resulting in an equilibrium interest rate of 4.5 per cent and a money stock of 1,250, as shown in Figure 4.10.

Secondly, the authorities could take steps to reduce the amount of cash available, perhaps by indulging in open-market operations in which securities were sold to the public. This would shift the supply curve to the left, just as it did in Figure 4.5. Thus it would force interest rates up and the money stock down. By choosing an appropriate level of sales, the authorities could force the supply curve to move from $M_s'$ to a position like that of $M_s''$ in Figure 4.10 which produces an equilibrium interest rate at 4.5 per cent and a money stock of 1,250. It might be thought that the banks would respond to any fall in cash holdings by using last resort lending facilities to restore their holdings, so that there would actually be no effect on the equilibrium position.

They might well make some use of the facilities temporarily, to maintain a reasonable cash ratio until deposits could be cut by reducing advances and selling securities. However, they would be unlikely to use these facilities on an indefinite basis to keep the money stock at 1,400 thereby keeping the interest rates on the securities they buy at the original level of 3 per cent. The principal reason for this is that the rate at which they can borrow these facilities is assumed to be 3.5 per cent, which would be above the level being earned on their securities.

Thirdly, the authorities could require the banks to have a cash ratio higher than the 8.33 per cent held at the (new) equilibrium E'. The simplest example to consider is to suppose the banks were required to hold a ratio of at least 10 per cent. They might respond by having a target ratio of exactly 10 per cent, for they could rely on the temporary use of last resort lending whenever the ratio fell below this level. Thus, in this example, it is supposed the banks will set the same 10 per cent cash ratio that they had before the last resort lending facilities were introduced.

As in Figure 4.7, the imposition of a cash ratio requirement would create a new supply curve with a kink in it. This new curve is shown as $M_s''$ on Figure 4.11 where $M_d$, $M_s'$, E and E' are reproduced from Figure 4.10. It will be seen that $M_s''$ passes the original equilibrium point E so that the new equilibrium would also be at E with an interest rate of 5 per cent and a money stock of 1,200. (The new supply curve would have to pass E, for that point shows the desired money stock at an interest rate of 5 per cent when the desired cash ratio is 10 per cent; but the new curve would actually be steeper than the original $M_s$ – shown in Figure 4.10 – to the right of E and so would not coincide with $M_s$ there, for $M_s$ reflects a willingness by banks to have cash ratios below 10 per cent at higher interest rates than 5 per cent, a strategy they would now not be allowed to pursue.)

Fourthly, the authorities could impose a credit ceiling on the banks. Thus if equilibrium was initially at E' and the banks were obliged to reduce their credit by 200, then the supply curve would have a kink at 1,200 as shown by $M_s''$ in Figure 4.11. The reasons for this effect on the supply curve are identical to those given when

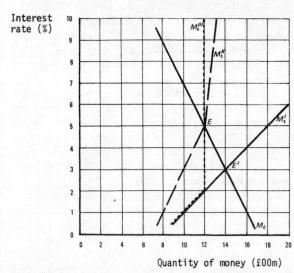

Figure 4.11

explaining the effect of such a ceiling in relation to Figure 4.9 in the last section. In the present example the money stock would settle at E with the money stock at 1,200 and with an interest rate of 5 per cent.

The final point made in the last section should be made again here, namely that if the authorities want to expand the money stock then they should take precisely the opposite actions to the contractionary ones just described. Thus they could seek to increase the cash available to the banks, reduce any cash ratio requirements imposed on them, ease any credit ceilings in force or reduce the interest rate charged on last resort lending facilities. As before though, it must be stressed that while contractionary measures can compel the banks to contract, or at least they can if the banks start off fully lent, expansionary measures merely permit expansion.

## Further aspects of monetary control

The last two sections have shown how the authorities can seek to change the money stock. In practice, the authorities seek not so much to reduce or raise the money stock but rather to reduce or, more rarely, to increase its rate of growth. However, although the previous two sections have indicated the principles of the main methods of monetary control, they embodied a number of assumptions whose significance must now be considered.

First, it was assumed that changes in the interest rate would not affect the demand curve for money. In practice, measures which reduce the money stock inevitably raise the rate of interest and, in turn, are likely to reduce the level of spending in the economy, particularly spending on investment goods and consumer durables. Consequently, such measures lead also to a fall in the overall level of income, and this fall in income is likely to lead to a fall in the demand for money – especially the transactions and precautionary demands on the Keynesian approach. This means that measures which shift the $M_s$ curve to the left are likely to create, in time anyway, leftward shifts in the $M_d$ curve. A glance at the diagrams will reveal that the subsequent leftward shifts in the $M_d$ curves will ease any rise in interest rates but reinforce any fall in the money stock caused by the shift in the $M_s$ curves. Conversely, steps to raise the money stock tend to reduce interest rates. This will raise spending and incomes, so shifting the $M_d$ curve to the right and thereby restraining the anticipated fall in interest rates but augmenting the anticipated rise in the money stock.

Secondly, it was assumed that the public's demand for cash would not be affected by changes in the level of their bank deposits. In practice, the public may tend to want more cash when deposits are high and less when they are low. Such behaviour would reduce the effects of any measures to cut the money stock except credit ceilings. The reason is straightforward. Once measures such as reducing the level of banks' cash holdings, imposing higher cash ratios or raising the terms offered on last resort lending start to cut deposits, so the public will place some of its cash holdings in the banks. This extra bank cash means the banks will not have to cut their deposits as much as earlier sections suggested. Of course, credit ceilings also reduce deposits and might lead to the public placing extra cash in the banks, but the banks would still be unable to allow their lending to exceed the ceiling levels. Conversely, action by the authorities to raise the money stock might have less effect than the analysis given earlier suggests if, as banks respond by expanding their deposits, they find the public withdrawing some cash, thereby reducing cash held by the banks. Incidentally, a tendency for the public to want more cash when deposits rise and vice versa is likely to make the money supply curves more inelastic; for attempts by the banks to raise the level of deposits when interest rates rise will be partially frustrated when the higher deposits result in the public wanting a little more cash.

Thirdly, it was assumed that the public would not react to falls (or rises) in their money holdings by selling (or buying) National Savings Certificates. This is a fairly minor point, but if the authorities embark on, say, a process of monetary contraction and the public seek to reduce its impact by selling National Savings Certificates – that is surrendering their certificates to the government in return for money – then they will receive cheques from the government which will be paid into their banks and increase the clearing banks' cash holdings. Consequently, the banks will be able to reduce their deposits by less than the previous analysis has suggested – unless they are subject to credit ceilings which cannot be escaped. Conversely, measures to increase the money stock might have less effect than suggested here if the public uses some of the increase to purchase National Savings Certificates, thereby reducing the cash holdings of the clearing banks.

Fourthly, it was assumed that there were no NBFIs. It was explained in the last chapter that when a saver switches funds from a bank to an NBFI this does not of itself affect the money stock. Nevertheless, NBFIs have major consequences which should be mentioned here. The key point is that if NBFIs, or at least deposit-taking NBFIs, were set up for the first time in a country, then their deposits might be seen to some extent as substitutes for bank deposits. Of course, NBFI deposits are not spendable money, so they are of limited use for funds held with a view to being spent soon, but they are well worth considering for funds that might not be spent for a few weeks or months. In other words, although NBFI deposits are not money, they are a form of 'near-money'. It follows that if such NBFIs were set up, then there could be a fall in the demand for money in the form of bank deposits. Consequently, interest rates would be reduced and, provided the money supply schedule is not vertical, the money stock would also end up somewhat lower.

To consider the implications of this point in the context of monetary control, imagine now that the initial $M_s$ curves in the diagrams in this chapter related to a country where such NBFIs exist, and so that initial interest rates were lower than they would have been if there were no NBFIs. Now attempts to reduce the money stock typically shift $M_s$ curves to the left. In turn they raise the interest rates on securities and bank loans and reduce the level of bank lending. Of course, higher interest rates on securities and bank loans mean that banks will be able to offer higher rates on interest-bearing deposits, and competition between banks for deposits will doubtless drive these rates up. At the same time, therefore, NBFIs must raise the rates on their deposits to prevent a mass switch of funds by depositors from NBFIs to the banks. The NBFIs will be able to meet the extra cost of deposits by increasing the rates charged on their loans which will be more in demand now that bank lending has decreased. In fact, it is perfectly possible that while bank lending will fall, NBFI lending will rise, or at least fall by less, and this growth in the relative importance of NBFIs could lead to a greater differential between the interest rates offered on their deposits and the rates on interest-bearing bank deposits. This could stimulate a fall in the demand for interest-bearing bank deposits and so a fall in the demand for money. In short, the existence of NBFIs means attempts to shift $M_s$ curves to the left will put some leftward pressure on $M_d$ curves, thus ameliorating any rise in interest rates though reinforcing any fall in the money stock (except in cases where the $M_s$ curve is vertical). Conversely, the existence of NBFIs means that attempts to raise the money stock might have more effect on the stock but less downwards effect on the interest rates than previous analysis suggests.

It can be seen that releasing any one of these assumptions means monetary controls tend to have less effect on interest rates than previous sections indicated. On the other hand, releasing some of them suggests that the effects on the money stock could be greater than indicated while releasing others means they could be less. Needless to say, though, the direction in which the money stock would change will remain the same no matter which of these assumptions is released.

This chapter ends with a final but critically important point. Despite the qualifications to the analysis raised in the last few paragraphs, the system will settle down at some point on the demand curve for money. The possible monetary measures examined in this chapter may induce some modest shifts in the demand curve, but in general the monetary authorities tend to regard the demand curve as reasonably stable and not under their direct control. In practice, then, they typically regard their monetary measures as enabling them to shift from one point on the demand curve to another. This means, of course, that they do not expect to be able to use monetary measures to secure an equilibrium position at a point off the demand curve. Suppose they reckon the demand curve is as shown in Figures 4.10 and 4.11, and reckon that monetary control measures would not move it much. It follows that if they are anxious to have a particular money stock, say, 1,000, then they *must* have interest rates around 7 per cent. On the other hand, if they want interest rates around 7 per cent, then they *must* have a money stock of 1,000. In short, the authorities can choose a particular level for interest rates or a particular level for the money stock, but they cannot choose particular levels for both.

# 5

# Controlling the money stock when last resort lending is done indirectly

## Introduction

Chapter 4 explained how the money stock could be controlled if there was no lender of last resort facility, and it also explained how it could be controlled if last resort lending was made available directly to the banks. The main purpose of this chapter is to explain how the stock could be controlled if, as in the UK, last resort lending facilities are made available indirectly via the discount houses. The chapter also allows for a rather greater variety of clearing banks assets than was considered in Chapter 4.

It is worth stressing two points at the outset of this chapter. First, by allowing for the existence of discount houses and for a greater variety of bank assets, the analysis is a little more complex than the analysis of Chapter 4; nevertheless, the basic underlying principles are generally much the same. Secondly, although the analysis gets closer to the realities of what happens in the UK, it should still be seen as a much simplified view of a very complex system. One consequence of a complex real-world situation is that the banks and discount houses may be able to react in a variety of ways to actions by each other and to actions by the monetary authorities. The reactions described here should be seen as illustrating plausible reactions but not as defining the only possible reactions.

As in Chapter 4, the discussion of monetary control will be based on four simplifying assumptions. The first is that the demand curve for money is assumed not to shift if interest rates fall. The second is that the public's demand for cash is not be affected by changes in their bank deposits. The third is that the public will not react to falls (or rises) in their money holdings by selling (or buying) National Savings Certificates. The fourth is that NBFIs can generally be ignored. The last section of the chapter recalls the effects of releasing these assumptions.

It is useful to begin by supposing that the system is initially in equilibrium and by presenting a combined balance sheet for all clearing banks showing their initial liabilities and assets. This is done in the top part of stage 1 in Table 5.1. The figures in this table are given in £m and have been chosen purely for convenience. The table shows a single entry for deposits of 1,000, but it shows four separate entries for assets. The first of these is notes and coin held on banks' premises shown at 20; to keep later analysis straightforward, it will be supposed that the banks would keep this figure at

20 unless the total level of deposits changes by more than 50. The second entry for assets comprises balances at the Bank of England; it is supposed that there are regulations which require banks to hold balances there equal to 0.5 per cent of their total deposits, and that they actually seek balances of 0.6 per cent in order that they could meet small falls in these balances without going below the mandatory limit. Next comes loans to the discount houses, or LDMA. For convenience, it will be assumed that these loans comprise the whole of the banks' money-at-call and it will be supposed that the banks are obliged to have money-at-call amounting to 5 per cent of total deposits but actually aim to have a level of 5.4 per cent, hence 54 here, so that they can meet small falls in these loans without falling below the obligatory 5 per cent level. Notice, then, that the banks like balances at the Bank of England plus money-at-call to equal 6 per cent of total liabilities. The remaining assets of 920 comprise securities and advances (other than loans to the LDMA).

There are two other aspects of the initial equilibrium to note. First, there is the combined balance sheet of the LDMA which is shown in the lower part of Table 5.1.

**Table 5.1**   The effects of reducing the cash available to the banks

| STAGE | 1 | 2 | 3 | 4 | 5 | 6 | 7 | 8 | 9 |
|---|---|---|---|---|---|---|---|---|---|
| Clearing bank liabilities | | | | | | | | | £m |
| Deposits | 1000 | 997 | 997 | 997 | 1000 | 1000 | 997 | 950 | 976 |
| Total | 1000 | 997 | 997 | 997 | 1000 | 1000 | 997 | 950 | 976 |
| Clearing bank assets | | | | | | | | | £m |
| Notes and coin | 20 | 20 | 20 | 20 | 20 | 20 | 20 | 20 | 20 |
| Balances with Bank of England | 6 | 3 | 3 | 6 | 6 | 6 | 6 | 5.7 | 5.8 |
| Market loans to LDMA | 54 | 54 | 54 | 51 | 54 | 54 | 51 | 51.3 | 52.2 |
| Securities and advances | 920 | 920 | 920 | 920 | 920 | 920 | 920 | 873 | 898 |
| Total | 1000 | 997 | 997 | 997 | 1000 | 1000 | 997 | 950 | 976 |
| LDMA liabilities | | | | | | | | | £m |
| Money-at-call | 54 | 54 | 54 | 51 | 54 | 54 | 51 | 51.3 | 52.2 |
| Total | 54 | 54 | 54 | 51 | 54 | 54 | 51 | 51.3 | 52.2 |
| LDMA assets | | | | | | | | | £m |
| Balances with Bank of England | 0 | 0 | 3 | 0 | 0 | 0 | 0 | 0 | 0 |
| Balances with clearing banks | 0 | 0 | 0 | 0 | 3 | 0 | 0 | 0 | 0 |
| Treasury bills | 14 | 14 | 14 | 14 | 14 | 14 | 14 | 14.3 | 15.2 |
| Other securities | 40 | 40 | 37 | 37 | 37 | 40 | 37 | 37 | 37 |
| Total | 54 | 54 | 54 | 51 | 54 | 54 | 51 | 51.3 | 52.2 |

This shows that their liabilities consist only of the 54 they have borrowed from the clearing banks, while their asset figures show they have used up 14 of this money-at-call on Treasury bills and 40 on other assets, notably, no doubt, commercial bills; the assets figures show also that the discount houses have accounts at the Bank of England, and with the clearing banks, though all these accounts are initially empty.

Secondly, there is the money stock and the rate of interest. The money stock comprises cash held by the public, taken to be 200, and bank deposits. It will be assumed that the central bank generally has no deposits other than those of the clearing banks, so that only the 1,000 deposits held at the clearing banks need to be included. Thus the money stock is 1,200. Figure 5.1 shows that this money stock can be taken to be at the equilibrium level, for the demand and supply curves ($M_d$ and $M_s$) intersect at the level 1,200. The intersection also indicates the equilibrium interest rate which is currently 10 per cent. It will be noted that the supply and demand curves used in this chapter are curved; it is unlikely that the curves in the real world are straight like the ones used in the last chapter.

Now the authorities can seek to control the money stock using the same methods discussed in the last chapter, though the precise mechanics are a shade more complex, and the analysis is a little different in the case of changing the interest rate charged on last resort lending facilities. This is particularly important as this is currently the pre-ferred method of control in the UK. This method will be considered last. Until then, it will be supposed that the Bank of England is always prepared to make last resort lending facilities available to the discount houses at an interest rate equivalent to the current rate available on Treasury bills; and it will be supposed, too, that this rate is the same as the rate on consols as determined by the intersection of the money demand and supply curves. It will be seen later that it is only when the Bank of England sets a higher rate than the Treasury bill rate that its choice of rate is likely to affect the money stock.

The following four sections show how the authorities could seek to reduce the

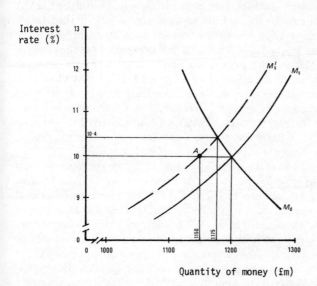

**Figure 5.1**

money stock by reducing the amount of cash available to the banks, by raising cash (or other) ratios imposed on the banks, by imposing credit ceilings and by raising the rate charged on last resort lending facilities above the Treasury bill rate. Naturally they could seek to expand the stock by increasing the amount of cash available to the banks, by reducing the cash (or other) ratios imposed on them, by relaxing credit ceilings or by reducing the rate charged on last resort lending facilities towards the Treasury bill rate. However, the contractionary and expansionary measures do not have perfectly symmetrical effects. Contractionary measures force contraction, or at least they do if the banks are initially fully lent, while expansionary ones merely permit expansion.

## Open-market operations

Consider, first, the effects of steps taken by the authorities to reduce the amount of cash held by the banks, perhaps as a result of open-market sales of securities by the Bank of England. Suppose the value of these sales is 3. Then the initial effects, shown in stage 2 of Table 5.1, are to reduce clearing bank deposits by 3, the deposits concerned being those of the security purchasers, and to reduce clearing bank balances at the Bank of England by 3. Why do these balances fall? It is because the clearing banks' depositors have paid money to the Bank of England, so the Bank takes money from the clearing banks by reducing the value of their deposits with it. (As far as the Bank of England is concerned, the fall in its liabilities resulting from smaller bankers' deposits would, of course, be matched by the fall in its assets resulting from the sale of some of its securities.)

Notice that there is no immediate effect on the discount houses. However, there will be an almost immediate effect on them, for the banks' deposits at the Bank of England have now fallen below 0.5 per cent of their liabilities, so the banks are likely to call in loans to the LDMA of about 3 to restore them. The banks will want the LDMA to pay in cash, the normal arrangement in the circumstances, and the LDMA will most probably raise the cash by selling bills, say commercial bills, to the Bank of England. The effects of these sales are, in the first instance, to reduce by 3 the holdings of 'other securities' by the LDMA and to give it deposits of 3 at the Bank, as shown in stage 3. The LDMA then arranges for the Bank of England to transfer these deposits to the clearing banks with the effects shown in stage 4. The LDMA loses 3 in assets (its deposit at the Bank of England) and 3 in liabilities (it now has fewer loans from the clearing banks) while the banks gain 3 in their deposits at the Bank in return for a fall of 3 in the size of their loans to the LDMA. Of course, steps 2 to 4 happen very quickly, but it is useful to break the process down into steps to see the precise order in which events take place.

However, stage 4 is not the end of the story. The banks have now got deposits at the Bank of just over their target of 0.6 per cent, but their loans to the LDMA now account for only 51 out of total liabilities of 997, that is about 5.1 per cent. This level is permissible as it exceeds the mandatory 5 per cent, but it is below the target level of 5.4 per cent that the banks are assumed to want. The most tempting response from the banks is to seek to restore loans to the LDMA to 54. Now the Bank effectively imposes limits on how much the LDMA can borrow by imposing upper limits to the level of assets they can have, a point considered more fully in Chapter 7. But even if their initial level of loans (54) was the maximum permitted, they could still borrow 3 more in the stage 4 position since their loans there are only 51. The initial effects of such a response are shown in stage 5, where it is supposed the houses have agreed to borrow an extra 3 and where their accounts at the clearing banks have accordingly been raised by 3 ready for them to spend. Perhaps the LDMA soon buy some commercial bills off other depositors at the banks with the results shown in stage 6. There is no change in the banks' balance sheets, because some depositors (the LDMA) have made purchases from others, but the LDMA gain bills for 3 at the expense of their short-lived deposits at the clearing banks. As a result of all this activity, the balance sheets of both the banks and the LDMA could end up in stage 6 just as they were in stage 1!

All of this suggests that the open-market operations have been ineffective in reducing the money stock. However, they can be made effective if the Bank of England takes steps to increase the supply of new Treasury bills in line with any increase in new loans made by the banks to the LDMA after stage 4. So if the banks raise these loans by 3, as in stage 5, then the Bank should at once offer new Treasury bills for sale. The effects of this action would actually be to create the situation shown in stage 7 rather than the stage 6 situation that the banks hoped for. How is stage 7 reached from stage 5? No matter who buys the new Treasury bills, the banks' deposits will fall by 3 to 997; and their balances at the Bank will fall by 3 from 6 to 3, and these must be at once be restored to 6 by calling in loans of 3 to LDMA which thus end up at 51. This calling in of loans from the LDMA could most easily be effected by removing the 3 in their clearing bank deposits that arose in stage 5.

In fact, it is possible that the new Treasury bills would have been bought by the LDMA themselves. After all they buy most new Treasury bills and *have* to buy any not bought by anyone else. However, if the LDMA did buy the new bills, then they would have used up their new loans of 3 by the time the banks demanded repayment of money-at-call for this amount. So the LDMA would have to get some money quickly and would obtain it from the Bank of England, probably by selling securities to the Bank. If these securities were Treasury bills, then there would be no effect on the stage 7 figures for the LDMA because, in effect, old Treasury bills were swapped for new ones; if the securities offered to the Bank were not Treasury bills, then the LDMA's holding of other securities would fall to 34 while its holding of Treasury bills would rise to 17.

The key point to grasp from stage 7 is that the clearing banks are in exactly the same position that they were in before in stage 4. Their problem in stage 4 was that their loans to the LDMA were below the 5.4 per cent of deposits they want. In practice, the banks know that any attempt to solve this problem by making new loans to the LDMA, as in stage 5, with the hope of reaching stage 6, where they are back in the original position, will be thwarted by the Bank selling new Treasury bills and so taking them to stage 7 which is the same as stage 4.

So what *does* happen after stage 4 if the Bank is determined the open-market sales will be made effective? The banks must accept that their total deposits at the Bank of England plus their loans to the LDMA are 57. They cannot in practice raise this figure, so they must make the combined new total of 57 for these items equal to the target 6 per cent of total liabilities by reducing total liabilities from 997 to 950. This they will do by selling securities and reducing the level of their advances so that those two items have a combined figure of 873, as shown at stage 8. This stage shows that the banks will actually raise loans to the LDMA just a little, in fact by 0.3, from 51 (in stage 4) to 51.3 (which is 5.4 per cent of 950); the Bank will accordingly sell Treasury Bills for this amount 0.3, probably to the LDMA, so the banks lose 0.3 in their deposits at the Bank which fall from 6 (in stage 4) to 5.7 (that is 6 per cent of 950) and the LDMA end up as shown in stage 8 with money-at-call and Treasury bill holdings both rising by 0.3 (from the stage 4 values). Stage 8 suggests that bank deposits, and hence the money stock, will fall by 50 from the initial stage 1 level. Indeed, it suggests a new money stock of 1,150, comprising 950 in bank deposits and 200 in publicly-held cash.

Actually, although the processes discussed in the moves from stage 1 to 4 and then to 8 may well occur, the results will not be as sizeable as the figures in Table 5.1 suggest. The point is that the fall in deposits of 50 between stages 1 and 8 would occur only if interest rates stayed constant. In turn, the level of the money stock desired by the banks would fall by 50 from 1,200 to 1,150 only if interest rates stayed constant. In fact, interest rates will rise. All this is shown by Figure 5.1. The authorities' action means the banks have a new supply curve, $M_s'$, and point A on this shows that the banks would want a money stock of 1,150 if interest rates stayed at the initial level of 10 per cent. But interest rates will rise to 10.4 per cent, the level where $M_s'$ cuts $M_d$, and so the banks will then want a money stock of 1,175.

The figures for stage 9 of Table 5.1 show how this might come about. First, higher interest rates could lead to higher rates on interest-bearing deposits so that maybe the public reduce their cash holdings by 1 (to 199) and increase bank-held cash by 1. Initially, the banks might add this to their Bank of England deposits, but stage 9 supposes they soon raise money-at-call by 0.9 (to 52.2) and that the LDMA spend their extra loans on newly-issued Treasury bills; accordingly, the banks lose 0.9 of the increase in their Bank of England deposits which thus rise in the end by only 0.1 (to 5.8) from the stage 8 level. Secondly, higher interest rates may induce the banks to operate with slightly lower ratios for their Bank of England deposits and loans to the LDMA. Stage 9 assumes they are happy to let securities and assets have a value of 898, so that total assets and liabilities can equal 976. They can be seen to accept Bank of England deposits at around 0.594 per cent of total liabilities (5.8 being around 0.594 per cent of 976) instead of the original 0.6 per cent, and to accept loans to the LDMA at around 5.35 per cent of total liabilities (52.2 being around 5.35 per cent of 976) instead of the original 5.4 per cent. Notice that the total level of deposits, 976, combines with the new level of publicly-held cash, 199, to give a money stock of 1,175 which squares with the new equilibrium shown in Figure 5.1. The upshot is that the authorities' action will raise interest rates and it will cut the money stock, but the money stock falls from 1,200 to 1,175, and clearing bank deposits fall from the original 1,000 in stage 1 to 976 in stage 9, a less significant fall than suggested by stage 8.

## Changing the minimum ratios banks are required to observe

Consider, next, the possibility of the authorities changing the ratios which the banks are obliged to meet. There are in fact two ratios in the present example, the 0.5 per cent for balances at the Bank of England and the 5 per cent for loans to the LDMA. In principle, the results would be much the same whichever ratio was changed. In practice, whenever this method has been used, it is, in effect the cash ratio which has been altered. The formal mechanism in the UK is that the clearing banks are required to open second *special deposits* at the Bank of England. Perhaps they would be required to keep special deposits there of 0.25 per cent of total liabilities, while maintaining a minimum of 0.5 per cent as before in their normal or 'other' deposits. Of course, the effect is identical to what would be observed if they were required to maintain just one deposit and to raise the amount held there from 0.5 per cent of total liabilities to 0.75 per cent.

Suppose, to start with, that the clearing banks and discount houses were in equilibrium with the figures shown in stage 1 of Table 5.2, which are the same as those shown in stage 1 of Table 5.1. There is no entry in Table 5.2 for LDMA deposits at the Bank of England as these will not be referred to in this section. It will be seen that the banks have 'other' deposits at the Bank of 0.6 per cent of their own total deposits and loans to the LDMA of 5.4 per cent. Recall that the banks maintain these two ratios a little above the minimums required in order to have a bit of room for movement, and that they are reckoned, for simplicity, to hold notes and coin at a constant value of 20 provided that total deposits do not change by more than 50. The equilibrium supply and demand curves for money are taken as $M_s$ and $M_d$ on Figure 4.2; these correspond to $M_s$ and $M_d$ in Figure 5.1 and give the same interest equilibrium interest rate of 10 per cent and money stock of 1,200, of which bank deposits account for 1,000 and publicly-held cash for 200.

The equilibrium is now disturbed by the requirement that the banks must keep new special deposits of 0.25 per cent of liabilities at the Bank of England. For simplicity, it will be assumed that the banks keep these deposits at precisely 0.25 per cent (rather than a shade above) and transfer money in and out of them from their 'other' deposits as often as needed. Initially, then, banks must put 2.5 in their new deposits. It will be supposed they acquire all the cash needed to do by calling in money-at-call, so that loans to the LDMA fall by 2.5 to 51.5 as shown in stage 2. The discount houses will be supposed to find the cash needed by selling commercial bills to the Bank of England, so stage 2 shows their holdings of these bills falling by 2.5, just as their loans from the banks do, when some money-at-call is repaid. (It would be possible to put on the table two short-lived intermediate stages in between stages 1 and 2, as was done between stages 1 and 4 of Table 5.1.)

At this point, stage 2, the banks are meeting both of their Bank of England deposit requirements, but they are not meeting their money-at-call target. This is because money-at-call is now 51.5 which is below the target level of 5.4 per cent of total deposits. In these circumstances, one option the banks might consider would be to create new loans of 2.5 to the LDMA, for in this way these loans would be restored to 54 as shown in stage 3. If they chose this option, then the banks would have to reduce by 2.5 their holdings of securities and (non-LDMA) advances so that the total for these items falls from 920 to 917.5 as shown in stage 3; this is so that the banks' total deposits stay at 1,000 which is the maximum their 'other' deposits of 6 and their loans of 54 to the LDMA can sustain at the banks' target ratios for these items. Stage 3 shows the situation for the discount houses before they have spent their new loans of 2.5. Now if they spend them on, say, commercial bills bought for 2.5 from the public, then their balance sheet would return to its stage 1 position. The banks and the LDMA would have no incentive for further change. Bank deposits would be 1,000, as shown in stage 3, which is the same as the initial level in stage 1, and the money stock would be 1,200 (once allowance is made for publicly-held cash of 200) which was its initial value. It seems changing the cash ratio is ineffective.

However, the changing ratio can be made effective in the same way that open-market operations were made effective, if the Bank of England matches any increase in loans by the banks to the LDMA made after stage 2 by issuing new Treasury bills. If they issued these bills just after stage 3, for a value of 2.5, then the banks would find their total deposits falling by 2.5 while their 'other' deposits at the Bank of England would also fall by 2.5. To restore those deposits to the 6 they want (strictly just under 6, as deposits would now be only 997.5) they would have to recall loans of 2.5 from the LDMA and reduce the total for these to 51.5 once again. By this means, the Bank of England can prevent money-at-call rising above the 51.5 shown in stage 2.

Deprived of this escape from stage 2, the banks must take other action. The only option in stage 2 is actually to reduce their holdings of securities and (non-LDMA) advances by 40 so that total liabilities fall from 1,000 to 960 as shown in stage 4. This requires a special deposit of just 2.4 (that is 0.25 per cent of 960) releasing 0.1 from the level of 2.5 shown in stage 2. This 0.1 will be transferred to the banks 'other' deposits at the Bank taking these from 6 to 6.1; however, for reasons explained in a moment, they are shown as 5.76, that is 0.34 less. The new 960 level for deposits leads to the banks seeking 'other' deposits of 5.76 (that is 0.6 per cent of 960) releasing 0.34 from the 6.1 level just noted. Finally, it leads to the banks seeking to raise their loans to the LDMA by 0.34 from 51.5 to 51.84 (which is 5.4 per cent of 960). Stage 4 assumes that the banks have made extra loans of this amount which the LDMA spent on extra Treasury bills issued by the Bank of England; this reduces the banks' deposits at the Bank of England by 0.34, but they would still be able to have the amounts desired (5.76) in these deposits. Thus stage 4 shows how the calling of special deposits can be made effective. It also suggests that the money stock will fall by 40 from 1,200 to 1,160 once publicly-held cash of 200 is taken into consideration along with bank deposits.

The authorities could have secured identical contractions in deposits from 1,000 to 960 if they had instead raised the mandatory level of loans to the LDMA by 0.25 per cent to 5.25 per cent, and had then 'soaked up' any extra loans to the LDMA by issuing new Treasury bills for the appropriate amount. Suppose this change occurred when the banks were at stage 1 so that their balances at the Bank of England plus their loans to the LDMA were 60. Initially, they were happy if these had a combined level of 6 per cent of deposits, that is 0.6 for the bankers' deposits at the Bank and 5.4 per cent for the LDMA loans. With the new rule for loans to the LDMA, they would want the combined level to be, say, 6.25 per cent, 0.6 still for deposits at the Bank, but perhaps 5.65 now for the LDMA loans. They could secure this by reducing other loans and security holdings by 40 from 920 to 880 as shown in stage 5, with total deposits falling by 40 from 1,000 to 960. They would want loans to LDMA to be 54.24 (that is 5.65 per cent of 960) and their Bank of England deposits to be 5.76 (that is 0.6 per cent of 960). Stage 6 supposes the banks create the extra 0.24 loans to the LDMA required (compared with stage 1) and that the discount houses then find they have to spend this sum on new Treasury bills which causes the banks' deposits at the Bank of England to fall by that amount. The new Treasury bills must be issued to make the changing ratio effective.

Actually, although the processes discussed in the moves from stage 1 to 4 or 5 will occur, the results will not be as sizeable as the figures in Table 5.2 suggest. The reasons are the same as those given in the discussion of stage 9 of Table 5.1. The point is that stages 4 and 5 show what would happen to deposits if the interest rate stayed constant as the initial 10 per cent level. This point is illustrated in Figure 5.2 where $M_d$ and $M_s$ represent the corresponding curves on Figure 5.1 and intersect at the initial equilibrium with the money stock at 1,200 (comprising deposits of 1,000 and

**Table 5.2** The effects of increasing the banks' mandatory ratios

| STAGE | 1 | 2 | 3 | 4 | 5 | 6 |
|---|---|---|---|---|---|---|
| Clearing bank liabilities | | | | | | £m |
| Deposits | 1000 | 1000 | 1000 | 960 | 960 | 981 |
| Total | 1000 | 1000 | 1000 | 960 | 960 | 981 |
| Clearing bank assets | | | | | | £m |
| Notes and coin | 20 | 20 | 20 | 20 | 20 | 20 |
| Special deposits with Bank of England | 0 | 2.5 | 2.5 | 2.40 | 0 | 0 |
| Other deposits with Bank of England | 6 | 6 | 6 | 5.76 | 5.76 | 5.84 |
| Market loans to LDMA | 54 | 51.5 | 54 | 51.84 | 54.24 | 55.16 |
| Securities and advances | 920 | 920 | 917.5 | 880 | 880 | 900 |
| Total | 1000 | 1000 | 1000 | 960 | 960 | 981 |
| LDMA liabilities | | | | | | £m |
| Money-at-call | 54 | 51.5 | 54 | 51.84 | 54.24 | 55.16 |
| Total | 54 | 51.5 | 54 | 51.84 | 54.24 | 55.16 |
| LDMA assets | | | | | | £m |
| Balances with clearing banks | 0 | 0 | 2.5 | 0 | 0 | 0 |
| Treasury bills | 14 | 14 | 14 | 14.34 | 14.24 | 15.16 |
| Other securities | 40 | 37.5 | 37.5 | 37.5 | 40 | 40 |
| Total | 54 | 51.5 | 54 | 51.84 | 54.24 | 55.16 |

publicly-held cash of 200). The effect of the changing cash ratios is to create a new supply curve $M_s'$. Point A and $M_s'$ shows that if interest rates stayed at 10 per cent then the money stock desired by the banks would be 1,160 comprising deposits of 960 (as shown in stages 4 and 5 of Table 5.2) and publicly-held cash of 200. However, the new equilibrium interest rate will actually be 10.3 per cent, where $M_s'$ cuts $M_d$, and the money stock will be 1,180.

Stage 6 of Table 5.2 shows how this modified result might come about if the authorities had raised the ratio for loans to the LDMA, and thus stage 6 shows better than stage 5 what the final effects might be. It is supposed that the rise in interest rates causes the public to deposit extra cash of 1 in the banks leaving their own holdings at 199; these combine with the 981 for deposits shown in stage 6 to give the final money stock of 1,180 shown in Figure 5.2. Stage 6 shows how the banks settle with deposits at 981. It supposes the banks keep 0.08 of their extra cash at the Bank of England, raising their 'other' deposits there to 5.84, and are happy at the higher interest rates

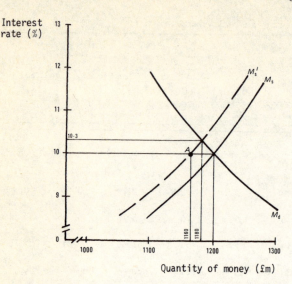

**Figure 5.2**

for these 'other' deposits to be 0.595 per cent of their own total deposits (5.84 being 0.595 per cent of 981) instead of the previous 0.6 per cent. The remaining 0.92 is taken to be used up by making higher loans for this amount to the LDMA – who are taken to use it to buy newly-issued Treasury bills from the Bank of England – raising the figure for these loans from 54.24 to 55.16 which is 5.62 per cent of deposits; again the banks are assumed to be happy with a lower percentage than the previous 5.65 because interest rates have risen. Securities and non-LDMA advances make up the remaining part of total assets of 981. Once again, the upshot is that the authorities' action will raise interest rates and cut the money stock, but the fall in the money stock is more modest than suggested in stages 5 and 6.

## Credit ceilings

A third way in which the authorities could alter the level of deposits, and so the money stock, would be to impose credit ceilings on the banks. Suppose, for instance, the banks and discount houses started in the same position as they did in Tables 5.1 and 5.2. The relevant figures as shown in stage 1 of Table 5.3. The table has no entries for LDMA deposits at the clearing banks as none will be needed in this section. Suppose, too, that the initial level of bank deposits, 1,000, combines with publicly-held cash, 200, to form a money stock of 1,200. This is consistent with the equilibrium given by the intersection of the supply and demand curves for money, $M_s$ and $M_d$, as shown in Figure 5.3 which reproduces them from Figures 5.1 and 5.2. The intersection of these curves shows also the initial equilibrium interest rate of 10 per cent.

Now bank credit covers all advances and securities and is initially 974; 54 of this is accounted for by loans to the LDMA and 920 by other advances and securities. Suppose the banks are asked to reduce their total credit by 36 to 938. They would

**Table 5.3**  The effects of credit ceilings

| STAGE | 1 | 2 |
|---|---|---|
| Clearing bank liabilities | | £m |
| Deposits | 1000 | 964 |
| Total | 1000 | 964 |
| Notes and coin | 20 | 20 |
| Balances with Bank of England | 6 | 6 |
| Market loans to LDMA | 54 | 52 |
| Securities and advances | 920 | 886 |
| Total | 1000 | 964 |
| LDMA liabilities | | £m |
| Money-at-call | 54 | 52 |
| Total | 54 | 52 |
| LDMA assets | | £m |
| Treasury bills | 14 | 14 |
| Other securities | 40 | 38 |
| Total | 54 | 52 |

doubtless be given a little time to respond, but might eventually react by cutting the two components shown in the balance sheet in (almost) identical proportions, so that loans to the LDMA would fall by 2 (a fraction over 3.7 per cent of the original level of 54) and other loans and advances by 34 (a fraction under 3.7 per cent of the original level of 920). Thus the new levels would be 52 and 886 as shown in stage 2. The fall in loans to the LDMA means, in effect, that the LDMA would be required to repay loans of 2. Suppose they were given a few days to respond, just as it has been assumed that the banks were given some time to fall into line. The LDMA might well react by waiting till the commercial bills nearest maturity actually mature, for then bank deposits would be transferred from the issuers of the bills to them. At this point, LDMA deposits at the clearing banks would rise from 0 to 2 while their holdings of 'other securities' would fall from 40 to 38; the LDMA could then repay loans of 2 from the banks by having their deposits with them reduced to zero. Stage 2 shows the effect when this process is completed. The fall in deposits from 1,000 to 964 suggests that the money stock will fall from 1,200 to 1,164 once publicly-held cash of 200 is allowed for as well as bank deposits.

As in previous cases, the initial discussion based on the table assumes that interest rates would stay at their initial level. In fact they would rise. This can be seen by looking at Figure 5.3. The effect of the credit ceiling is to produce a new supply curve, $M_s'$, which follows $M_s$ at low interest rates and then kinks upwards at the 1,164 level, that is at a level 36 below the original money stock level. This kink arises because the money stock cannot exceed this level as the clearing banks are not allowed to create the extra deposits that would be needed for it to exceed that level. Now the

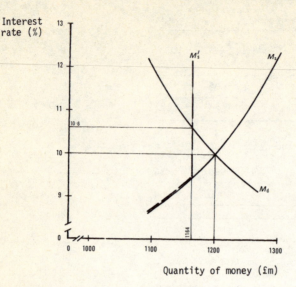

Interest rate (%)

Quantity of money (£m)

**Figure 5.3**

new equilibrium is where $M_s$ intersects $M_d$ and it can be seen that this produces a new equilibrium interest rate on securities of 10.6 per cent, noticeably above the original 10 per cent.

In previous cases, this rise in the equilibrium interest rates on securities has been held likely to lead to a rise in the rates on interest-bearing bank deposits and so lead to a small movement of cash from the public to the banks. In the present case, though, the rates paid on interest-bearing deposits might not rise so that there might be no such movement of cash.

Ordinarily, banks pay as high interest rates as they can afford because they compete with each other for deposits. Any bank which offered a lower rate than its rivals would be liable to lose deposits to them, as people decided to switch their accounts to other banks, and so it would lose cash to other banks and, in turn, would have to cut back on lending in order not to fall foul of the ratios imposed by the authorities. Accordingly, any rise in the interest rates shown on the diagrams, which relate to the returns that can be obtained on securities, will enable banks to pay more on deposits (which are effectively loans to them made by the public) and competitive pressures will result in these rises occurring. In the present case, though, the banks would not mind losing some deposits to others and so losing some cash, for they are not allowed to be fully lent. In other words, they could lose some cash without falling foul of the ratios imposed by the authorities. Accordingly, rates paid on interest-bearing accounts might not rise. The upshot of the credit ceilings, then, is that interest rates on securities will rise, though the rate on interest-bearing bank deposits may not, and the fall in bank deposits, and in turn the money stock, may well be the 36 shown by stages 1 and 2 of Table 5.3.

## Interest rate control

The final method of controlling the money stock to be discussed here is often termed interest rate control. This is brought about by the central bank changing the terms on which it will conduct its last resort lending activities with the discount houses. So far, it has been assumed that the authorities set these terms at the same rate as is currently available on Treasury bills, and it is useful to consider first the implications of this arrangement.

Suppose this arrangement is in force, and that the banks, the discount houses and the money market are in the initial equilibrium positions noted in the previous three sections. These positions are reproduced in stage 1 of Table 5.4 and are reflected by the intersection of the demand and supply curves $M_d$ and $M_s$ of Figure 5.4 which correspond to the curves in Figures 5.1 to 5.3. Note that if this initial position really is an equilibrium one, then the discount houses' assets are likely to be at a level close to the maximum level permitted, for otherwise banks would have an incentive to create more money-at-call and, in turn, more deposits. The figure shows that the equilibrium interest rate, or more specifically, the equilibrium rate on consols, is 10 per cent. As the interest rates on all financial claims tend to be closely related, it is worth considering what the rates will be on the assets and liabilities of the discount houses. All rates in this section are expressed in per cent per annum.

The discount houses' assets comprise chiefly bills, both Treasury and commercial bills. Now Treasury bills, like consols, have negligible risk of default and are likely to have very similar interest rates. However, it was explained in Chapter 2 that short-term interest rates are often a little below long-term ones so it will be supposed that the Treasury bill rate is initially 9.5 per cent. Commercial bills are riskier than Treasury bills and carry higher interest rates; suppose these average 10.5 per cent. On the liabilities side, it would be expected that the rate on money-at-call would be lower than the lowest rate earned on assets, that is the 9.5 per cent on Treasury bills, because discount houses would not want to lend except at a higher rate than the one at which they borrow. Suppose the call-money rate is 9.25 per cent. It might seem odd to find that this rate is *below* the rates on government securities such as consols and Treasury bills, for no claim has less risk of default than these. However, call-money, too, has negligible risk of default to the lenders (the clearing banks) because the borrowers (the discount houses) can always borrow from the Bank of England to repay their loans. At the same time, call-money is actually more liquid than government securities because the banks can demand repayment in a matter of hours.

Another interest rate which will be below the Treasury bill rate of 9.5 per cent is the rate offered by the clearing banks on interest-bearing deposits. They can secure these deposits at low rates by allowing almost instant access to depositors who are effectively permitted to spend the deposits at any time by cheque, though at the loss of a few days' interest. The rate on these accounts can be taken to be 8 per cent. Now any shift in the demand or supply curve in Figure 5.4 will alter the interest rate in consols. In turn, the rates on other claims are likely to move in the same direction, and for simplicity the rates on other claims will be taken to move up or down by the same absolute amount as the rate on consols.

It is useful to look closely at the position of the discount houses in stage 1 of Table 5.4. They have borrowed 54 at 9.25 per cent, and have used these funds to buy Treasury bills worth 14 and other securities, say commercial bills, worth 40 with returns of 9.5 per cent and 10.5 per cent respectively. The returns do not come as interest as such, but by buying each bill at a discount and either selling it later for a higher price or waiting for redemption at face value on maturity. Now suppose for some reason that the banks suddenly insist on repayment of call-money for 4. The discount houses

**Table 5.4**   The effects of interest rate control

| STAGE | 1 | 2 | 3 |
|---|---|---|---|
| Clearing bank liabilities | | | £m |
| Deposits | 1000 | 1000 | 943 |
| Total | 1000 | 1000 | 943 |
| Clearing bank assets | | | £m |
| Notes and coin | 20 | 20 | 20 |
| Balances with Bank of England | 6 | 10 | 9 |
| Market loans to LDMA | 54 | 50 | 51 |
| Securities and advances | 920 | 920 | 863 |
| Total | 1000 | 1000 | 943 |
| LDMA liabilities | | | £m |
| Money-at-call | 54 | 50 | 51 |
| Total | 54 | 50 | 51 |
| LDMA assets | | | £m |
| Treasury bills | 14 | 10 | 14 |
| Other securities | 40 | 40 | 37 |
| Total | 54 | 50 | 51 |

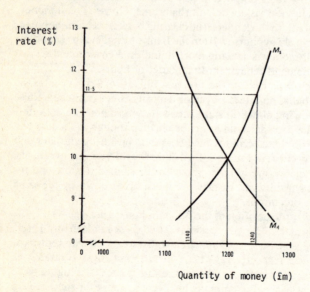

**Figure 5.4**

will probably sell bills, either Treasury bills or commercial bills, for this amount to the Bank of England, thus acquiring 4 in their deposits there which they immediately lose by transferring 4 to the clearing banks to meet the repayment demanded. Thus the banks and the LDMA move to the position shown at stage 2. Notice, incidentally, that with rates on Treasury bills of 9.5 per cent, a discount house would offer about £977 on a new three-month bill with a face value of £1,000 and would expect it to be worth about £984 after one month; so the Bank of England would give it £984 for a one-month-old Treasury bill if it made last resort lending facilities available at this rate.

The only effects on the discount houses of moving from stage 1 to stage 2 are that their assets are now some way below the maximum allowed and that they are now making less profit each day than before, for they are now borrowing less money and lending less money. They will not like this, but there is little they can do. Each house might be tempted to offer less money for bills in future in order to secure higher returns, but it might then be outbid by its rivals who will be anxious to restore their assets to the maximum levels allowed!

Now return to the original stage 1 situation, and suppose the Bank of England declared that last resort lending facilities would in future be made available only at a rate of 11 per cent, that is 1.5 per cent above the Treasury bill rate. In these circumstances, the facilities are said to be available at a penal rate. The discount houses would now be very much more worried about the possibility of banks suddenly wanting repayment of some money-at-call. Suppose, once again, that the banks demanded repayment of 4 and that the discount houses sold Treasury bills for 4 to the Bank, then stage 2 would reappear. (Actually, the discount houses would have to sell rather more bills this time to raise the money, as the Bank is offering lower prices consistent with a higher discount rate, and so the houses would be left with a holding of a little under 10, say 9.9; so if the tables in this chapter included all the items of the houses' balance sheets, then this fall in assets at stage 2 from 50 to 49.9, would be matched by a fall of 0.1 in the revaluation reserve on the liabilities side. However, the point made here is ignored in the following paragraphs as it complicates the argument without changing the essential analysis.)

The trouble with stage 2 for the discount houses now is that they have had to repay loans of 4 which they borrowed at 9.25 per cent by selling Treasury bills on which they actually secured a much lower return. To see this, suppose they sold a one-month-old Treasury bill to the Bank. The Bank would now offer only some £982, in order to secure an 11 per cent return for itself before maturity. This means that the discount house has sold for £982 something which it bought a month before for £977, and this represents a rate of return of around 6 per cent. The result is that each time money-at-call is recalled, the discount houses will find they have borrowed money from the banks at a higher rate than the one at which they lent it, and so they have made a loss. At least, this is what they would find if they took no action.

In practice, they will take action, and this will take the form of offering less for bills in future so that they get a higher return on them. Suppose they offer so much less that they secure 11 per cent on Treasury bills, then they will not make any loss in future if bills are suddenly sold off to the Bank at prices which reflect this rate. For instance, they would now offer about £973 for a new £1,000 bill; if this was sold for £982 after one month, then the return would still be 11 per cent. Of course, the discount houses would now want some 12 per cent on commercial bills since they want 1 per cent more on these than they get on Treasury bills to cover the extra risk.

In principle, this strategy of offering lower prices, and so, in effect, raising the interest they charge when they lend by buying bills, faces two threats. To see the first of these threats, consider an individual discount house. If it lowers its offer price for bills, then it could be outbid by its rivals. However, such outbidding is unlikely to occur. If one rival takes this action, then it will increase its slice of the total amount of money-at-call and hence increase its slice of any repayments demanded by banks. In turn it will increase its losses if it has to give a proportion of its call money back at short notice by selling bills to the Bank at a penal rate. Rivals would be much better advised to lower their bids too!

A more serious looking threat comes from the possibility that sellers of new bills, faced with substantially lower offers by the discount houses, will try to sell them elsewhere for only a little less than before. At first sight, it seems quite possible that the bill sellers could do this. Thus it seems that it would be difficult for the houses to lower their offers and still end up with a reasonable number of bills at all. However, there are reasons why their peculiar position in the system takes the sting out of this threat. The key point to grasp is that if the discount houses ended up with fewer bills, then they would want less money-at-call, and the banks, who are obliged to have call-money at a minimum level of 5 per cent of deposits, would have to cut back on their lending and so make less profit. Thus the banks will take whatever action is needed to prevent other institutions or people buying bills in place of the discount houses.

Who might buy more new bills if their prices were slightly reduced? The most likely candidates would seem to be the banks, NBFIs and the general public. The banks, though, will not buy any more than they would have bought anyway, because they want the houses to carry on buying bills as before and so to keep up their need for money-at-call. How can the banks stop the NBFIs and the general public from stepping in?

Consider, first, the NBFIs. Suppose that the interest rate the NBFIs initially paid on their deposits meant that they could not make a profit on commercial bills if these had rates under 11 per cent. The implication is that the NBFIs would not have any commercial bills in the initial situation when the actual rate on them just was 10.5 per cent. Now, though, the discount houses want 12 per cent on commercial bills, so the NBFIs seem well able to undercut them. In other words, the possibility has now arisen that the NBFIs will drive the discount houses out of the commercial bill market by offering higher prices for new bills than the discount houses are prepared to pay. As it happens, the banks can prevent this from happening by raising the rates on their interest-bearing deposits by 1.5 per cent. This will force the NBFIs to raise their deposit rates by a similar amount to prevent a sudden rapid drain caused by their depositors switching funds out of NBFI deposits into bank deposits. In turn, it means that the NBFIs would now need 1.5 per cent more on commercial bills, that is 12.5 per cent, to make a profit. Consequently, they will be unable to undercut the discount houses who need only 12 per cent!

Next, consider the possibility of increased bill purchases by the general public. A slight fall in bill prices might on its own encourage them to buy more. In practice, though, any increased enthusiasm the public might have for buying bills will be largely, perhaps, wholly, damped out by the increased attractiveness of deposits at both banks and NBFIs since the interest rates on all these deposits have risen.

It follows that the banks can ensure that the discount houses are not driven out of the bill market simply by raising the rates offered on their interest-bearing deposits. However, the banks must also raise the interest rates on their advances, for they are now paying higher rates on their interest-bearing deposits, and they must always lend at higher rates than they pay in order to make a profit. The rates of return on securities other than bills are also likely to rise, for higher rates on deposits at banks and NBFIs make securities initially less attractive than before, and this will cause their prices to fall, and so cause their effective returns to rise until their relative appeal has been restored. In short, interest rates everywhere are likely to rise, and they will probably rise by roughly 1.5 per cent.

It is useful to consider what the effect of the rise in the terms offered on last resort lending has in Figure 5.4. Nothing so far described has suggested that the banks will be any less willing to create deposits. On the contrary, if interest rates can be regarded as rising by 1.5 per cent, then the rate on consols, shown on the figure, is also likely to rise by this amount from 10 per cent to 11.5 per cent, and the slope of $M_s$ shows that banks would actually like to create more deposits at these higher rates. There is no reason for supposing the schedule will shift. This is a significant difference from the case where last resort lending facilities are offered directly to the banks, for then (as discussed in relation to Figure 4.10) a rise in the terms offered *will* shift the supply curve to the left.

However, the effects of the action are really very similar in either case. In Figure 4.10, the action caused the supply curve to shift to the left and so, in due course, it cut the stock of money and raised interest rates. In the present case, the action raised interest rates immediately and it will rapidly reduce the amount of money demanded. Indeed, with an interest rate of 11.5 per cent, the amount demanded falls to 1,140, and the money stock will fall to this level. The banks would like to see a much higher stock at this interest rate, indeed a stock of 1,240, but they cannot take action to generate it. This is because any action taken by the banks to raise their deposit levels will put downward pressure on interest rates, and they cannot allow this to happen in the present circumstances. Notice that the final interest rate and money stock combination, 11.5 per cent and 1,140, is not at the intersection of the final supply and demand curves.

The final position of the banks' balance sheets could be as shown in stage 3 of Table 5.4. This should be compared with stage 1 which shows the initial situation before the rate of interest on last-resort lending facilities rose. The higher interest rates are here presumed to have caused the public to deposit more cash of 3 with the banks, so reducing publicly-held cash from 200 to 197, and the banks are reckoned to have deposited the extra cash at the Bank of England so their deposits there rise from 6 to 9. The fall in publicly-held cash to 197 means bank deposits will be 943 given that a money stock of 1,140 is demanded at the present level of interest rates. It is further supposed that the banks reduce their money-at-call loans to 51, just about the desired 5.4 per cent of total deposits, and that the discount houses react by holding 3 less commercial bills. The discount houses might prefer to have fewer Treasury bills, but they may have little choice if the Bank of England wants them to hold 14 because they are obliged to buy any Treasury bills not bought by others. With notes and coin of 20, Bank of England deposits of 9 and loans to the LDMA of 51, the remaining 863 of assets will be accounted for by securities and advances.

Notice that the banking system is now not fully lent. For example, the discount houses have assets of 51 while it has been assumed they are allowed to have assets of 54, so there is scope for more money-at-call. Also, the banks have deposits at the Bank of England of 9 while they only want about 5.7 (that is 0.6 per cent of 943). In practice, the Bank of England might well reinforce its efforts to reduce the money stock by open-market selling operations of, say, 3.3, for this would reduce the banks' cash holdings to 5.7 and reduce any temptation they might have to expand deposit levels.

## Further aspects of monetary control

This final section considers briefly the effects of releasing the main simplifying assumptions made in the analysis. Four of these assumptions were made in Chapter 4 and the effects of releasing them are explained further in the last section of that chapter.

First, it has been assumed that the demand curve for money will not shift if interest rates change. In fact, rises in interest rates are likely to reduce spending and hence incomes and, in turn, the demand for money. Consequently, the contractionary measures illustrated in the diagrams could in time lead to the $M_d$ curves shifting to the left, and these shifts would reinforce any fall in the money stock but ease any rise in interest rates.

Secondly, it has been assumed that the public's demand for cash is not affected by the level of their bank deposits. In fact, a fall in bank deposits caused by the contractionary measures discussed above is likely to lead to the public wanting less cash. Any unwanted cash deposited in the banks will enable the banks to contract less than suggested and so the $M_s$ curves would generally tend to shift less than shown. In turn, the money stock would fall less and interest rates would rise less. However, this qualification to the results is not applicable to the case of credit ceilings, where the banks are unable to create more money no matter how much extra cash they acquire, nor is it applicable in the case of interest rate control where $M_s$ did not alter and where, in any case, the final equilibrium is not dependent on the position of the supply curve.

Thirdly, it has been assumed that the public would not respond to any falls in their money holdings by selling National Savings Certificates. If they do, then their banks will acquire extra cash so that the fall in the money stock and the rise in interest rates will be less than previously implied.

Fourthly, it was generally assumed that there were no NBFIs. The implications of NBFI existence are discussed more fully in Chapter 4. The basic point is that because attempts to reduce the money stock reduce bank lending, so they are also likely to encourage more activity by NBFIs. Consequently, NBFI deposits are likely to have more attractive interest rates vis-a-vis bank deposits than they had before. This could cause the $M_d$ curves to shift to the left and so, in turn, reinforce the fall in the money stock (except in the case of credit ceilings where the vertical $M'_s$ means a leftward shift in $M_d$ has no effect on the money stock) and ease the upward pressure on interest rates.

One final simplifying assumption in the earlier analysis of this chapter was that the banks would maintain constant levels of notes and coin on their premises. In reality, these levels are likely to be kept at some small proportion of deposits. Consequently, when measures other than credit ceilings are used to secure a reduction in deposits levels, the banks can release some stocks of notes and coin to put in their central bank deposits and so will be able to reduce deposits a little less than earlier sections suggested. In other words, releasing this assumption means the $M_s$ curves will move less than suggested so that monetary control measures have less effect than implied on both interest rates and the money stock.

# 6

# International aspects of money

## Introduction

The discussion in the last two chapters has been concerned only with those aspects of banking and money that would arise in a country whose citizens undertook no transactions with citizens in other countries. The present chapter focuses on those aspects of banking and money which relate specifically to transactions between citizens of different countries. The first section considers the basic financial mechanism which is involved when money passes from one country to another, while the second looks at exchange rates. The following sections consider the implications of international money flows on a country's money stock and its interest rate. The final two sections consider the possibility of the citizens of one country having deposits of foreign currencies at banks in their own country, and the related topic of Euro-currencies.

## International transactions

There are two key distinguishing features of transactions between citizens in different countries. First, the transactions involve people who ordinarily use different currencies. Secondly, they involve banks which form part of separate monetary systems. Of course, international trade took place long before banking systems became well developed, and merchants have adopted different ways of handling the problems of varying currencies. In the days when coins were the sole type of money, traders would often take merchandise with them, sell it in a foreign country for foreign coins and then use those coins to purchase items which could be sold again in their own countries. One reason for individual traders engaging in two-way trade was that countries often made the export of their coins illegal. Such a rule was effective in the UK from 1390 until 1819 and similar rules were found elsewhere. Accordingly, merchants may have found they had little scope for taking money in or out of different countries and so had to pay for the goods they bought in each with the proceeds of other goods which they sold there.

There was actually an advantage in two-way trade even for those traders who were not bound by laws over coin imports and exports and also for those who ignored the laws! The point is that such an arrangement avoided the need for exchanging different currencies. This was generally desirable from the traders' point of view. The reason was that there were always many different countries and, indeed, cities with their own mints all producing coins from different metals (or different alloys) with different degrees of purity and different degrees of clipping. Money-changers existed but would naturally charge a fee for their expert knowledge as well as for taking the risk that the demand for some foreign coins bought today might fall before they were sold and hence mean they would have to be sold for a lower price than the one the changers had paid. On the whole, money-changers probably made handsome profits by charging significant fees. It was therefore in the merchants' interests to do as little money-changing as possible to minimize the amount of fees they had to pay.

However, merchants did not always want to do the same amount of exporting and importing in each country which they visited, and by the thirteenth century, at least, their problems were eased by the development of bills (Morgan, 156). These bills were noted in Chapter 1, and it must be recalled that until laws against usury were relaxed, some centuries later, bills were not meant to be sold for a discount. The basic idea was that a dealer from York selling exports in, perhaps, Rheims might accept a bill made out by the French importer promising to pay, say, 1,000 livres (an old French coin) in three months' time. The York dealer could then return home, without having to make any purchases in France, and he could sell the bill for an agreed sum in pounds to a trader from Norwich who did want to make some purchases in France. This Norwich trader could then make his purchases, perhaps in Nice, by giving the bill to a French manufacturer there. The Nice manufacturer would actually get the livres he wanted from the importer in Rheims when the bill matured.

It will be noticed that using the bill meant that neither of the Englishmen ever had to touch French currency – other than for travel expenses, of course – and neither of the Frenchmen had to touch English currency. More generally, the use of bills greatly reduced the need for money-changers. It will also be noticed that the men from York, Norwich and Nice might have to wait some time between acquiring the bill and actually getting any money. In effect, each lent money for a while to the man in Rheims. While interest and discounting as such might be prohibited, returns for lending were possible as the exchange rate terms agreed between the two parties each time the bill changed hands could be arranged in a way which gave some benefit to each of the three lenders at the expense of the borrower.

One apparent inconvenience of this system would be the need for each of the purchasers of the bill to know how reliable the Rheims business was. Another would be the need for the York man to find someone interested in buying a bill made out by someone in France. Over the years, specialist concerns called accepting houses, or merchant banks, evolved and they set out to remove these inconveniences. One function they perform is the accepting of bills. Thus the Rheims concern might have its bills accepted, or endorsed, by a French merchant bank which would agree to pay the holder on maturity. The merchant bank risked making a loss if the Rheims concern did not then reimburse it, but merchant banks charged fees for accepting bills which, typically, more than covered any losses they made. The Rheims merchant gained, of course, because he would find that people like the man from York would be much more willing to be paid in bills instead of cash if his bills were accepted by a well-known merchant bank. Now another function of merchant banks is buying and selling second hand bills. Thus the York man could sell his bill to a merchant bank in

England, and the Norwich man could buy it there, and in this way English traders would not have to seek each other out. Of course, the English merchant bank might itself hold the bill till maturity and then seek payment in some form from the French merchant bank who had accepted it. In practice merchant banks typically owed each other substantial amounts of money, but the payments needed to clear their net debts might be small.

The use of bills for settling international payments continued to be the main system until around the end of the last century, being substantially unaffected by the developments of paper money and commercial banking. In the present century, however, banks have stolen the scene. Perhaps the most important ways in which a bank can participate in the system of international payments are to open up accounts at banks in other countries and to open up branches of its own in other countries. Consider the first option. For simplicity, suppose there are just two countries, the United Kingdom and the United States, and suppose the exchange rate between the two currencies is £1 = $1.50. The factors determining the exchange rate will be considered later.

Next consider two banks, UKX and USX, and suppose their initial balance sheets are as shown in column (1) of Table 6.1 where the item cash covers notes and coin plus balances at the banks' respective central banks. It can be seen that the banks each have cash ratios of 5 per cent of total liabilities, and it will be assumed for simplicity that they always seek 5 per cent ratios as a matter of prudence. Suppose Bank UKX decides it wants to have a (dollar) deposit at an American bank and selects USX for this purpose. Bank UKX will open an account at USX and USX would be said to be a correspondent bank for UKX.

An easy way of UKX acquiring a balance at USX would be for UKX to wait until one of its depositors received a cheque from a US bank – called, say, bank USY – perhaps from the sale of an export worth $30 (or £20). The customer will present the cheque to UKX, just as she would if she had received a cheque from another UK bank. So she would expect her deposit to rise by £20 and expect her bank to claim £20 from the purchaser's bank. Certainly UKX will raise the deposit of its customer by £20 as shown in column (2). Also, UKX will certainly want $30 (or £20) from USY, but it will not expect a transfer from USY's deposit at the Bank of England to its own deposit there, for USY probably has no Bank of England deposit. Instead, UKX asks USY to transfer $30 to UKX's deposit at USX, and this explains the change in UKX's assets in column (2). As for USX, one of its customers, UKX, has received $30 from a depositor at another bank, USY, so USX's deposits rise by $30 and its balance at the American central bank rises by $30 (and USY's deposit there falls $30). This explains USX's column (2) figures.

The column (2) figures show a temporary phase only. UKX finds that its £100 in cash is under 5 per cent of its total £2,020 liabilities, so it will seek to reduce its holdings of securities and advances by £20 and thus end up as shown in column (3). USX finds that its $230 cash exceeds 5 per cent of its total $4,030 liabilities, and so may well consider expanding its holdings of securities and advances. However, column (3) imagines for simplicity that, shortly after column (2) is reached, other USX customers pay $30 to depositors at other US banks so that USX loses deposits and cash of $30 to reach, in column (3), the same figures that it had in column (1).

Now suppose that USX decides it wants to open an account at a British bank and selects UKX, and suppose an American exporter banking at USX receives a cheque for £30 (or $45) from a depositor at a UK bank called, say, UKY. The column (4)

**Table 6.1**   Banks with deposits at overseas banks

Bank UKX

| Column | (1) | (2) | (3) | (4) | (5) |
|---|---|---|---|---|---|
| Liabilities | | | | | £m |
| Deposits | 2000 | 2020 | 2000 | 2030 | 2000 |
| Total | 2000 | 2020 | 2000 | 2030 | 2000 |
| Assets | | | | | £m |
| Cash | 100 | 100 | 100 | 130 | 100 |
| Deposits at overseas banks | 0 | 20 | 20 | 20 | 20 |
| Securities and advances | 1900 | 1900 | 1880 | 1880 | 1880 |
| Total | 2000 | 2020 | 2000 | 2030 | 2000 |

Bank USX

| Column | (1) | (2) | (3) | (4) | (5) |
|---|---|---|---|---|---|
| Liabilities | | | | | $m |
| Deposits | 4000 | 4030 | 4000 | 4045 | 4000 |
| Total | 4000 | 4030 | 4000 | 4045 | 4000 |
| Assets | | | | | $m |
| Cash | 200 | 230 | 200 | 200 | 200 |
| Deposits at overseas banks | 0 | 0 | 0 | 45 | 45 |
| Securities and advances | 3800 | 3800 | 3800 | 3800 | 3755 |
| Total | 4000 | 4030 | 4000 | 4045 | 4000 |

situation will be reached as USX raises its customer's deposit by $45 and asks UKY to pay £30 into USX's deposit at UKX. Of course, UKX raises USX's deposit from zero to £30 and gets £30 added to its Bank of England deposit (where UKY's deposit will fall by £30). USX finds that its cash is below 5 per cent of its liabilities and so cuts back on securities and advances to reach the column (5) figures. UKX could expand, but it is supposed for simplicity that any efforts to do so are frustrated by other customers who, shortly after column (4) was reached, pay £30 to depositors at other UK banks, so that UKX ends up in column (5) with the same figures that it had in column (3).

With a deposit at a US bank, UKX is now able to handle its depositors' transactions with US citizens. If, for instance, a depositor receives a cheque for $15 (worth £10), then UKX will raise his deposit by £10 and arrange for the bank on which the cheque is drawn to pay $15 into UKX's deposit at USX. If another depositor wants to pay $15 to an American, then UKX will reduce his deposit by £10 and arrange for $15 to be taken out of its deposit at USX and given to the bank of the American concerned (which will add $15 to his deposit).

Now compare the balance sheets in columns (1) and (5). It can be seen that UKX and USX have sacrificed some of their income-earning assets of securities and advances in return for deposits at banks abroad. Although they may be able to get some interest paid on these deposits, the yield is likely to be much lower than the yield on the lost securities and advances. It seems, then, that placing themselves in a position to handle international transactions is likely to reduce their income. However, banks charge a fee to depositors when international transactions are involved. In the example of Table 6.1, for instance, UKX will charge the depositor who receives $30 a fee for 'converting' this to the £20 added to her deposit, while USX will charge the depositor who received £30 a fee for 'converting' this to the $45 added to his deposit. Inverted commas are used for the word converting as UKX actually held on to the $30 and USX held on to the £30.

Banks will set their fees at a level to compensate themselves for having fewer income-earning assets than they might have had, and also for taking the risks involved in having a mismatch of currencies between assets and liabilities. To see how there is a risk, consider UKX and suppose the exchange rate of the dollar (in relation to the pound) fell. In that case, the sterling value of UKX's assets shown in its balance sheet would fall. (This would be matched on the liabilities side by a fall in the revaluation reserve which, as explained in Chapter 1, would appear on a complete balance sheet for UKX but not on the simplified one used here.)

Irrespective of the level of fees they charge, banks naturally like to keep their foreign currency deposits at as low a level as possible. Typically, banks will enter reciprocal arrangements with their correspondent banks to help keep these deposits low. Thus UKX may arrange with USX that if UKX's dollar deposit gets close to zero, then USX will give UKX a loan. This loan would raise UKX's assets in the form of a higher dollar deposit, and it would raise its liabilities in the form of a loan made to it, though loans to banks have not been listed under liabilities in the simplified balance sheets used so far. Alternatively, if UKX found its dollar deposit getting very low while another bank, UKY perhaps, found its dollar deposit getting larger than needed, then UKX might arrange to borrow dollars from UKY. By these methods, foreign currency deposits are often kept so low that published bank balance sheets do not record them as a separate item but instead add them in under another more important heading and indicate in a footnote that this has been done.

## Exchange rate regimes

The last section explained why banks want to keep their deposits of foreign currencies as small as they can manage. Now there are, of course, almost countless transactions between citizens of the UK and the US every day, so at the end of any given day some UK banks will naturally end up with larger dollar deposits than they had at the start of the day with while others will end up with smaller ones. These daily fluctuations can generally be smoothed out by means such as inter-bank loans. However, there are inevitably some days when UK banks as a whole find their dollar deposits rising or falling. These deposits fall, of course, on days when UK citizens between them have typically made more purchases requiring dollars than US citizens have made requiring pounds. Just as the UK banks find their dollar deposits falling on such a day, so US banks will find their sterling deposits rising.

Now all these banks are participants in what is called the foreign exchange market, and as such they all need stocks of foreign currencies, so the UK banks will be concerned about the possibility of their dollar stocks running out while the US banks will be concerned about their sterling stocks reaching unnecessarily high levels. The obvious strategy for all banks in this situation is to start offering a different exchange rate between sterling and the dollar. Perhaps they could set the rate at, say, £1 = $1.40. By changing the rate so that £1 now buys less US currency than before, they would hope to reduce the value of dollar purchases made by UK citizens and so reduce their demand for dollars; while by making sterling cheaper in terms of dollars, they would hope to stimulate sterling purchases by Americans and so raise the demand for sterling.

In the absence of government intervention, this is exactly what banks would do. It would be expected that the exchange rate between any pair of currencies would change quite frequently. A situation in which exchange rates fluctuate without government intervention is defined as one where exchange rates are freely (or cleanly) floating. However, the UK has never had such an exchange rate regime. Instead, the UK operates for sterling a system known as a managed (or dirty) float. Before looking at the present UK system, it is useful to consider briefly the regimes that have been used in the past.

Consider, first, the days before paper money and banking developed in the seventeenth and eighteenth centuries. Coins were the only form of money and coins had a precious metal content. Now if, for instance, the French livre contained twice as much gold as the Italian lira, then the exchange rate was likely to be stable at around 1 livre = 2 lira. If Italian merchants were demanding so many livres, and French merchants so few lira, that exchange dealers seemed likely to run out of livres and to amass large stocks of lira, then their best policy was not to alter the exchange rate but rather to melt down the lira and take the gold to the French mint to make them some more livres. Of course, the dealers would face transport costs and seignorage charges in such activities and therefore might be willing to sell lira at a rate of a little under the rate of 1 lira = 0.5 livre and to buy livre for a little more than the rate of 1 livre = 2 lira, but such discrepancies from the ratio of bullion content would be modest.

However, it should not be thought that exchange rates were stable throughout the medieval period. The relative bullion content of different currencies changed as a result of varying rates of debasement and varying 'normal' amounts of clipping and sweating, and exchange rates followed suit. Moreover, different metals might be in use in different countries, so that exchange rates could be affected by changes in the relative bullion price of different metals. This happened, for example, when gold became relatively cheaper following the Spanish discoveries of gold in South America.

The evolution of paper money issued by individual banks did not of itself change matters greatly since banks were always obliged to convert their notes into coins. The replacement of paper money issued by individual banks with a system of bank deposits and paper money issued by a central bank, as happened in England, did not necessarily change matters much either. Bank deposits could always be withdrawn in note form, and what mattered was what could be done at the Bank of England with the notes. It is clear that if all central banks stood prepared to convert their notes into gold coins or gold bullion at standard rates, then variations in exchange rates would be very limited.

In fact, such a situation did come about towards the end of the nineteenth century and it was known as the gold standard. In 1914, for instance, the amount of gold for which dollars and sterling could be exchanged was such that the exchange rate would be expected to be fixed at £1 = $4.87. The value of £1 actually varied by two or three cents either way. Why did it vary at all? The reason was this. If dealers in, say, London found their stocks of dollar bills (notes) or their dollar bank deposits in New York rising, then they could indeed take their bills to the US central bank – or transfer their own bank deposits of dollars to it by cheque – and then demand gold, ship the gold to the UK and convert it into sterling at the Bank of England. However, the shipping costs involved meant that it was not worth doing all this unless sterling's value had risen a few cents above $4.87. In its hey-day, however, the gold standard brought greater exchange rate stability than had existed before.

The gold standard regime did not come about as soon as paper money and banking developed. For the regime to work as outlined above, it was necessary for all countries to agree to convert their currencies into a single metal, and yet both gold and silver were still commonly used for currency for much of the last century. It was also necessary for all countries to adhere to convertibility at constant rates, yet convertibility was not always maintained; indeed, the UK itself, the most important trading country of the last century and a champion of convertibility into gold, withdrew convertibility on the normal basis from 1797 until 1821 owing to the Napoleonic Wars. Moreover, it was necessary for all countries to permit the export of bullion derived from melting down coins and/or the export of coins themselves; even in Britain, such exports were prohibited until the nineteenth century.

Needless to say, the First World War wreaked havoc with the international monetary system, as with so much else, and the gold standard system collapsed as all the fighting countries in Europe suspended convertibility. Attempts were made after the war to restore the old system, and Britain resumed convertibility in 1925 at the same price for gold that it had used in all periods of convertibility since it was fixed by Sir Isaac Newton in 1719. In the event, this value turned out to be too high, which means to say that foreign exchange dealers amassed large amounts of sterling which they converted into gold at the Bank of England, thereby threatening to deplete its gold stocks.

Of course, throughout the period of the gold standard there had been times when the demand for sterling was low so that the Bank of England's gold stocks declined and vice versa, and in any such periods before 1914 the Bank of England had typically raised the Bank Rate, that is the rate at which it made last resort lending facilities available; as explained in the last chapter, this tended to raise UK interest rates in general, and consequently increased the demand for sterling as foreigners decided to invest more money in the UK and needed to convert their currencies into sterling to buy, say, bonds or equities in London. Now rises in interest rates tend to reduce investment and so, in turn, to reduce output and incomes and raise unemployment. The fall in incomes would be likely to cut the demand for imports and so reduce the demand for foreign exchange by UK citizens which would help ease the pressure on the Bank of England's gold stock. However, the very high unemployment levels in the late 1920s and, especially the early 1930s, made a high interest rate policy unacceptable at that time. Accordingly, the UK came off the gold standard in 1931. Other countries followed suit, and the short interwar period of a gold standard regime came to an end. Exchange rates fluctuated widely in the 1930s.

Mindful of the economic crises of the 1930s, there was a desire after the Second World War that the world should recreate the stability of the gold standard period. With this in mind, the major allied powers met at Bretton Woods in the US in 1943, and again in 1944, to work out an international monetary system for the post-war period. In the system which evolved, countries once again fixed the values of their currencies in terms of gold, but now most countries undertook actually to convert them into US dollars rather than gold. However, the US authorities agreed to convert dollars into gold at $35 an ounce, so that the system was in effect very much like the old gold standard system. Individual countries decided their target exchange rates – or 'parity' rates – against the dollar and agreed to keep the actual rates within 1 per cent of the target value.

Why did countries prefer to maintain convertibility into dollars rather than gold? The reason was that countries could see that the value of international payments had risen over previous years and was likely to increase over future years, whereas the volume of the world's gold was rising very slowly. Why was this a problem? To understand that, suppose one country, perhaps the UK, persisted in maintaining convertibility into gold. Next, suppose that in 1870 the demand for sterling in foreign exchange markets had fallen short of the supply by 1 per cent. The UK authorities might have found that all the people with excess sterling wanted to exchange it into gold; the UK authorities could no doubt have managed this, although there would have been a significant cut in their gold reserves. But what could have happened if the supply of sterling had exceeded the demand by 1 per cent of 1970? The answer is that as the demand and supply were then both so much bigger, so a 1 per cent excess supply would also have been much bigger; and if all the people with excess sterling had then wanted to convert it into gold, then the authorities might have found it very hard to meet their demands. In 1968, for example, the excess supply of sterling was £1,410m while the UK's gold stocks were just £614m!

It is clear that maintaining convertibility into gold would become progressively more difficult, but the monetary authorities in the UK – and elsewhere – thought they could continue to offer convertibility into dollars. They thought this because they expected their holdings of dollars would rise roughly in line with the value of international payments. They expected such a rise because the US was a wealthy country making substantial purchases from the rest of the world. These purchases led to UK banks amassing substantial dollar deposits which they then sold for sterling to the UK monetary authorities.

Despite allowing countries to use dollars rather than gold, the founders of the Bretton Woods system realized that some countries might have difficulty meeting a demand for dollars if foreign exchange dealers amassed unwanted sums of their currencies and sought to convert them into dollars. It was hoped that such countries would take steps to prevent this happening, either by raising interest rates to stimulate purchases of their currency by foreigners, or by such means as tax increases which would reduce the ability of their citizens to finance imports. In addition, the International Monetary Fund was established, and this organized arrangements whereby countries which were short of dollars were able to borrow them from countries which had plenty. Even so, it was recognized that individual countries might have difficulty maintaining their exchange rates, and indeed some individual countries, notably France and the UK, did devalue from time to time, while others, notably West Germany, had occasional revaluations. The UK, for instance, devalued in 1949 by reducing the value of £1 from $4.03 to $2.80, and again in 1967 by reducing the value from $2.80 to $2.40.

The Bretton Woods system did promote stability of exchange rates, though it must be said that the tendency for countries such as the UK to have to endure periodic bouts of high interest rates and high tax levels to sustain stability was a very unfortunate cost of that stability. However, the system had one fundamental problem which was that the US sought to maintain convertibility of the dollar into gold even though the amount of dollars held by central banks around the world was growing rapidly when US official reserves of gold were not. In a sense, the US authorities were like a bank which finds its cash ratio progressively diminishing; this does not matter if few people want cash, but is potentially critical if many want cash. The US authorities found there was no problem until the late 1960s, for it had no difficulty meeting the relatively modest demands for gold made on it until then. But in the late 1960s foreign exchange dealers found themselves amassing unwanted dollars and it became clear that there might be a 'run for gold' which the US authorities could not meet. Consequently, dollar convertibility was suspended in 1971, and soon afterwards the value of the dollar fell by around 7 to 9 per cent against other currencies. Incidentally, one result of the US authorities no longer being willing to supply gold at $35 an ounce was that the price of gold on bullion markets rose very rapidly.

With the dollar at a more realistic level, it would in principle have been possible for countries to adhere to a system of fixed exchange rates, albeit punctuated by occasional devaluations and revaluations. However, this did not happen. Instead, countries have generally allowed their exchange rates to float, though the floats are 'managed' rather than 'free' inasmuch as central banks sometimes use their reserves of dollars – or other foreign currencies – to buy their own currencies rather than let them fall too low, and at other times they sell their own currencies – in return for others – rather than let them rise too high.

One reason for this recent acceptance of floating, after a century or more in which stability was highly prized, was to avoid the costs of stability noted above. Another was that the high but varying rates of inflation which were characteristic of the 1970s meant that the real values of currencies were changing rapidly in relation to one another, and it is impossible for countries with relatively high inflation to try to maintain constant exchange rates. Furthermore, the enormous rises in oil prices that occurred in the early 1970s made it impossible for some oil-importing countries to maintain fixed exchange rates. Perhaps the most important attempt at stability today is represented by the European Monetary System. In this, most EEC members – though not the UK – try to keep their exchange rates with each other as stable as they can, while allowing the group of currencies concerned to rise or fall against other currencies.

# International money flows and the domestic money stock

It is now necessary to consider what effect international transactions undertaken by a country's citizens have on their country's money stock. It is worth noting that there are three types of international transaction concerned: first, purchases and sales of goods and services, that is imports and exports; secondly, payments and receipts of what is termed property income, which includes interest, dividends and other profits; and, thirdly, what is termed foreign investment, which comprises, for example purchases of plant, buildings, vehicles and machinery or financial claims, notably, of course, securities. Flows of money relating to imports, exports and property income are termed current flows while flows relating to investment are termed capital flows.

To see the effects of these transactions on a country's money stock, it is useful to consider a combined balance sheet for all its banks, and this is done in the lower part of Table 6.2. The upper part of the table shows the balance sheet for the Bank of England, or, more precisely, the balance sheet for its Banking Department alone. The starting position is shown in column (1). In the interests of simplicity, the Bank of England has been assumed to have no assets of cash and no deposits apart from public deposits and bankers' deposits. Public deposits have been divided into two items, one item containing a deposit belonging to what is known as the Exchange Equalization Account and the other containing remaining public sector deposits. The purpose of the Exchange Equalization Account will become clear shortly.

As far as the clearing banks are concerned, liabilities comprise deposits which are divided into two groups. These are UK deposits, which belong to UK citizens and institutions, and overseas deposits, which belong to foreigners and will be taken here to belong wholly to foreign banks. On the assets side, it is assumed for simplicity that clearing banks have just one ratio to concern themselves with, namely a cash ratio, and in this example it is assumed that for reasons of prudence they have a target ratio of 6 per cent, keeping half their cash as notes and coin and half in deposits at the Bank of England. Thus loans to the LDMA are assumed here to have no special importance and so get included under securities and advances. The only other bank assets are balances at banks abroad.

The money stock needs to be defined with some care. On the basis of definitions used earlier in this book it might be calculated as being equal to total bank deposits – 50 at the Bank of England plus 1,000 at the clearing banks – less bankers' deposits at the Bank of England, 30, plus cash held by the public, say 245; this makes a total of 1,265 (all figures being given in £m). However, it is now necessary to note that measures of the UK money stock actually seek to measure the amount of money held by UK residents. Accordingly, they exclude deposits at UK banks that are held by foreign residents. Thus the UK money stock excludes the deposits worth 15 that are so held, and it actually has a total of 1,250.

Now suppose that column (1) represents the position one morning when banks open for business. Suppose, too, that one bank depositor is an importer who has paid £1m by cheque to a foreign exporter, and suppose the exporter gives the cheque to his bank overseas called, say, OSB. OSB will raise the exporter's deposit by £1m worth of local currency, and it may seek to match this by a £1m increase in its deposit at its UK correspondent bank called, say, UKB. Imagine, then, that soon after banks open for business, UKB demands £1m from the importer's UK bank. As far as total UK bank assets are concerned, there will be no change; all that happens is that the Bank of England deposit of the importer's bank falls by £1m and the Bank of England deposit of UKB rises by £1m. Likewise, the total liabilities of the UK banks must remain unaltered, although £1m passes from the importer's deposit to OSB's bank deposit at UKB. The upshot is shown in column (2) where it can be seen that the only change from (1) is that domestic deposits have fallen by £1m while foreign deposits have risen by £1m. Thus the purchase has the effect of raising overseas banks' sterling deposits by £1m and cutting the UK money stock by £1m. There is no necessary impact on the Bank of England.

As it happens, OSB might have credited the exporter's deposit with £1m worth of local currency and then, instead of asking for £1m more in its deposit at UKB, agree with UKB to reduce UKB's deposit at OSB by £1m worth of local currency. UKB might then seek to have its deposit at OSB replenished by the importer's bank, asking his bank to pay £1m worth of foreign currency from its deposit in the country concerned to UKB's deposit at OSB. If this had happened, then the result would have been as shown in column (3). As far as clearing bank liabilities are concerned, the importer's bank would reduce his deposit by £1m, but there will be no change in foreign banks' deposits at UK banks. As for assets, there is a fall of £1m in UK banks' overseas deposits, for the importer's bank has lost £1m worth of currency in its deposit in the country where the imports originated. Once again the money stock will fall by £1m as UK deposits have again fallen from 985 to 984. This time, though, the fall is matched by a fall in UK deposits held in overseas banks rather than by a rise in deposits held in the UK by overseas banks. Again, there is no necessary impact on the Bank of England.

The point of exploring in detail the effects of this expenditure by a UK citizen is that it shows what tendencies would arise if, during the morning which began with the situation shown in column (1), UK citizens as a whole made out more cheques in favour of foreign citizens than they received from foreign citizens. The UK money stock would fall, UK bank deposits of foreign currencies would fall and overseas bank deposits at UK banks would rise. This situation is shown in column (4) where it is supposed that soon after the day concerned in column (1) began, UK citizens spent £4m more abroad than they received from abroad, and that the net fall in UK sterling deposits by 4 from 985 to 981 was matched partly by a fall in 2 of UK bank deposits abroad and partly by a rise of 2 in overseas bank deposits in the UK. The UK money stock, of course, will have fallen by 4 in line with the fall in UK deposits. Now suppose that banks in the UK and abroad started the day with their holdings of foreign currency deposits at the levels they desire. Then the UK banks would get steadily alarmed by the fall in their holdings of foreign currencies, and overseas banks would get steadily irritated by the rise in their holdings of sterling. (Remember that banks like to keep foreign currency holdings as low as possible.)

There is one obvious course of action for the banks, and this is to change the exchange rate between sterling and other currencies so that foreigners find sterling cheaper while UK citizens find foreign currencies dearer. As noted earlier, this should encourage foreigners to do more spending in the UK and so to want more sterling, and it should encourage UK citizens to do less spending overseas and so to want less foreign currency. It can be seen, then, that left to their own devices bankers will adjust exchange rates continually to ensure that their deposits of foreign currencies actually remain very stable, which means ensuring that the amount of money spent abroad by UK citizens equals the amount they receive from abroad. In other words, exchange rates will fluctuate so that the figures shown in column (1) persist, and this means that the UK money stock will not be raised or cut as a result of international transactions. To be more precise, the money stock may change slightly from hour to hour, but such changes will induce exchange rate adjustments which bring it back to its original level. (The description given here somewhat over-simplifies real-world actions in the interests of clarity. In practice, bankers may be prepared to accept small fluctuations in their stocks of different currencies and so they may not always react to fluctuations by adjusting exchange rates. Thus small net flows of money may occur into or out of a particular country so that its money stock may not be quite as stable as suggested here.)

The analysis in the last paragraph applies to a situation of freely floating exchange rates where the monetary authorities in the different countries allow exchange rates to be established by market forces. Suppose, though, that the UK monetary authorities see downwards pressure on sterling soon after the column (4) figures are reached, and suppose they are anxious to prevent any fall in sterling. Such anxiety is quite possible as a fall in sterling will, for example, raise the sterling price of imports such as food and raw materials, and that in turn will raise prices in UK shops and raise the costs faced by UK industry. Anxiety is not inevitable, however, as a fall in sterling will make UK exports cheaper in terms of foreign currencies and will raise the level of exports, and that in turn will raise the levels of UK output and employment. In the present example it is supposed that the disadvantages of a fall in sterling are held to outweigh the advantages. How can the authorities prevent a fall? In other words, how can they fix the exchange rate?

The answer is that the authorities must help UK banks to build up their foreign currency deposits and help overseas banks to reduce their sterling deposits. The necessary action will be taken by the government which must buy sterling from UK banks and overseas banks. Of course, the government must give these banks some-thing in exchange for sterling, and it holds a range of assets which it can give them. Actually, these assets are recorded in the name of what is termed the Exchange Equal-ization Account (EEA) which was set up by the government for the purpose in 1932, shortly after the UK left the gold standard. It should be noted that the activities of the EEA are handled on the government's behalf by the Bank of England, though the Bank naturally handles them in the way required by the government of the day.

Now the EEA holds some foreign currency deposits, generally at foreign central banks, but most of its assets are securities, generally short-term government securities such as bills, which are held in many different countries. In time, each of its bills matures in the appropriate currency, and the proceeds are used to buy new bills. Although the EEA's assets are mostly in the form of securities rather than bank deposits, they represent the government's holdings, on the country's behalf, of what is termed the country's official reserves of foreign currencies. The EEA also holds the country's reserves of gold which could be sold for foreign currencies if need arose. In addition to its assets held abroad and its holdings of gold, the EEA has an account at the Bank of England, as shown in Table 6.2. The value of this is assumed to be 5 in columns (1) to (4).

What must the EEA do, faced with the column (4) situation, to avoid a fall in the value of sterling? It must first offer to buy sterling from the banks and to sell them for-eign currencies. Recall that UK banks have £2m less in foreign currencies than they want. The EEA can sell them £2m worth of foreign currencies in exchange for £2m of sterling with the effects shown in column (5). By making purchases from the EEA, a depositor at the Bank of England, the banks will lose 2 from their deposits at the Bank, so these fall to 28 while the EEA's deposit rises to 7. In return, the banks will be given £2m worth of foreign currencies which the EEA will have transferred from its bank accounts in the countries concerned to the UK banks' accounts there. Accord-ingly, UK banks' foreign currency deposits rise from a value of 8 to a value of 10, as shown. Of course, the EEA's foreign currency holdings, and so the UK's official reserves, both fall by £2m although there are no items on Table 6.2 to reflect this.

The EEA must also sell foreign currencies to foreign banks for sterling, as foreign banks have £2m more sterling than they want. The effects of doing such deals for £2m can be seen by comparing columns (5) and (6). The EEA will ask foreign banks for £2m from the overseas sterling deposits they hold at UK banks. This reduces these deposits from 17 to 15 and so reduces total UK bank deposits from 998 to 996. It also reduces UK bank deposits at the Bank of England by 2 from 28 to 26, because depositors with the clearing banks are paying money to the EEA which keeps its account at the Bank. Conversely, the EEA's deposit there rises by 2 from 7 to 9. Simultaneously, the EEA has money transferred from its accounts in foreign central banks to the accounts of those foreign banks which have purchased foreign currencies from it. Again, such transfers out of EEA accounts held abroad represent a fall in UK reserves of foreign currencies.

The initial effects of the EEA's actions can be seen by comparing columns (6) and (4). Overseas bank deposits in the UK have been restored to the desired level of 15 while UK bank deposits abroad have been restored to the desired level of 10. Thus the threat of a fall in the value of sterling should have been successfully removed. At the same time, it appears that the UK money stock has been increased by 4 to its original level of 1,250; this is the sum of UK deposits at clearing banks of 981, deposits at the Bank of England of 50, less bankers' deposits of 26 plus publicly-held cash of 245. The increase in the money stock by 4 from column (4) is entirely attributable to the fall by 4 of bankers' deposits at the Bank of England.

However, the ultimate effect of the EEA's actions on the money stock will not be to create a small rise but rather to create a sharp fall. This is a direct result of the fall in the clearing banks' deposits at the Bank of England. These deposits form part of the banks' reserves of cash, and their total cash holdings are now 56 which is less than their target ratio of 6 per cent of deposits. In fact, therefore, it seems banks will have to reduce their holdings of securities and advances by some 63 to 867, thus reducing total liabilities by 63 to 933, for their cash of 56 will then be just about 6 per cent of total liabilities. In turn, the money stock will fall by 63 from 1,250 to 1,187.

It follows from this analysis that banks can be persuaded to hold exchange rates stable in a period when a country's citizens spend more abroad than they receive, for in this example UK citizens spent in foreign currencies £4m, worth more than foreigners spent in sterling. In other words, a country's exchange rate need not fall when it has what is termed a balance of payments deficit, provided that its monetary authorities undertake perfectly offsetting currency transactions. In this example they sold foreign currencies held in the official reserves for £4m in sterling. However, such offsetting action seems likely to cause a multiplier contraction in the money stock of the country concerned. Conversely, a country's citizens can spend less than they receive, and so create a balance of payments surplus, without the exchange rate for their currency being raised, provided their monetary authorities undertake perfectly offsetting currency transactions by buying foreign currencies so raising official reserves. Such action would be expected to cause a multiplier expansion in the money stock of the country concerned.

It will be realized that the monetary authorities in a country will have some difficulty maintaining a fixed exchange rate if a balance of payments deficit is sustained for a long period, for the authorities will be continually using their foreign currency reserves to buy their own currency, and reserves are necessarily limited in amount. Eventually the authorities may be forced to devalue – that is to accept a lower exchange rate – but there are various ways in which they can try to hold on even when reserves are limited. Three ways will be indicated here.

First, they can seek to borrow foreign currencies which they can then spend purchasing their own currency. Secondly, they can introduce exchange controls which limit the purposes for which citizens at home are allowed to buy foreign currencies. Thus there could be a limit on how much foreign exchange people could buy for foreign holiday purposes or a limit on how much money can be held in foreign

**Table 6.2**    The effects of international transactions on banks

**Bank of England**

| Column | (1) | (2) | (3) | (4) | (5) | (6) | (7) |
|---|---|---|---|---|---|---|---|
| Liabilities | | | | | | | £m |
| Exchange Equalization Account | 5 | 5 | 5 | 5 | 7 | 9 | 5 |
| Other public deposits | 15 | 15 | 15 | 15 | 15 | 15 | 15 |
| Bankers' deposits | 30 | 30 | 30 | 30 | 28 | 26 | 30 |
| Total | 50 | 50 | 50 | 50 | 50 | 50 | 50 |
| Assets | | | | | | | £m |
| Securities and advances | 50 | 50 | 50 | 50 | 50 | 50 | 50 |
| Total | 50 | 50 | 50 | 50 | 50 | 50 | 50 |

**Clearing banks**

| Column | (1) | (2) | (3) | (4) | (5) | (6) | (7) |
|---|---|---|---|---|---|---|---|
| Liabilities | | | | | | | £m |
| UK Deposits | 985 | 984 | 984 | 981 | 981 | 981 | 985 |
| Foreign deposits | 15 | 16 | 15 | 17 | 17 | 15 | 15 |
| Total | 1000 | 1000 | 999 | 998 | 998 | 996 | 1000 |
| Assets | | | | | | | £m |
| Notes and coin | 30 | 30 | 30 | 30 | 30 | 30 | 30 |
| Deposits at Bank of England | 30 | 30 | 30 | 30 | 28 | 26 | 30 |
| Balances at banks abroad | 10 | 10 | 9 | 8 | 10 | 10 | 10 |
| Securities and advances | 930 | 930 | 930 | 930 | 930 | 930 | 930 |
| Total | 1000 | 1000 | 999 | 998 | 998 | 996 | 1000 |

currency bank deposits or used to buy securities abroad. Naturally such controls are likely to reduce the demand for foreign currency. Various controls have often been imposed by the UK authorities, but there have been none since 1979. Thirdly, they could introduce a multiple exchange rate system whereby, in effect, purchases of foreign currencies for some specified purposes are subjected to a tax; this means that the price of foreign currencies will vary according to the purpose for which it is needed. Incidentally, actions like these by the monetary authorities may be backed up by government policies such as tariffs or quotas or tax rises designed to discourage imports or interest rate rises to induce a net capital inflow.

## Sterilization and Domestic Credit Expansion

In practice, the authorities in the UK can prevent exchange rate fluctuations by taking the action described in the last section, and they can simultaneously ensure that such action need not cause changes in the money stock after all. In other words, the authorities can complement the action described so far with further measures which offset or sterilize their likely effects on the money stock. To see how they can do this, look again at Table 6.2 and notice that the steps taken to prevent sterling's value falling resulted in the figures of column (4) being replaced by those in column (6). It is true that the clearing banks' holdings of cash have fallen by 4, so that a contraction in the money stock seems imminent. However, the EEA's deposit at the Bank of England has risen by 4 and it is necessary to consider what it will do with this new found sterling.

Remember that the EEA's money belongs to the government, and remember that the government has a continuous problem of raising enough by way of taxes and loans to finance its expenditure. Suppose, for simplicity, that the government raises 10 each day by way of taxes and loans and has to finance a daily expenditure of 10. In the course of a normal day, then, bankers' deposits at the Bank of England fall by 10, as some depositors pay money to the government, only to rise again by 10 when other depositors receive money as a result of government expenditure. In short, bankers' deposits at the Bank actually stay at a stable level.

Now on the particular day considered in column (6), the government's deposits have actually risen by 4 as a result of sales of foreign currency so it could in time raise 4 less by way of taxes and loans to finance its normal expenditure. The likely outcome is that, in the near future, the EEA deposit will be transferred to other public deposits and spent, and that the government will borrow 4 less than it would have done if the foreign currency sales had not taken place. In other words, the government will in the near future spend 4 more than it receives so that bankers' deposits at the Bank of England will rise by 4. The consequences are shown in column (7). The EEA deposit falls by 4, as funds have been transferred to other public deposits. However, these other public deposits do not rise because the funds are spent without any offsetting receipts from taxes or loans to the government; instead, bankers' deposits rise by 4. As for the clearing banks, their depositors receive 4 from the government to match the rise in bankers' deposits. The result is that the banks are in the identical position that they had in column (1) and the money stock reverts to its original level.

It can be seen, then, that if a country's citizens have a balance of payments deficit which reduces domestic bank holdings of foreign currencies and raises foreign bank holdings of domestic currencies – as occurred when the column (4) figures replaced the column (1) figures – then the government can prevent a change in the exchange rate by selling an appropriate offsetting amount of foreign exchange – as occurred when the column (6) figures replaced the column (4) figures. This action will, of itself, reduce banks' cash holdings and threaten to lead to a cut in the money stock, but the contractionary effect will be sterilized or neutralized, that is eliminated, if the government uses its receipts from the foreign currency sales to undertake in its own country some expenditure that is not financed by taxation or borrowing – as occurred when the column (7) figures replaced the column (6) figures.

Actually, a government may find sterilization less feasible than this description of the mechanics suggests. Suppose a country is running a balance of payments deficit and that each day citizens spend more abroad than they receive from abroad. Suppose, too, that its monetary authorities are preventing a decline in its exchange rate by selling foreign exchange reserves. If the authorities decide not to sterilize the monetary effects, then the money stock will fall, and so, for reasons explained in the last chapter, interest rates will rise. This, in turn, is likely to result in the balance of payments deficit reducing and eventually ceasing, for higher interest rates will reduce capital outflows and increase capital inflows, and they are likely also to reduce overall spending levels and hence reduce incomes and imports. If, instead, the monetary authorities opt for complete sterilization, then interest rates will not rise and the deficit is likely to persist. However, it cannot persist indefinitely, for the government will not be able to sell reserves indefinitely since reserves will eventually run out. Thus it may, eventually, decide to let the exchange rate fall. It may, instead, take action to reduce the deficit, and in that context it is likely to stop sterilizing the monetary effects and so allow interest rates to rise.

Return to Table 6.2, and suppose the government decided not to sterilize when the column (6) figures were reached. What would it have done with the deposits of 4 in the EEA? It would have used them to buy government securities for 4 from the Bank of England, to reduce the need to pay interest to the Bank. The Bank of England would find both its liabilities and assets falling by 4, for the reduction to zero of the EEA deposit would be matched by a fall of 4 in the Bank's holdings of securities. The banks would have remained with cash of 56 and would have had to start reducing their deposit levels.

It has been seen that sterilization eliminates the tendency for a balance of payments deficit to reduce the money stock. In turn, sterilization prevents from working forces which would eliminate the deficit. Sterilization is, in fact, the antithesis of what was meant to happen in the days of the gold standard, at least according to some textbooks. To see what was meant to happen then, suppose the UK had a deficit. Then foreign banks would amass unwanted sterling in their deposits at UK banks while UK banks would find their foreign currency deposits at overseas banks diminishing. The foreign banks would use their sterling deposits to buy gold from the Bank of England, for they could then ship the gold to other countries to buy currencies for which they had more need; these foreign banks would use cheques instructing their UK banks to pay money to the Bank of England, so UK bankers' deposits at the Bank would fall. Also, the UK banks would buy gold from the Bank of England, for they could then ship this to other countries to buy currencies for which their stocks were low; their deposits at the Bank would be reduced in payment for the gold. In short, the deficit would result in a fall in banks' deposits at the Bank of England, and by the process outlined in the last chapter this would cause a fall in the money stock.

A further point to notice about this gold standard situation is that the fall in the Bank of England's gold holdings would cause a fall in the ratio of these holdings to the total issue of its notes. The ratio might improve in time if falls in the money stock led to falls in the public's demand for cash. However, the Bank of England might have to take further measures to contract the money stock and so reduce the demand for cash in order to restore the original ratio. Central banks were often at pains to keep to some particular ratio, partly out of prudence since they were meant always to be willing to exchange gold for notes, and sometimes in order to meet requirements imposed on them by their governments.

It has been seen that under the gold standard a balance of payments deficit should lead to a fall in the money stock. Now the lower money stock was expected to reduce spending levels and so lead to downward pressure on prices. By making domestic industries more competitive in terms of price, there should be a fall in imports and a rise in exports and hence an end to the deficit. No doubt a mechanism such as this was at work much of the time in the gold standard era. In many countries, though, the effects of a deficit on the money stock were often sterilized. One way in which this could be done was for their central banks to undertake open-market purchases of securities at a time when there was a deficit. This policy would mean that any tendency for bankers' deposits at the central bank to fall as a result of people buying gold from the bank could be offset. Of course, the resulting stability in the money stock would certainly mean that the central bank had a lower ratio of gold to issued notes, but with careful management this fall could be accommodated. For instance, if there was a minimum permitted ratio, then the authorities might allow the actual ratio to rise in a period of balance of payments surplus, so that the ratio could fall for some time in a period of deficit before the note issue had to be reduced.

One final point about Table 6.2 should be stressed. Over the period of time which elapsed between column (1) and column (7), the country's citizens spent £4m more abroad than they received from abroad, yet they ended up with the same amount of money in their bank deposits that they started with! How can this paradoxical result be explained? It arose because – between columns (6) and (7) – the government gave them £4m in return for goods and services supplied, and financed its purchases by selling – between columns (4) and (6) – some of its foreign currency reserves. It would be fair to say that during the period covered by column (1), and then columns (4) to (7), the citizens acquired an extra £4m of money to spend, by selling goods and services to the government, and that by spending £4m abroad more than they received from abroad, they ensured that there was no increase in their deposits to show up when the money stock figures at the beginning and end of the period were compared.

It can be seen that comparisons of the money stock figures can give a misleading impression of the extent to which the amount of money which people can spend has changed over a period of time. For this reason, the concept of Domestic Credit Expansion (DCE) was devised. It was brought into prominence in the late 1960s and early 1970s. DCE seeks to show the extent to which people have had access to more (or less) money over a period of time. Clearly it should be £4m in the period elapsing between columns (1) and (7). It can be found from the formula $DCE = \Delta M - \Delta R$, where $\Delta M$ is the change in the recorded money stock (zero in this example) and $\Delta R$ is the change in official foreign currency reserves (they fell by 4 in this example, so the change was $-4$). In this example, then, $DCE = 0 - (-4)$ so that $DCE = 4$.

The use and measurement of DCE is equally appropriate if sterilization does not take place. Suppose it had not occurred so that the period started with the column (1) figures and ended with the column (6) ones. In that case, the money stock would fall by 4. On the other hand, DCE would be zero because, in the absence of the sterilization moves, there was no change in the amount people could spend. These observations are consistent with the formula $DCE = \Delta M - \Delta R$ since this would now give DCE as $-4 - (-4) = 0$. In fact, if no sterilization occurred, then for the reasons explained earlier the banks would soon take actions to ensure that the level of deposits fell by a further 63 to 933. When the cuts were complete, then a comparison with the starting position would show $\Delta M$ to be $-67$ and DCE to be $-63$.

Of course, in a period when exchange rates float freely, $\Delta R$ is always zero so that $DCE = \Delta M$. In these circumstances $\Delta M$ *does* give a correct view of the extent to which the authorities are changing the amount of money citizens can spend. Accordingly, there is no need to produce figures for DCE. Since the early 1970s, the UK's exchange rate has floated quite widely, if not wholly freely, and figures for DCE have not varied greatly from figures for $\Delta M$. For this reason, the authorities have ceased publishing DCE figures.

# International monetary flows and interest rates

The last two sections have shown the effects that international flows can have on a country's money stock. It is useful to consider briefly their implications for a country's interest rate. In fact they make it hard to sustain for long any change in a country's interest rate. This result is clearly different from the situation in a closed economy, considered in the last chapter, where it seemed that expansionary and contractionary monetary policies could shift the $M_s$ curves to secure any desired interest rate. Furthermore, it is a result that arises whether exchange rates are fixed or floating.

Suppose, first, that one country, X, has a fixed exchange rate. Suppose, too, that its $M_d$ and $M_s$ curves have determined an interest rate which happens to be similar to interest rates in other countries; the importance of this assumption will become clear shortly. The $M_d$ and $M_s$ curves will also determine an equilibrium money stock. Suppose that the actual money stock equals the equilibrium stock. Finally, suppose that there is equilibrium on the balance of payments.

Now consider what might happen if the government wants to cut interest rates. On reading the last chapter, it might imagine that any measures designed to shift right-wards the $M_s$ supply curve – say open market purchases of bonds – could achieve this result. So they could, but only for a while. Why is this? The point is that interest rates in X will be falling below those found elsewhere, so there will be a tendency for those who own securities in X to sell their securities in X and to buy securities abroad, and there will be a tendency for people with money in interest-earning deposits in X to remove it from those deposits and place it in interest-earning deposits abroad. In short, X will soon have a balance of payments deficit. The size of the deficit is likely to be smaller if there is a system of exchange controls or multiple exchange rates which reduces the extent to which X's citizens can move funds into other currencies, but there will still be a deficit, partly because such measures are unlikely to prevent all moves by X's citizens and partly because they cannot be used to stop overseas citizens shifting funds from X to other countries.

To maintain its fixed exchange rate, X's monetary authorities must sell foreign exchange to its banks whose foreign currency deposits with their correspondent banks abroad will be falling, and it must buy X's own currency from foreign banks whose deposits with their correspondent banks in X will be rising. This action will tend, as explained earlier, to reduce the central bank deposits of X's banks, and this in turn causes the $M_s$ curve to shift to the left. This shift will raise interest rates again and so tend to end the capital outflow from X and hence end its balance of payments deficit. X's authorities may seek for a while to sterilize the monetary effects of their purchases of X's currency, but by doing so they will continue to create low interest rates and a deficit, and will therefore have to carry on selling their foreign exchange. Since their stocks of foreign exchange reserves will be limited, they cannot maintain low interest rates for ever.

Of course, attempts to raise interest rates have converse effects to those just described. They create a balance of payments surplus, and unless X's government wants to carry on buying reserves indefinitely, it will eventually have to let interest rates fall. However, there is admittedly a less clear cut limit to the amount of reserves which can be bought than there is to the amount which can be sold.

Next, suppose the situation starts with the same equilibrium as before, that the government again takes steps to raise the money stock in order to reduce interest rates, but suppose this time that the exchange rate floats freely. In this case, the capital outflow will result in the exchange rate falling. This will tend to lead to a rise in exports and a fall in imports and so to higher output and incomes in X. In turn, the $M_d$ curve will shift rightwards as the increase in incomes causes the transactions and precautionary demands for money rise. This shift will cause interest rates to rise once again, perhaps ending up close to, or even at, their original levels. Conversely, attempts to cut the money stock in order to increase interest rates will raise the value of X's currency, and so cut its exports and raise its imports; in turn, output and incomes will fall, $M_d$ will shift leftwards and interest rates may end little higher than they started. In short, attempts to alter interest rates may, in the end, have as little effect when the exchange rate floats freely as they have when it is fixed.

Although the authorities were unable to have much effect on interest rates in either case, there are two important differences in the situations with fixed and floating exchange rates. To see the first difference recall that, with fixed rates, the effect on interest rates of the initial shift in $M_s$ was undone by a subsequent move in $M_s$ in the opposite direction. Consequently, not only were interest rates unaltered, so too was the equilibrium level of the money stock. With floating rates, however, the effect on interest rates of the initial shift in $M_s$ was undone by a subsequent move in $M_d$ in the same direction that $M_s$ had moved. Consequently, although interest rates were little altered, there was likely to be a significant change in the equilibrium level of the money stock. The second difference is that shifts in the $M_s$ curve lead to changes in the exchange rate, when the exchange rate floats, and so, in turn, lead to changes in output and incomes. No such shifts occur when the exchange rate is fixed. In short, changes in the $M_s$ curve have modest and only temporary effects on the economy when exchange rates are fixed, but they have important and lasting effects on the exchange rate, output and incomes – but not on interest rates – when exchange rates float.

This analysis has effectively assumed that there would be capital inflows if interest rates in X exceeded levels elsewhere and outflows if they were below. Thus interest rates have not been able to settle down except at levels equal – or at least close – to those elsewhere. In fact, there are several reasons why the level of interest rates in country X may have to settle at a point above the general level elsewhere. They would have to settle at a relatively high level if securities in X were thought generally riskier than those elsewhere or if X's exchange rates, whether or not theoretically fixed, were thought likely to fall (thereby reducing the purchasing power of X's currency in world markets); clearly no one would want securities in X unless interest rates there compensated for these disadvantages. Conversely, interest rates in X might settle at a relatively low level if securities in X were thought to have particularly low risks or if the value of X's currency was thought likely to rise. A further complication arises if countries restrict the activities of people who want to switch their funds from country to country. If X makes it hard for funds to leave while other countries make it hard for funds to enter, then the forces tending to make interest rates in X resemble levels elsewhere will clearly be much reduced, and significant differentials could emerge between countries.

# Foreign currency deposits

Previous sections have implied that only banks and the EEA hold deposits of foreign currencies, and they have also implied that deposits of foreign currencies are necessarily held at foreign banks. In fact, many people – or, more usually, businesses – hold foreign currency deposits, and it is perfectly possible to hold such deposits at a UK bank. These two possibilities will be considered in turn.

The possibility of UK citizens holding deposits of foreign currencies in foreign banks can arise very easily. Suppose a UK exporter sells goods for $1.5m to a US importer and that the exchange rate is $1.5 = £1. The exporter will receive a cheque from the importer. As suggested in earlier sections, he may well take the cheque to his UK bank and ask them to raise his deposit, and thus their liabilities, by £1m. The bank will initially match this by a rise in its assets secured by arranging for its deposit at a US bank to rise by $1.5m, representing a transfer from the US importer's bank deposit of this amount. The effect on the quantity of the sterling money stock depends on the factors outlined earlier. If the exchange rate floats freely, then this receipt of funds will soon be offset by matching outflows and there will be no effect, but if the exchange rate is fixed, then the stock will rise by £1m unless the authorities take steps to sterilize the rise.

However, the exporter might decide instead to open up an account of his own at a US bank and have the cheque paid into his deposit there. If so, the payment merely represents a transfer of US dollars from the US importer's US deposit to the UK exporter's US deposit and no UK bank is involved. In this case, the amount of money held by UK citizens would rise, but the quantity of the sterling money stock would obviously be unaffected. Why might the exporter want to keep his funds in dollars? One very possible reason is that he might want soon to spend $1.5m buying goods from another American. By keeping his funds in dollars he can be sure of having the dollars needed. If, instead, he had opted to convert them into £1m and subsequently the exchange rate for sterling had fallen to, say, $1.4 = £1, then his £1m would buy only $1.4m worth of goods. Of course, converting the dollars into pounds means he would gain if sterling appreciated, but the attraction of a dollar deposit is that it offers certainty in place of uncertainty.

As it happens, the exporter has yet another option, which is to take the cheque to his UK bank and ask them to open a dollar deposit for him and credit it with $1.5m in his name. Once again he has security against changes in the value of the dollar, and once again the sterling money stock would be unaltered, though the amount of money held by UK citizens would rise. As in the first case, his bank would arrange for the $1.5m to be credited to its US bank deposit, but a key difference from that case is that there the $1.5m in assets was matched by a rise in sterling liabilities, denominated by £1m, while here it is matched by a rise in dollar liabilities, denominated by £1.5m.

There is another key difference from the first case. In that case, the UK bank probably had all the dollars it wanted to begin with. It acquired some more because the exporter presented it with his dollars which he converted to sterling, and the bank, having acquired surplus dollars, would probably want to dispose of them shortly for sterling. In the new case, though, it can be inferred that the bank wants more dollars and that it will not sell them for sterling. How can this be inferred? To answer this, consider why the exporter has placed his dollars with the UK bank instead of a US bank. The only possible advantage a UK bank could offer him would be to pay some interest on its dollar deposits, or at least more interest than US banks pay, but a UK bank will not offer any interest at all on dollars unless it actually wants dollars. Why might it want dollars? Presumably it wants dollars so that it can lend them, believing that it can lend them for a higher rate than it pays on the deposit. For the moment it will be assumed that it expects to lend them to someone in the US, perhaps a business wanting to borrow to buy some raw materials.

The dollar deposits at the UK bank are known as Euro-dollars. In fact, the term Euro-dollar is used to describe US dollars deposited at any bank outside the US, and such a bank is known as a Euro-bank whether or not it is in Europe. It should be stressed that many of the banks outside the US where Euro-dollars are deposited are actually subsidiaries of banks in the US. The term Euro-sterling is used to describe UK currency deposited at any bank outside the UK. More generally, the term Euro-currency describes any currency deposited at any bank other than banks in the country where the currency is used. In practice, though, Euro-dollars are by far the most important of the Euro-currencies. Note that Euro-banks will not lend all the dollars they acquire but will keep a prudent percentage on deposit at US banks in case some of their depositors wish to withdraw their dollars.

There were few Euro-dollars, or indeed any other Euro-currencies, until 1960, but there has been an almost explosive growth since. The reasons are best explained in the case of Euro-dollars, though the numbers used in the explanation will be imaginary. Suppose, for simplicity, that there are initially no Euro-dollars, that US banks are lending at interest rates of 10 per cent and paying 7 per cent on all their deposits, competition for deposits keeping the rates paid on deposits high. It can be taken that the banks regard the 3 per cent margin as adequate to cover the risks and administration costs of lending. Next, suppose, the US monetary authorities introduce restrictions on US banks. Imagine, for instance, that US banks are forbidden to pay interest on deposits at rates in excess of 4 per cent and that, simultaneously, credit ceilings are introduced which reduce the level of their loans and cause the banks to raise lending rates to 12 per cent. There is now an 8 per cent margin.

Now some banks outside the US may decide to attract dollar deposits by offering 5 per cent on such deposits, and they may be able to find US borrowers prepared to pay 11 per cent. Such action could yield handsome profits. Before long, more banks outside the US may decide to do likewise. In the end, competition between the Euro-banks may cause them to end up paying 7 per cent on deposits and lending at 10 per cent on loans. This will force US banks also to lend at 10 per cent, though they will not be permitted to raise interest rates on deposits. However, even though the US banks may pay less on deposits than Euro-banks, they need not actually fear a mass loss of deposits from the US. The point is that when depositors switch funds from a US bank to a Euro-bank, the Euro-bank will initially hold the funds itself in a deposit at a US bank, and then it will lend them to borrowers who typically will also keep them in US banks.

Incidentally, if the Euro-banks are liable for lower taxes than the US banks, or if their dollar activities are not constrained by any mandatory cash ratios, then they may be willing to end up with margins of under 3 per cent. Thus they could end up setting deposit rates of 8 per cent and lending rates at 9 per cent and still find the resulting 1 per cent margin profitable. Nevertheless, there is clearly a limit to the extent to which they can expand their activities while still making profits.

The development of Euro-dollars did arise chiefly because of the US authorities' controls on US banks, and other Euro-currencies have developed chiefly because of restrictions elsewhere. Such developments tend to push interest rates down. How can this be explained in terms of the $M_s$ and $M_d$ diagrams of Chapter 4? The $M_s$ curves show the amount of money a country's banks want people to hold in the country while the $M_d$ curves show how much money people want to hold in the country. When the

Euro-dollar option was opened, the demand for deposits in the US fell, so $M_d$ shifted to the left. It might be thought that the Euro-banks wanted to hold dollars in the US, but actually they wanted to get rid of them in loans; and it might be thought that the borrowers want to hold them but actually they wanted to spend them. So when the $M_d$ curve shifted to the left, the US money market did not reach a new equilibrium until interest rates fell enough to persuade people to hold all the dollars the banks wanted them to hold. This would have been at a smaller quantity of dollars than before if $M_s$ was not vertical. Of course, the lower interest rates were likely to stimulate extra investment in the US; this investment will have raised incomes and so in time shifted $M_d$ a little to the right.

Although the analysis in previous paragraphs sums up the key effects of Euro-currencies, three points need to be made. First, Euro-banks accepting deposits transferred from US banks do not ordinarily lend them *directly* to US borrowers. The reason is that such deposits, though invariably time deposits, are usually repayable within days while borrowers want to borrow for some months. To avoid the risks that direct lending to final borrowers would entail, a Euro-bank in receipt of a new deposit will generally lend it to another bank, perhaps insisting on repayment within two weeks of request, while that bank may lend it to another insisting on repayment within four weeks of request. In this way a whole chain of Euro-banks may be involved between the initial deposit and the final loan. Each bank along the chain will pay a little more in interest for its deposit, as each movement along the chain makes the deposits a little less liquid; but each bank will charge a little more for its loan as loans also become less liquid with each move along the chain. Thus each bank can make a little profit margin. This process means that the total value of Euro-dollar claims may be huge, and is far larger than the value of final loans handled by the Euro-banks. Consider a chain of 10 banks who receive an initial deposit of $1m and, ultimately, lend $0.95m to a US firm, keeping $0.05m in deposits at US banks out of prudence. Although approaching $10m of claims will be made by the chain, the true amount of dollars created will be $0.95m since that is the amount of extra dollars available for final borrowers. Thus the credit multiplier figure would be a modest 0.95. More generally, it appears that the Euro-currency multiplier must be $(1 - r)$ where r is the dollar deposit ratio desired by Euro-banks.

The second point to note is that the credit multiplier could actually be higher than $(1 - r)$. Accordingly, it could exceed 0.95 if Euro-banks seek a ratio for dollar deposits to final loans around 5 per cent. To see the reason for this, it is simplest to assume that all final loans are made by the bank receiving the initial deposit. The implication of the previous paragraph was that the bank would make a loan of $0.95m to a US citizen who would spend the money and thus cause it to be lost from the deposit of the Euro-bank leaving it with just $0.05m. More generally, it was assumed that dollars loaned by Euro-banks are instantly withdrawn from them. This need not be the case. For instance, some US borrowers may make purchases from other US firms who then deposit the money with Euro-banks once again. Alternatively, a Euro-bank might lend dollars to a Spaniard who would then use them to repay a loan to a Turk who decided to deposit the money at another Euro-bank. Suppose, for a moment, that all Euro-dollar loans were redeposited at Euro-banks. Then an initial $1m could support a loan of $0.95m, which in turn could support a loan of some $0.90m, which could support another of $0.86m and so on. The credit multiplier would be given by $(1 - r)/r$ when r is the dollar ratio desired; if that was 5 per cent, then the credit multiplier would be 19. In fact, though, 'leakages' to US citizens who do not redeposit in the Euro-dollar market are very high. When the fraction of each loan leaked is x, then the multiplier is actually given by $(1 - r)/(r + x)$. Real world values of r are very small and x tends to be nearly one, so in practice the multiplier has a value of around one.

Thirdly, an important final point should be made about Euro-currencies for the benefit of readers tempted by the high rates offered on deposits. The minimum deposits accepted are usually for values equivalent to $1m!

## The implications of international monetary transactions

Suppose, now, that the world has settled down with a system of Euro-currencies, and suppose a number of citizens and institutions in each country have Euro-currency deposits in their own currency, Euro-currency deposits in other currencies, and deposits of foreign currencies held in banks in the countries where these currencies are used. Finally, suppose the money stock of each currency, and the Euro-currency stock of each currency, is at an initial equilibrium level. How, if at all, does this affect the implications of international transfers considered earlier?

One area of change is that new types of transaction can occur. For instance, UK citizens may wish to move sterling out of deposits in the UK into Euro-sterling deposits. As outlined in the last section, such moves may reduce interest rates in the UK while having little initial effect on the UK money stock. Of course, a fall in interest rates here will lead to capital outflows and so to either a fall in the money stock, if the exchange rate is fixed, or a fall in the exchange rate if it is floating. Eventually, UK interest rates must rise almost to their initial levels while interest rates in other countries may fall a minute fraction as a result of the capital inflow to them! The remaining examples will focus entirely on the initial consequences. Each time subsequent events must bring UK interest rates back into line with world levels for reasons explained earlier.

Another possibility is that UK citizens will wish to switch from sterling – or Euro-sterling – deposits to foreign exchange deposits. This will reduce the demand for sterling and increase the demand for foreign exchange and so have essentially the same effects as other transactions such as purchases of imports or foreign securities financed from sterling – or Euro-sterling – deposits. These effects are to depress the exchange rate if it floats, so stimulating offsetting inflows and causing the money stock in the UK to stay constant; and they are to make the UK monetary authorities buy sterling for foreign exchange if the exchange rate is fixed, so cutting the UK money stock, unless the authorities sterilize this increase. In short, the effects are as discussed in earlier sections. Needless to say, switches from foreign currency deposits to sterling or Euro-sterling deposits, like purchases by foreigners of UK goods and services or securities, have precisely the opposite effects.

There is one further possibility. UK purchasers of foreign commodities or securities can now use appropriate foreign currency deposits to finance these purchases. These result in deposits of foreign currencies changing hands and have no effect at all on sterling. Likewise, foreigners can use their stocks of sterling to finance purchases in the UK. Such deals will result in sterling deposits changing hands, but they will not alter the total amount of sterling held. Accordingly, these transactions have no effect on interest rates. It should be noted, though, that while such transactions do not alter the total stock of sterling that is held, they do alter the amount of sterling held by UK citizens, and so they do affect published money stock figures which concentrate on the money held by UK citizens.

Finally, it should be observed that countries will still have to have interest rates close to world levels, subject to the factors noted earlier. Indeed, the whole thrust of the analysis of the effects of attempts to change interest rates by changing the money stock is unaltered.

# 7

# The main financial institutions in the United Kingdom

The key elements of a banking system were outlined in Chapter 3. The present chapter builds on the material given there and in Chapters 4 and 5 to give further details of the activities of the main financial institutions in the UK. The first section looks at the Bank of England. The following sections take in turn the discount houses, the retail or primary banks, the wholesale or secondary banks, and NBFIs (non-bank financial intermediaries). It is worth noting that, with one exception, there are broadly comparable institutions in most other Western countries. The exception is provided by the discount houses. In other countries their functions are usually performed by the retail banks – and for this reason last-resort lending facilities are generally made available directly to the banks.

## The Bank of England

As earlier chapters have explained, the Bank of England is in many ways similar to a normal commercial bank except that its main depositors are the government and banks. To get a clearer idea of the Bank of England's activities, it is useful to look at its balance sheet. This is published regularly in the *Bank of England Quarterly Bulletin* and it is divided into two parts headed 'Issue Department' and 'Banking Department'. The Banking Department will be considered first, and its balance sheet for 29 October 1986 is given in Table 7.1. In common with all the balance sheets given in this chapter, Table 7.1 records all the assets and liabilities of the concern under consideration. It was explained in relation to Table 1.1 that, when this is done, then total liabilities and total assets must be equal.

Because Table 7.1 includes all the Banking Department's liabilities, it includes some items which have been omitted in the simplified bank balance sheets of earlier chapters. On the liabilities side, it includes items equivalent to the 'capital and reserves' that appeared in Table 1.1. For the privately owned company in Table 1.1, 'capital' represented the initial sums put up by the private shareholders when they first bought their shares; for the Bank of England, which is owned by the government, 'capital' can be taken to represent the initial value of the holding of the sole 'shareholder' which is the Treasury on behalf of the government. The liabilities

**Table 7.1**   Balance sheet for the Bank of England Banking Department on 29 October 1986

£m

| Liabilities | | Assets | |
|---|---|---|---|
| Public deposits | 92 | Notes and coin | 7 |
| Bankers' deposits | 962 | Government securities | 688 |
| Special deposits | — | Advances and other accounts | 833 |
| Reserves and other accounts | 1,986 | Premises, equipment and other | |
| Capital | 14 |    securities | 1,525 |
| Total | 3,054 | Total[1] | 3,054 |

Source: *Bank of England Quarterly Bulletin*, December 1986, Table 1.
[1]Total subject to rounding errors

side also covers the Bank's deposits. Public deposits and bankers' deposits are shown separately. The term 'special deposits' appears too, and its presence highlights the possibility, considered in Chapter 5, that the Bank might from time to time require other banks to maintain some special deposits in addition to their normal bankers' deposits. There was no such requirement in October 1986, and indeed there has been none since July 1980. There is no real need for special deposits to be shown separately from other bankers' deposits, but there are two advantages in distinguishing them. First, it is easy to see when such deposits are being required – and hence to see when the Bank is using them to restrain the money stock – and, secondly, such deposits differ a little from ordinary bankers' deposits in that 'special deposits' are entitled to interest, usually at the rate on the most recently issued Treasury bills (rounded to the nearest 1/16%), while 'bankers' deposits' are not.

On the assets side, Table 7.1 includes notes and coin, securities and advances, as have most bank balance sheets in earlier chapters. However, Table 7.1 also includes the value of fixed physical assets which are covered by the terms premises and equipment. Of course, as the Bank is not a producer which uses raw materials, there is no equivalent of the item 'stocks and work in progress' shown in Table 1.1.

Perhaps the two most striking facts revealed by Table 7.1 are the small level of public deposits and the miniscule level of the Banking Department's cash ratio. The reasons for the usually small level of public deposits were explained in Chapter 2. In fact, though, these deposits have occasionally risen to very large levels in recent years, being, for instance, over £6,000m in July 1985. Such surges have generally followed a major sale of public assets by the government, such as the sale of British Telecom (which in fact took place in three instalments). These sales have given rise to large sudden influxes to the government's account, but the funds tend to disappear over a period of months as government spending continues with less need for borrowing than there would otherwise have been. Incidentally, these sales of public assets threaten to drain bankers' deposits entirely, perhaps several times over, and this situation calls for substantial special last-resort assistance by the Bank. Much of this assistance has actually taken the form of the Bank of England buying securities off the other banks, paying for its purchases simply by raising the recorded sums in bankers' deposits. The securities are gradually sold back as the other banks' cash position improves following subsequent government spending.

**Table 7.2**   Balance sheet for the Bank of England Issue Department on 29 October 1986

£m

| Liabilities | | Assets | |
|---|---|---|---|
| Notes in circulation | 12,623 | Government securities | 3,469 |
| Notes in Banking Department | 7 | Other securities | 9,161 |
| Total | 12,630 | Total | 12,630 |

Source: *Bank of England Quarterly Bulletin*, December 1986, Table 1.

The result is that the Bank's security holdings have also been very volatile in recent years.

The ability of the Bank to survive with a miniscule cash ratio – just over 0.2 per cent in Table 7.1 – is explained by the fact that cash chiefly takes the form of Bank of England notes which the Bank can itself print! Formally, the Banking Department must obtain any extra notes needed from the Issue Department, and this department must now be examined. The Issue Department's balance sheet for 29 October 1986 is shown in Table 7.2. In many respects, its balance sheet resembles the one for the simple note-issuing bank considered in Tables 1.4 to 1.6, and it is helpful to contrast the situation of that bank with the Issue Department.

The bank in Table 1.6 accepted deposits of coins and gave depositors IOUs in return. It was always obliged to give coins back to anyone coming in with an IOU, but as its own IOUs could be used as money such withdrawals were rare. Accordingly, it was able to print new IOUs and lend them. The extra IOUs became extra liabilities and were matched by the loans which were assets. Now the Issue Department issues notes or IOUs – indeed it is the only English bank allowed to issue notes – and its liabilities are represented by its issued notes. As Table 7.2 shows, some of these notes were held by the Banking Department on 29 October 1986 but most were in circulation with the public.

The Issue Department's assets comprise securities and these, of course, can be regarded as loans to whoever issued them. The key difference between the Issue Department and the simple bank of Chapter 1 is that the Issue Department has no asset comparable with the coins held by that bank. The reason is simply that there is no need for such an asset. The bank in Chapter 1 was obliged to exchange notes for coins but the Issue Department has no comparable obligation. There was, as explained in the last chapter, a long period when it was obliged to exchange notes for gold, and accordingly it had to hold some gold; but that obligation has long ceased and the Issue Department no longer has to hold any gold.

The fact that Issue Department is not obliged to convert its notes into anything raises the question of what limit there is to the number of notes it issues. Its note issue is known as the fiduciary issue because people accept its notes on faith that the notes will continue to have a value as a medium of exchange for they know that they cannot demand notes to be converted to gold or coins. For many years, the size of the fiduciary issue was limited to a maximum value laid down by Parliament, but it is now under the general discretion of the Bank of England. Of course, the value has to be raised from time to time. In practice, the Issue Department issues notes to the Banking Department alone, and it always issues them as and when required. In turn, the Banking Department asks for notes only when its depositors want so many that its own stock is felt to be too low. The customers most likely to want notes are the clearing banks, and they want them only when their depositors' demands for cash cause these banks to withdraw some of their bankers' deposits in cash form.

It can be seen, then, that the issue of bank notes is really determined by the public in that the Bank of England undertakes to supply via the clearing banks whatever amounts they want. However, the Bank will take some interest in the amount demanded by the public. Suppose, for instance, that the public's demand for notes suddenly rose by £500m. Table 7.2 shows notes in circulation to have a value of £12,623m so this would be a sizeable rise, but it is the sort of rise which could easily occur over a short period of time. The public will withdraw £500m cash from their clearing bank deposits. The clearing banks will initially deplete the stocks of cash held by their branches, but they will be supposed to replenish these stocks by reducing their deposits at the Bank of England and asking for £500m in notes. Table 7.1 shows these deposits to be worth £962m, so it will be seen that a modest rise in the demand for cash could have a drastic effect on these deposits. Of course, the Banking Department does not initially have £500m worth of notes, but it could acquire them rapidly from the Issue Department. To do so, it would give the Issue Department £500m worth of government securities and ask for £500m worth of notes to be printed and given in exchange. The effect on the Issue Department would be a rise in liabilities of £500m in the form of extra notes in circulation – since the new notes would go to the clearing banks and would not stay in the Banking Department – matched by a rise in assets of £500m in the form of extra government securities. In contrast, the Banking Department's assets would fall by £500m when it gave securities to the Issue Department and its liabilities would fall by £500m when bankers' deposits were withdrawn.

However, there would be further more significant effects. The clearing banks would find their bankers' deposits had just about halved. It was noted in Chapter 5 that these deposits must form at least 0.5 per cent of the banks' total liabilities. The banks would presumably seek to restore them as quickly as possible by seeking repayment of £500m money-at-call from the discount houses who would doubtless seek to raise this sum by selling Treasury bills or other securities to the Banking Department. This move by the discount houses would eventually raise the Banking Department's assets by £500m, as a result of its purchases of securities, and its liabilities by £500m, as bankers' deposits rose once again. But now the banks' money-at-call will have fallen by £500m and this asset is meant to equal at least 5 per cent, or one-twentieth, of the banks' total liabilities. It might seem that if the value of the banks' call money fell by £500m, then the banks would have to take rapid steps to contract their total liabilities by 20 times as much, that is by the very substantial sum of £10,000m. At least, this might be the expected result unless the banks' initial amounts of call money had been some way in excess of the minimum required. However, it was explained in Chapter 5 that the banks could seek to avoid such contraction by giving new advances, of £500m in this case perhaps, to the discount houses who might use the new loans to purchase commercial bills. In this way, call money could be restored to the initial level.

The only threat to this ploy would come if the monetary authorities took steps to make it useless as far as the banks were concerned by issuing £500m new Treasury bills and obliging the discount houses to buy them instead of commercial bills. For this would result in the discount houses making out cheques in favour of the Bank of England, thereby reducing bankers deposits once again. Would the authorities take such action? They would probably not seek to issue £500m worth of new

Treasury bills, and thereby insist on a possible £10,000m contraction in bank liabilities and deposits, for to do so would mean allowing a modest rise in the demand for cash to have a big effect on the money stock and so on interest rates and the economy. But they might issue some new Treasury bills and seek some contraction. Their enthusiasm for so doing might well depend on why the demand for notes rose in the first place. If it rose for seasonal reasons, as tends to happen before Christmas and during the summer holiday period, then the Bank would probably want the rise to have no impact on the total money stock or interest rates. Accordingly, it is unlikely to be much worried by clearing bank attempts to replenish their money at call; though it might want the total level of money-at-call to fall very slightly so that, in turn, bank deposits had to fall by just enough to offset the rise in publicly-held cash and thereby produce a stable money stock overall. On the other hand, if the demand for notes had risen as a result of a general inflationary rise in prices, then the Bank might well sell a substantial quantity of Treasury bills in order to reduce the money stock and so create a rise in interest rates. In this way it would hope to create some restraint in spending and so ease inflationary pressure in the economy.

This discussion of the note issue emphasizes a point made in Chapter 2, namely that while issued notes represent assets to their holders they represent liabilities to the Bank of England or, more specifically, the Issue Department there. It is worth pointing out that the same characteristics apply to issued coins. There is no difficulty understanding that these represent assets to their holders, but why are they liabilities to the Bank of England? To see this, suppose the clearing banks find that their depositors want an extra £½m in the form of coins and withdraw coins to that value. The banks will find their coin stocks falling and may decide to withdraw £½m from their bankers' deposits at the Bank of England in coin form. Now it might be inferred from Tables 7.1 and 7.2 that the Banking Department has no assets in the form of coins, for its assets of notes and coin are shown as £7m in Table 7.1 while the liabilities' side of Table 7.2 shows that the Banking Department has £7m in notes. Of course both these figures are rounded to the nearest £m and the Banking Department will have some coins. Suppose for simplicity it has £½m which it gives to the banks.

Naturally, the Banking Department will want to replenish its stock of coin. It does so by purchasing more, say £½m worth, from the Royal Mint. The Mint is a government department and sells the coins at face value. Accordingly, a purchase of £½m worth adds £½m to the assets of the Banking Department – in the form of coins – and £½m to its liabilities – in the form of higher public deposits as the Mint's deposit there will have risen by £½m. In this way, any issue of new coins by the Mint always causes a rise in the Bank's liabilities. Notice that when the Bank hands the coins to the clearing banks by the mechanism outlined in the last paragraph, the coins naturally become assets of the clearing banks rather than the Bank, but the liability of the Bank to the Mint, generated when it acquired the coins, remains. In fact, the Bank's liability to the Mint could subsequently fall if the Mint used cheques to purchase metal or labour from depositors at clearing banks, but the Bank's total liabilities would be unaltered since such purchases would, in fact, merely transfer funds from public deposits to bankers' deposits.

This discussion of the Bank of England can be concluded with a few observations about its security holdings. One point to appreciate is that the value of these securities fluctuates over time as their stock exchange prices rise and fall. Any rise or fall in the value of the Banking Department's securities will be matched by an equal rise or fall in its (revaluation) reserve which is included in the item 'reserves and other accounts'; the reasons for this were discussed in relation to Table 1.1. However, the Issue Department's liabilities do not have a 'reserve' item. Its balance sheet is drawn up once a quarter, and if the value of its assets is found to exceed the value of its liabilities then the excess value of assets is given to the Treasury. If the value of its assets falls short of the value of its liabilities, then the Issue Department is, in effect, given extra securities by the Treasury to restore equality.

A related issue arises with the interest (or dividends) accruing from security holdings. When these payments accrue to the Banking Department, then there is a rise in its 'profit and loss a/c' liability (see discussion of Table 1.1) which is included in 'reserves and other accounts'. This will be matched by a fall in bankers' deposits if the interest is paid in respect of non-government securities, since the people paying money to the Bank will typically do so with cheques drawn on their clearing banks; and it will be matched by a fall in public deposits if the interest is paid by the government on government securities. Again, though, the Issue Department has no appropriate liability item to adjust. In fact, it is not paid interest on its government securities, and it at once passes any interest on its other securities to the government. In this way, receipts by the Issue Department of interest on non-government securities actually cause a rise in public sector deposits and a fall in bankers' deposits for the Banking Department but they do not affect the Issue Department's balance sheet at all.

## The discount houses

It was noted in Chapter 3 that there are nine discount houses that are members of the LDMA, that is the London Discount Market Association. It is useful to describe the activities of the LDMA by referring to the balance sheet for all its members taken together. Table 7.3 shows the balance sheet for 29 October 1986. It will be seen that the balance sheet includes both sterling and non-sterling items on both sides, though the value of the non-sterling items is actually given in sterling by converting their values in dollars, marks, yen and so on at the appropriate current exchange rates. Some implications of this feature of the balance sheet will be explored later. For the moment it is enough to notice that total liabilities equal total assets even though total sterling and non-sterling liabilities do not respectively equal total sterling and non-sterling assets.

On the liabilities side, it will be noticed that the discount houses acquire their funds almost wholly in the form of loans. Obviously they seek to lend the money thus acquired as soon as possible, and the ways in which they lend will become clear shortly in the discussion of their assets. Occasionally they borrow from the Bank of England, for instance when the Bank chooses to help them with loans in its capacity as lender of last resort, and the LDMA had some loans from the Bank on the day covered by Table 7.3. However, most loans come from institutions in the UK monetary sector other than the Bank of England. Now the UK monetary sector includes all banks along with accepting houses and discount houses. As far as the LDMA is concerned, though, most of the £6,722m loans from this sector are made to it by banks, and most of these bank loans are made on a money-at-call basis. The LDMA also accept loans from other (non-monetary sector) bodies in the UK as well as some loans from abroad. As it happens, some of these other loans are also made on a money-at-call basis. Indeed, the total value of money-at-call loans on the day shown in Table 7.3 was £8,030m. (This figure is not shown in Table 7.3 but is taken from the source used for that table.)

It will be noticed that some of the loans made to the discount houses are made in foreign currencies. These can come about in two main ways which can be explained by considering, say, US dollar loans. First, the discount houses may have some bank accounts in the US and they may place in these accounts dollars borrowed from other holders of dollars in the US. These could be US holders, in which case the loans would go under the item 'loans from overseas', and they could be non-US foreign holders in which case they would go in the same heading; or they could be UK holders, in which case they would go under loans from the UK monetary or non-monetary sector as appropriate. Secondly, the discount houses may have some dollar accounts at UK banks, that is to say Euro-dollar accounts. Again, they could place in them dollars borrowed from foreign or UK holders of Euro-dollars. Of course, the houses will want to acquire income-earning assets with any foreign currencies they borrow just as rapidly as they want to acquire income-earning assets with any UK currency they borrow.

The final item on the liabilities side is 'other liabilities' and it comprises, principally, 'capital and reserves'. As explained in relation to Table 1.1 in Chapter 1, these terms cover all money put up by shareholders, along with retained profits after allowing for depreciation and also the revaluation reserve. The revaluation reserve rises and falls in line with any rise or fall in the market value of the discount houses' holdings of securities, and it rises in line with any rise in the value of their land and buildings. This item also covers adjustments which may be required as a result of exchange rate changes, a point which will be considered shortly.

Turning to the assets side, the first item covers cash ratio deposits at the Bank of England. All monetary sector institutions are now required to hold some deposits at the Bank of England though the amount is trivial in the case of discount houses; this item will be considered further in the discussion of banks where it is more significant. Over half of the discount houses' assets are in the form of securities. These are split into two groups in the balance sheet. The first group comprises bills, and it can be seen that 'other bills' (essentially commercial bills) predominate there. It should be added, though, that the LDMA's Treasury bill holdings were at an exceptionally low level on the day concerned in Table 7.3; these holdings fluctuate a good deal, typically between £20m and £200m. The second group of securities comes near the bottom of the table and covers all securities other than bills.

The discount houses do not spend all the money they borrow on securities. They use some to make loans, and the balance sheet gives the loans made by them under seven headings. Four of these headings are self-explanatory: these are loans to the UK monetary sector, loans to UK local authorities, other UK loans and loans overseas. The other three headings refer to CDs, that is certificates of deposit, and these must now be explained.

Earlier discussions of banks and other deposit-taking institutions, that is NBFIs, have indicated that some deposits may be withdrawn on demand while notice is needed for withdrawing other deposits, and they have indicated, too, that time deposits attract interest while demand deposits tend not to attract interest. In general, interest rates are highest on the least liquid deposits. Banks and NBFIs offer high rates on such deposits to encourage depositors to place their funds in

**Table 7.3**   Balance sheet for the discount houses on 31 October 1986

£m

Liabilities

| | Sterling | Other currencies | Total |
|---|---|---|---|
| Loans from Bank of England | 142 | — | 142 |
| Other loans from UK monetary sector | 6,722 | 104 | 6,826 |
| Loans from UK non-monetary sector | 1,776 | 114 | 1,890 |
| Loans from overseas | 17 | 87 | 104 |
| Other liabilities | 315 | — | 315 |
| Total | 8,972 | 305 | 9,277 |

£m

Assets

| | Sterling | Other currencies | Total |
|---|---|---|---|
| Cash ratio deposits at Bank of England | 8 | — | 8 |
| UK Treasury bills | 7 | — | 7 |
| UK local authority bills | 5 | — | 5 |
| Other bills | 4,619 | 104 | 4,723 |
| Loans to UK monetary sector | 390 | — | 390 |
| UK monetary sector CDs | 2,581 | — | 2,581 |
| Building society CDs and time deposits | 320 | — | 320 |
| Other CDs | — | 78 | 78 |
| Loans to UK local authorities | 80 | — | 80 |
| Other UK loans | 306 | — | 306 |
| Loans overseas | 55 | — | 55 |
| UK government securities (except Treasury bills) | 26 | — | 26 |
| UK local authority securities (except bills) | 11 | — | 11 |
| Other securities | 487 | — | 487 |
| Other assets | 73 | 127 | 200 |
| Total | 8,968 | 309 | 9,277 |

Source: *Bank of England Quarterly Bulletin*, December 1986, Table 4.

them, for the more these institutions can persuade people to hold their funds in time deposits, the less risk there is of a sudden widespread demand for cash which the institutions would be hard-pressed to meet. Of course, the situation facing depositors is that they can secure high interest rates only if they are prepared to leave their deposits alone for some time.

Now certificates of deposit can best be seen as a relatively new sort of high interest rate time deposit, not mentioned so far, which is attractive to both the deposit-taking institution and the depositor. Essentially, a depositor agrees to place a deposit for a relatively long period, anything perhaps from three months to five years. As evidence of this deposit, he is given a certificate of deposit (CD) rather than a normal bank statement. These CD deposits are very satisfactory to the deposit-taking institution, for the more deposits it has in this form the less need it has for low yielding highly liquid assets. Accordingly, the institutions offer relatively high interest rates on CDs. The rates on some CDs are fixed at the time of issue while the rates on others 'float' in line with other rates. The rates may be individually negotiated, a point which might suggest that operating CD deposits would entail high administrative costs, but these deposits are issued only to selected depositors, usually businesses or other bodies wishing to deposit £50,000 or more, so large sums can be involved with relatively few negotiations. It might be wondered why CDs are attractive to depositors, for they seem to have secured high interest only by tying up their funds for long periods. The answer is that CDs can be bought and sold second-hand. Thus an insurance company, say, might buy a new three-year CD at an attractive interest rate, and then sell it a few weeks later if it needed to spend its funds quickly. One final point to note is that UK monetary institutions were not allowed to issue sterling CDs until 1966, though they were allowed to issue dollar CDs from 1961.

Returning to Table 7.3, it can be seen that the discount houses buy sterling CDs from UK monetary institutions and also from building societies who have started to issue them. In addition, the discount houses buy some CDs in foreign currencies. The final item on the table is 'other assets'. The sterling component chiefly comprises physical assets of land, buildings and equipment. The foreign currency component seems longer but in fact comprises chiefly various loans and securities which – if more details were available – would actually be included in various items higher up the other currencies column in the table.

One possible surprise in the assets may be the lack of any reference to bank deposits other than at the Bank of England. The discussion of liabilities showed that the LDMA acquire funds by loans which are initially placed in clearing bank deposits both at home and overseas. Although they then spend the funds as rapidly as possible, a small amount of funds is retained in bank deposits. These deposits are actually included as loans, chiefly 'loans to UK monetary sector'.

The assets in Table 7.3 are listed in five groups which correspond broadly to their order of liquidity. Bank of England deposits are obviously fully liquid. Bills are highly liquid since the discount houses are able to rediscount (that is sell) them at any time to the Bank of England by special arrangement as explained in Chapter 3. Loans are generally less liquid, though loans include small amounts in highly liquid bank deposits, as explained in the last paragraph. Physical assets, of course, are much less liquid than any of the others.

Looking down the list of assets, it can be seen that the discount houses will acquire pieces of paper such as securities or CDs in respect of practically every item. Of course some assets are loans which do not result in the discount houses being given a security or a CD, but even so there will naturally be some document to prove a loan has been made. Now it might be thought that the houses would hold on to these documents themselves, but in fact they give most, if not all, to the institutions from whom they themselves borrow, thereby using them as a form of security, or collateral, to encourage these institutions to make the loans. In fact, the normal practice is for the value of the collateral to exceed slightly the value of the loan. How can the houses produce pieces of paper with a market value exceeding the total amount they borrow? The answer is that they have pieces of paper covering just about their entire asset value, but they need loans for less than their entire liability value since some liabilities are in the form of capital and reserves. This can be put more simply. They can finance some of the loans they make from their own capital and reserves, so they do not need to borrow the full amount that they lend; thus the value of the loans they lend, for which they have pieces of paper, exceeds the value of the loans they borrow.

The discussion in the last paragraph is useful in showing how the scale of a discount house's activities are limited. Suppose, for simplicity, that a discount house has all its assets in the form of bills and that these have a value of £105m; and suppose it has just two types of liability, namely capital and reserves worth £5m and call-money loans worth £100m. Suppose also that banks lending call-money insist on having collateral in the form of securities and want these securities to have a market value of £105 for each £100 lent. In that case, the discount house considered here would have placed all its £105m bills with the banks to secure its £100m loans. It could not borrow any more money because it has no securities left to give to lenders as collateral. Thus even if there were no officially imposed limits on the discount houses, there would still be an effective limit. In the present example, a discount house's total liabilities, and hence its total assets, would be limited to £105 for every £5 it had in capital and reserves.

In fact, there are two officially imposed limits about the level which discount house assets can have in relation to their capital and reserves. These limits do not relate to the actual levels shown on the balance sheet; instead they relate to adjusted levels of assets, that is to say to actual levels as adjusted according to rules laid down by the authorities. A discount house's adjusted level of assets is higher than its actual level of assets because 'risky' assets – essentially ones with more than a few months to maturity – are included at two, three or five times their present market value, depending on how risky they are deemed to be.

The rules state first that a discount house's adjusted assets must not exceed 40 times its capital and reserves, and secondly that the differences between its adjusted assets and its actual assets must not exceed 15 times its capital and reserves. To see how these rules operate, suppose that a discount house has capital and reserves of £50m. The first rule means that its adjusted assets must not exceed 40 times this amount, that is £2,000m. The second rule means that the gap between its adjusted assets and its actual assets must not exceed 15 times this amount, that is £750m. Suppose it has an adjusted assets level of the maximum £2,000m allowed. Then its actual assets could be as much as £2,000m if all its assets were non-risky ones, but they could be as little as £1,250m if it has as much in risky assets as allowed.

Now that the whole balance sheet has been outlined, it is possible to consider the impact of exchange rate changes. Suppose, for simplicity, that one discount house starts with no assets and no liabilities in 'other currencies'. Since total assets must equal total liabilities, it follows that this house must start with total sterling assets equal to total sterling liabilities. Say both are equal to £1,000m. Next, suppose it now borrows $210m in the US and immediately lends all these dollars to someone in the US. Other currency liabilities and assets will now both equal $210m, and these sums could be recorded under 'loans from overseas' and 'loans overseas'. However, they will be recorded at their sterling value, so if the exchange rate is £1 = $1.50 then the foreign currency entries in the balance sheet will both be £140m (as \$210m = £140m). What would happen if the value of sterling fell, perhaps to £1 = \$1.40? The sterling value of both the dollar entries would *rise* to £150m as the dollars would now be worth more pounds. Thus both liabilities and assets would rise by £10m and there is no difficulty in seeing that the balance sheet would still balance.

The situation would be more interesting if the discount house decided to convert from one currency to another. Return to the starting position and suppose the discount house borrowed the \$210m at the initial exchange rate and then lent \$105m in the US but converted the other \$105m into £70m and lent that in the UK; note that \$105m = £70m at the initial exchange rate of \$1.50 = £1. In this case, other currency loans from overseas would equal \$210m and would be written down on the liabilities side of the balance sheet as £140m as before. On the assets side, though, other currency loans overseas would equal just \$105m, or £70m, so that other currency liabilities would now exceed other currency assets. But the rise of £140m in liabilities would be matched not only by the £70m of loans overseas but also by £70m of, perhaps, 'other UK loans' in sterling.

What would happen now if the exchange rate fell to £1 = \$1.40? The value of other currency liabilities would rise by £10m to £150m as before. The sterling value of other currency assets would rise from £70m to £75m – as the sterling value of the \$105m loans would then rise – but of course the sterling value of the £70m extra 'other UK loans' would be unaffected. It seems, therefore, that total liabilities would rise by £10m while total assets would rise by just £5m. In fact, though, equality would be restored by reducing the value of the revaluation reserve by £5m. This item is included in 'other liabilities', so a fall in them of £5m means that total liabilities would actually rise by £5m rather than £10m. This fall in the revaluation reserve would reflect the unfortunate fact that the value of what the house owes rose by £10m while the value of what it owns rose by just £5m!

This discussion of the discount houses will end by looking at their day-to-day role in the UK monetary system. It will be recalled that the bulk of their liabilities are in the form of call-money from UK clearing banks. This call-money actually plays an important part in the clearing operations between the banks. Consider, first, a day in which the flows of money from clearing bank depositors to and from the government – and other central bank depositors – just balance out so that there is no need for the combined Bank of England balances of the clearing banks to alter. Now it is probable that there will be net flows of funds between individual clearing banks. Thus customers of Barclays Bank may spend £10m more in favour of customers of Lloyds Bank than they receive from customers of Lloyds. The initial effect is that Barclays must give £10m to Lloyds which it will do via the Bank of England where Barclays balance will fall by £10m while Lloyds' balance will rise.

However, Barclays will wish to increase its Bank of England balance again, as this will now be closer to the minimum level permitted, while Lloyds' balance at the Bank will have £10m surplus to its requirements, so it will want as soon as possible to use this money to acquire interest-earning assets. The traditional arrangement is for Barclays to call in £10m call-money from the discount houses and for Lloyds to lend £10m as extra call-money, and this traditional money market exercise takes place each day. The mechanics are that the discount houses will be given an advance by Lloyds which they use to meet the demand for repayment by Barclays, so that there is now a counter-flow of £10m from Lloyds to Barclays. Thus each bank's balance at the Bank of England will return to its original level. However, it will be noted that, in this example, Barclays ended up with £10m less call-money while Lloyds ended up with £10m more. In due course, therefore Barclays will have slightly to contract its operations so that it retains a satisfactory ratio of call-money to total liabilities, while Lloyds can slightly expand, but the present discussion is concerned solely with the immediate moves.

Consider, next, a day on which there are no significant net flows between the clearing banks, but when clearing bank depositors as a whole are paying more to central bank depositors than they receive from them. On such a day it could well be that each clearing bank finds its Bank of England deposit falling, so they will each be calling in some call-money loans from the discount houses. This puts the houses in the position of having to use last resort lending facilities, whereby they will probably sell bills to the Bank of England. This gives the discount houses larger deposits at the Bank, and they can then instruct the Bank to pay money to the clearing banks whose Bank of England deposits will rise while the discount houses' deposits there fall again. Note, though, that the clearing banks will have less call-money, and this is likely to stimulate a contraction in the money stock for the reasons outlined in Chapter 5.

Now the Bank of England may not want a contraction in the money stock, and it may take steps to prevent it in the interests of keeping both the money stock and interest rates stable. For instance, on days when it notices that clearing bank deposits at the Bank are falling, it may ease matters by open-market purchases of securities. These raise the clearing bank deposits of the security sellers, and the clearing banks will match this rise in their liabilities by higher assets in the form of higher Bank of England deposits. Alternatively, the Bank may seek to buy Treasury bills direct from the banks who then find their Bank of England deposits rising in exchange for the bills. Either way, there will be less need for the banks to call in loans from the discount houses.

Finally, consider a day when the clearing banks' customers receive more money from the Bank of England's depositors than they pay to them. The banks will find their Bank of England deposits rising and they may well seek to raise their loans to the discount houses by almost as much as these deposits rise. Typically, the Bank will then offer to sell securities, probably bills, to the discount houses which will result in clearing bank deposits at the Bank falling as the discount houses pay money in their clearing bank deposits to the Bank. Of course, the banks now have more call-money than they started with, as well as slightly higher deposits at the Bank of England, so the money stock is likely to expand unless the Bank takes counter-measures such as open-market sales of securities. However, these expansionary forces will be smaller than they would have been if the Bank had not sold securities to the discount houses, for then the clearing banks would have retained all the initial increase in their deposits at the Bank as well as acquiring more money-at-call. Thus the Bank's tendency to offer securities to the discount houses when the banks are seeking to lend more to the houses can be seen as part of a general Bank policy of promoting monetary stability.

## The retail or primary banks

It has so far been assumed that there is only one sort of bank which, among other things, handles small deposits for private individuals – and so presumably has an

extensive branch network – and which also participates directly in clearing arrangements by means of a Bank of England deposit. In practice, banks take a variety of
forms. This section looks at those banks which the Bank of England terms retail
banks, but which are also often referred to as the primary banks. The key common
feature of these retail banks is that they are willing to handle small deposits. The
following section looks at other banks which are often termed wholesale or secondary
banks.

The best known primary banks in the UK are the 'big four' English banks, which
also dominate the retail banking scene in Wales. These are Barclays Bank, Lloyds
Bank, the Midland Bank and the National Westminster Bank. Along with two other
English banks, Coutts and Williams & Glynn's, the big four are often referred to as
the London Clearing Banks because they are members of the London Bankers'
Clearing House. The members of this institution work out their net debts daily and
arrange for suitable payments between themselves to be made by means of their
Bank of England deposits. Thus these banks conform fully to the image of banks
portrayed in earlier chapters.

Since 1981 another bank has joined the London Bankers' Clearing House and this
is the National Girobank. This was actually set up in 1968 with the chief aim of
attracting as depositors private individuals who did not have accounts at other
banks. It does not have premises of its own but instead operates through Post
Offices. In this way it can be said to have far more branches than any of the 'big
four', but in terms of assets and liabilities it is relatively very small. It may be added
that, compared with other banks, the National Girobank's assets contain proportionately more government securities and fewer advances.

There are further retail banks in England and Wales which have branch networks
but which do not really count as clearing banks since they do not operate their
clearing arrangements directly with Bank of England deposits. Instead, these banks
use accounts which they hold in their own names at the clearing banks. The best-
known banks in this group are the Co-operative Bank, the Yorkshire Bank and the
Trustee Savings Banks (TSB). The TSB were originally saving institutions where
people placed interest-bearing time deposits alone, but since 1965 they have
operated sight deposits and issued cheque books. They were originally very
numerous and worked on a non-profit basis for their depositors or members, but
there is now a single TSB in England and Wales, and dividend-earning shares have
recently been sold to the public.

Clearing arrangements by these further retail banks are very simple. If one such
bank, A, has a deposit at, say, Barclays and another, B, has one at Lloyds, and if A
owes money to B, then A instructs Barclays to transfer money from its account there
to B's account at Lloyds. The effect is the same as any other payment by a Barclays
depositor in favour of a Lloyds depositor, and of course affects the calculations on
which clearing between Barclays and Lloyds themselves will be made. The implications of this type of clearing arrangement are discussed further in the next section in
the context of wholesale banks which act in a similar way.

The London clearing banks are not the only UK retail banks that are also clearing
banks. There are in addition the three Scottish banks, namely the Bank of Scotland,
the Clydesdale Bank and the Royal Bank of Scotland. These do use deposits at the
Bank of England for clearing purposes, but they use these deposits only for clearing
net debts between each other. For all their other clearing purposes they use deposits at
the London clearing banks and so act like the banks described in the last paragraph.

The banks described so far cover most of those which are included as retail banks by the Bank of England, but there are five more. Four of these are the Northern Irish Banks. These are Allied Irish Banks, the Bank of Ireland, the Northern Bank and the Ulster Bank. These do all their clearing by means of accounts with the London clearing banks. The fifth is the Bank of England's own Banking Department which has already been discussed. This has few private individual depositors and few branches, and is really included among the retail banks for convenience. Nevertheless, it is perhaps less unlike the retail banks than it is unlike the wholesale banks!

Although the decision to include the Banking Department among the retail banks is debatable, it has little effect on the figures in Table 7.4 which present a combined balance sheet for all the retail banks on 31 October 1986. For at that time the Banking Department's total liabilities were just about £3,000m (see Table 7.1) which is well under 2 per cent of the total in Table 7.4. Incidentally, Table 7.4 excludes the assets and liabilities of any subsidiaries set up overseas by UK retail banks. Notice that like Table 7.3, Table 7.4 gives figures for sterling and other currency assets and liabilities, the value of the latter being converted into sterling at the appropriate exchange rates. Also, as in Table 7.3, total sterling and non-sterling liabilities do not respectively equal total sterling and non-sterling assets, though total liabilities equal total assets, as is the case with all balance sheets.

On the liabilities side, it will be seen that the first three items cover conventional deposits. These are not broken down here into sight deposits and other deposits, as was done for example in Table 3.6, though it is worth noting that about half of the sterling deposits were sight deposits (this figure is derived from the same source as the table). In principle, it is only sight deposits that banks customers can use for immediate spending. In practice, however, as explained in Chapter 3, banks often allow immediate access to at least some time deposits, though they generally impose a penalty such as deducting the interest which accrued to the withdrawn funds in their last week in the time deposit.

It is worth considering the various ways in which people can spend the money they hold in their bank deposits. Previous chapters have suggested that one depositor, X, who wished to pay from his deposit the sum of, say, £100 to another depositor, Y, could do so in two ways. First, X could withdraw £100 in cash from his bank and give the cash to Y who might then deposit it in his own bank. Secondly, X could give Y a cheque for £100 that Y could take to his bank which would credit his deposit; Y's bank would then send the cheque to X's bank, along with a demand for £100 in clearing operations, and X's bank would in turn reduce X's deposit by £100. However, there are other methods by which people can spend the money held in their bank deposits, most notably the system of credit transfers. In this case, X fills in a credit transfer slip in favour of Y and sends it to his (X's) own bank rather than giving it to Y. X's bank deducts £100 from X's deposit and sends the slip to Y's bank with a note to say that it owes Y's bank £100 in clearing operations. Y's bank then credits Y's deposit with £100. A very similar arrangement operates with bankers' orders whereby X might fill in a form instructing his bank to effect credit transfers regularly to some institution to whom he makes regular payments. Another system is known as 'direct debits' whereby X might fill in a form authorising his bank to make any payments demanded from his deposit by a named person or institution; this can be a very convenient time-saving way for X to pay regular but unequal bills to a body such as a club.

Instead of giving a breakdown of deposits into sight and time deposits, Table 7.4 divides them into UK monetary sector deposits, public and private and overseas deposits, that is deposits belonging to foreigners. The UK monetary sector deposits will include deposits at retail banks by other retail banks – notably by retail banks which do not do their clearing by means of Bank of England deposits – and also deposits by wholesale banks, as explained in the following sections. It will be seen that, unsurprisingly, most UK deposits are in sterling while most overseas deposits are in foreign currencies. In addition to these conventional deposits, the banks have substantial deposits in CD form, as shown in the table.

It may be surprising to some English readers to see the item 'notes issued' appearing on the liabilities side, especially if it is recalled that the table does not cover the Bank of England Issue Department even though it does cover the Banking Department. However, the Scottish and Irish banks are still allowed to issue notes, and their note issues must be included under these liabilities, just as the notes (or IOUs) issued by the bank in Tables 1.4–1.6 were included in its liabilities. It might be thought that the ability of these Scottish and Irish banks to print their own notes means they need not worry about how much they create in the way of deposits by buying securities or giving advances, since no matter how large their deposits then became they could still meet any widespread demand for cash from their depositors. They seem to be in a different position from the bank in Tables 1.4–1.6 which had always to be prepared to give coins in return for its IOUs.

In fact, the Scottish and Irish banks do not derive much advantage from the right to issue notes. An important reason is that they have to own and hold Bank of England notes to 'cover' just about the whole of their own issue of notes. In other words, they cannot issue notes of their own beyond their holdings of Bank of England notes. Thus they are in much the position they would be in if they issued the Bank of England notes to depositors wanting cash rather than issuing their own notes. This arrangement means, of course, that there is a large stock of Bank of England notes belonging to these banks. These are special large denomination notes held, for safe-keeping, at the Bank of England. They appear under assets of notes and coin in the balance sheets of the Scottish and Irish banks.

Even if the Scottish and Irish banks did not have their note issue restricted in this way, their ability to issue notes would still be of limited help. To see this it is helpful to compare a Scottish bank, say the Bank of Scotland, with an English bank, say the Midland Bank, and to suppose that the Scottish bank does all its clearing by means of a Bank of England deposit. Suppose, for simplicity, that the Bank of Scotland and the Midland Bank each have balance sheets showing deposit liabilities of £100m matched by assets of £95m in securities and advances and £5m in cash. The cash will be in the form of deposits at the Bank of England along with stocks of Bank of England notes plus coin. Notice that the Bank of Scotland would not include any stock of unissued Bank of Scotland notes in its balance sheet; the reason for this is explained later.

Now suppose that both these banks consider adding £100m to the level of their advances, thereby also adding £100m to the level of their deposits. It is clear that if the Midland Bank took this action, then it would have a cash ratio of 2.5 per cent; it might regard this as imprudently low and decide against the expansion. The Bank of Scotland would also have a 2.5 per cent cash ratio if it took the action; but if it was allowed to meet any demand for cash simply by printing Bank of Scotland notes, then it might be tempted to undertake the expansion. However, it would still run into trouble if it did, for a large slice of the new deposits, say £80m as a conservative estimate, is likely to be spent by the borrowers in favour of depositors of other banks, and these banks will in turn demand money from the Bank of Scotland. These banks will actually want paying through the normal clearing arrangements, not in Bank of Scotland cash. The Bank of Scotland could not possibly meet such a demand since the deposit it holds for clearing purposes, plus its other recorded cash assets, is only £5m! The upshot of this discussion is that Scottish and Irish banks cannot really expand any more than non-note-issuing banks for which the constraints were explained a little more fully in relation to Table 3.3.

The item 'other liabilities' includes capital and reserves, as was the case for the equivalent item in Table 7.3. Thus this item includes the revaluation reserve which, as with discount houses, will fluctuate to keep total liabilities equal to total assets whenever there are changes in the market value of the banks security holdings and whenever adjustments are needed as a result of exchange rate fluctuations. However, the 'other liabilities' figure in 7.4 is substantially augmented by what are termed 'items in suspense and transmission'. Essentially, these items cover cases of recent payments by depositors where the payers' banks have deducted the appropriate amounts from the payers' deposits but where the payees' banks have not yet added the appropriate amounts to the payees' accounts. Thus these items include sums which should be included among the various groups of deposits but which have not yet been processed and divided into the appropriate groups.

Most of the items on the assets side are fairly self-explanatory in the light of earlier discussion, but some comments are needed on the first two items. The first item is 'notes and coin' and it should be noted that although this relates to cash held by the banks themselves it excludes unissued Scottish and Irish notes in the vaults of the issuing banks. One reason for the omission is that the banks could always run the presses to augment their stock of unused notes; if these extra notes were added to assets then the balance sheet would cease to balance since there would be no corresponding rise in liabilities. Another reason relates to the points made earlier, namely that these banks' own notes have rather limited value as assets.

The second item covers the banks' deposits at the Bank of England. In fact, a bank may have as many as three separate deposits at the Bank of England. First and most important is its cash ratio deposit, on which no interest is paid. At present, all retail banks must have such a deposit equal to 0.5 per cent of what are termed their eligible (sterling) liabilities. To understand how the composition of eligible liabilities is arrived at, it is helpful to recall first that the origin of compulsory cash ratio deposits was, at least in part, to protect the general public from imprudence by bankers, and to recall secondly that the Bank is itself concerned only with the ability of banks to honour their sterling obligations. Thus the Bank is not specially concerned that the banking system should have a prudent level of cash ratio deposits in relationship to total liabilities, but it does want the system to have a prudent level of such deposits in relationship to sterling liabilities to the general public.

Now suppose Bank A lends £100 to a private citizen by raising the value of his deposit. In this case, the banking system has £100 more liabilities to the private sector and no more cash. Next, suppose that Bank A decides instead to lend £100 to Bank B which then lends £100 to the same citizen (the reasons why one bank might lend to another are discussed later). In this case, recorded total bank liabilities will rise by £200. Why is this? The point is that Bank A may decide to place its £100 loan to B in an interest-bearing account at Bank B. Bank B will ask the Bank of

**Table 7.4**   Balance sheet for the retail banks on 31 October 1986

£m

Liabilities

| | Sterling | Other currencies | Total |
|---|---|---|---|
| UK monetary sector deposits | 10,756 | 7,026 | 17,782 |
| UK public sector deposits | 2,894 | } 6,007 | 105,143 |
| UK private sector deposits | 96,242 | | |
| Overseas deposits | 12,009 | 31,585 | 43,594 |
| Certificates of deposit | 7,593 | 6,801 | 14,394 |
| Notes issued | 1,026 | — | 1,026 |
| Other liabilities | 35,317[1] | 0[2] | 35,317 |
| Total[3] | 165,837[4] | 51,419[5] | 217,257 |

£m

Assets

| | Sterling | Other currencies | Total |
|---|---|---|---|
| Notes and coin | 2,091 | — | 2,091 |
| Balances with Bank of England | 704 | — | 704 |
| Secured money with LDMA | 4,241 | — | 4,241 |
| Other loans to UK monetary sector | 19,505 | 12,611 | 32,116 |
| UK monetary sector CDs | 3,766 | 342 | 4,108 |
| Market loans to UK local authorities[6] | 1,460 | — | 1,460 |
| Market loans overseas | 2,846 | 0[7] | 2,846[8] |
| Treasury bills | 84 | — | 84 |
| Local authority bills | 192 | — | 192 |
| Other bills | 3,601 | 644 | 4,245 |
| Other UK government securities | 6,929 | — | 6,929 |
| Other securities | 3,431 | 6,364 | 9,795 |
| Advances to UK public sector | 347 | 174 | 521 |
| Advances to UK private sector | 84,250 | 5,004 | 89,254 |
| Advances overseas | 4,246 | 36,574[9] | 40,820[9] |
| Other assets | 17,853[1] | 0[2] | 17,853 |
| Total[3] | 155,545[4] | 61,713[5] | 217,257 |

Source: *Bank of England Quarterly Bulletin*, December 1986, Table 3.2.

[1]Includes some items in 'other currencies' – amount unspecified in source.
[2]Actual figure not zero but amount is unspecified in source; *see* note 1.
[3]Totals subject to rounding errors.
[4]Figure overstates total; *see* note 1.
[5]Figure understates total; *see* note 2.
[6]Includes only money lent indirectly via other monetary sector institutions.
[7]Actual figure not zero but amount is included in 'advances overseas'.
[8]Excludes foreign currency market loans overseas; *see* note 7.
[9]Includes market loans overseas; *see* note 7.

England to transfer £100 from A's deposit there to B's, and the initial effect on A's balance sheet is to leave its total assets and liabilities unaltered but to reduce its Bank of England deposit by £100 while raising its 'other loans to UK monetary sector' by £100. Bank B will find its liabilities rising by £100 in the form of Bank A's deposit, and its assets rising by £100 in the form of its Bank of England deposit. If B now lends £100 to the private citizen, then Bank B's assets will rise again, this time in the form of 'advances to UK private sector' and its liabilities will rise again, this time in the form of the citizen's deposit. Now although total liabilities will rise by £200 in this case, total liabilities to the public will rise by only £100 and the Bank of England will be no more concerned than it would be if Bank A had made the loan directly as in the first case.

It follows that the Bank of England is not concerned when total bank lending rises as a result of one bank lending to another. Accordingly, when deciding on how much cash the system as a whole should place at the Bank of England, the Bank is concerned only with their total liabilities less the value of inter-bank lending. If it thinks that cash ratio deposits should equal 0.5 per cent of this total, then it could secure the amount needed by asking each bank either for that fraction of its total liabilities less the amount it has borrowed from other banks, or for that fraction of its total liabilities less the amount it has lent to other banks. It uses the latter approach since this favours banks who lend to others at the expense of those who borrow from others, a reasonable approach since it is the latter, like Bank B in the example above, who ultimately create the liability to the public.

In practice, the calculation of eligible liabilities is rather more complex than suggested here. For instance, banks are allowed to deduct the value of any liabilities which had an initial maturity of over two years – these liabilities will be chiefly in the form of CDs – and there are further minor adjustments. The upshot on the day of the balance sheet in Table 7.3 was that the retail banks held eligible liabilities of £98,489m (this figure is not shown in the table but is taken from the same source). This implies a need for cash ratio deposits of some £492m. However, a final complexity is that the Bank works out the required deposits only twice a year, in May and November, and requires from each bank 0.5 per cent of its average level of eligible liabilities in the previous six months.

It seems clear, though, that the actual £704m level of the retail banks' Bank of England balances exceeded their cash ratio deposit requirements. In principle the extra amounts held in these balances might have been accounted for by so-called special deposits which were discussed in Chapter 5. These can be demanded from time to time and have the contractionary monetary effect of raising the banks' effective mandatory cash ratio. As noted earlier, they attract interest at about the current rate on Treasury bills. However, there have been no calls for special deposits since July 1980 so there were none on the day covered by Table 7.4 The modest excess of bank deposits at the Bank of England above the cash ratio deposit requirement was therefore all attributable to so-called operational deposits on which no interest is paid. These operational deposits comprise, essentially, deposits that are maintained by those banks which use Bank of England deposits for clearing purposes. However, this is not the only reason why these banks like to have some operational Bank of England deposits; they can also withdraw some of these deposits in cash form whenever they need more cash themselves.

Few comments are needed on the remaining assets most of which are generally self-explanatory. Details of 'secured money with the LDMA' were given in Chapter

3. 'Other loans to UK monetary sector' include deposits with other banks as well as more conventional loans. 'Market loans overseas' chiefly comprises loans to foreign banks. 'Other assets' includes the value of the banks' land, buildings and equipment.

However, some comment is perhaps needed for the item 'UK monetary sector CDs'. It is clear that these represent deposits in the form of CDs, but why do the banks simultaneously issue sterling CDs to the tune of £7,593m and then buy sterling CDs worth £3,766m? After all, consider what would happen if they decided to pay less interest on the CDs they issue. They might end up attracting fewer CD deposits, say £3,766m less. This means that they would pay much less in interest since they would have fewer CDs to service and would be paying less interest on those that remained. At the same time they could sell off all the £3,766m worth of CDs they own. The loss in income resulting from holding no CDs should be just about offset by the fact that they would themselves be paying interest on fewer CDs. It seems, then that cutting interest rates on CDs should raise profitability since the interest payments on the remaining CDs issued should fall and administration costs should fall also.

However, there are a number of reasons why no bank would cut the rate offered on its CDs in pursuit of this sort of strategy. One reason is that the banks are in competition for funds, so any one bank which cut its CD rates would soon find that it lost all its CD customers, and this would seriously reduce the funds available to it. Another reason is that the simultaneous issuing and holding of CDs by a bank actually has two advantages.

First, the average maturity on the CDs issued could be longer than the average maturity on the CDs held. This is particularly likely if banks tend to buy and hold CDs nearing maturity. There is much to be said from a bank's point of view in arranging for its issued CDs to have an average maturity of, say, two and a half years while holding CDs with an average of, say, one year, for this eases one of the big problems for banks which is that most deposits can be withdrawn very quickly while most assets are not very liquid.

Secondly, CDs can be used as a way of transferring funds from banks which have surplus Bank of England deposits to those which are short. In the last section an example was taken where, on a given day, Barclays customers spent £10m more in favour of Lloyds customers than they received from them. Barclays' Bank of England deposit fell £10m while Lloyds' rose £10m. Barclays then resorted to calling in call-money to replenish its deposit while Lloyds used its surplus funds to lend more call-money. This method of transferring funds is termed using the traditional money market. However, an alternative would be for Lloyds to use its £10m to buy second-hand CDs from Barclays. The presence of such an alternative is termed using a parallel money market and eases the pressure on the traditional money market.

CDs are not the only mechanism available for a parallel money market. The most likely alternative would be for Lloyds to deposit £10m in an interest-bearing account at Barclays. This procedure is known as using the inter-bank market. The development of a parallel money market was stimulated in the 1960s and 1970s by a growth in banking activity, especially of secondary banks which are the subject of the next section. The traditional money market, involving the discount houses, is no longer the main mechanism for facilitating transfers between banks, but it is still of crucial importance in handling the situations which arise when there is a net flow of funds between the Bank of England and the other banks.

It is appropriate to conclude this discussion of bank assets with a comment on the biggest item which is advances. Advances come in two main forms known as loans and overdrafts. Consider a student who finds she has £20 left in her deposit on 25 November and wants to borrow £100 from her bank for one month when she anticipates a generous Christmas cheque from her parents. She could ask her bank for a 'personal loan' of £100. If they agreed, they would at once add £100 to her deposit. The banks' liabilities would at once rise by £100 in the form of deposits while its assets would rise by £100 under the heading of advances. Of course, both liabilities and assets would subsequently fall each time the student withdrew cash or made out cheques in favour of depositors at other banks. It will be recognized that the procedure outlined here is identical to that outlined in relation to Tables 1.8 and 1.9. However, this procedure has the disadvantage for the student that she will have to pay interest on the whole £100 for the full month even though she probably does not need to spend £100 right away.

To ease this problem she could ask for an 'overdraft facility' of £100. If the bank agreed, then it would actually add money to her deposit – up to a maximum of £100 – only when her payments meant that her deposit would otherwise be less than zero. For instance, if her first payment after 25 November was a cheque for £25 presented on 28 November, then the first addition to her deposit would be £5 that day taking her deposit momentarily to £25. Of course, her deposit would then fall by £25 as soon as the cheque was processed! Thereafter, additions would be made in values equal to any subsequent cash withdrawal or cheque payments. The advantage for the student is that she is liable for no interest until 28 November, and she may not be liable for the interest on as much as, say, £90 until 23 December; indeed she may never actually borrow the full £100.

The descriptions in the last two paragraphs show that in balance sheet terms both loans and overdrafts result in the assets and liabilities of the student's bank rising, though these would fall again whenever she withdrew cash or made out cheques in favour of depositors at other banks. There is, though, one possible source of confusion in the case of overdrafts. The successive additions to the student's deposits from 28 November onwards were offset by deductions resulting from the student's subsequent payments. Consequently, her deposit had a constant value of zero. This value would be the one included in the bank's balance sheet which shows the total value of all deposits held there. However, if the student asked for a statement during this period, then it would not show a zero number. Instead it would show a negative number which really indicates how much she has borrowed by the date of the statement. Thus a statement late on 28 November would show a balance for the student of – £5. This procedure makes it clear at a glance to overdrawn depositors how much they have borrowed, but it also means that their statements no longer show the true value of their deposits in the bank's own records which, in the circumstances, are always zero.

# The wholesale or secondary banks

The key common feature of all the retail or primary banks discussed in the last section – with the exception of the Banking Department of the Bank of England which is included with the others for convenience only – is their willingness to handle the small deposits of private individuals. The key common feature of all the wholesale or secondary banks considered in the present section is their unwillingness to handle small deposits. Generally they accept customers only if their deposits reach some stipulated minimum such as £50,000 or £100,000. Thus they confine their depositors almost entirely to businesses and other institutions.

A further characteristic of the wholesale banks is that all of them maintain deposits at the clearing banks, rather than at the Bank of England, to handle their own clearing requirements. It is worth considering the implications of this arrangement before looking at the wholesale banks in more detail. The most interesting issue which this arrangement raises is whether the monetary authorities are likely to lose control of the money stock.

To see the issue more clearly, suppose that there are initially six banks in a country, one being the central bank and the other five being clearing banks, that is to say banks which maintain deposits at the central bank for clearing purposes. Also, suppose for simplicity that negligible use is made of cash so that banks keep negligible amounts of notes and coin. Finally, suppose the clearing banks voluntarily keep their central bank deposits at 5 per cent of their total liabilities, for clearing purposes, and suppose their deposits at the central bank have an initial value of 50; in these circumstances, given this prudent ratio of 5 per cent, the banks will keep their liabilities to a maximum of 1,000 (all figures can be taken as £m).

Suppose, next, that a set of new banks is established in competition with the existing clearing banks which will now be termed the old banks. The new banks might succeed in persuading a lot of old bank depositors to transfer their deposits from the old banks to the new ones. They could do this by offering some (or more) interest on deposits, the main method used by UK wholesale banks, but they could also set up more convenient branches for some depositors or, perhaps, set out to woo customers with friendlier staff. Suppose they succeed in securing half the initial deposits of 1,000. Now the new banks could, in principle, open deposits at the central bank and demand that the old banks transfer 500 into these deposits, but this would be impossible as the old banks' deposits at the central bank have a total of only 50!

Instead, the new banks could open up accounts for themselves at the old banks and ask the old banks to place 500 in these accounts. In this case there would be no significant effects to begin with on the old banks. Their deposit levels would stay at 1,000, though 500 of these would now belong to the new banks and the other 500 to the loyal depositors who stayed with them. As for the new banks, they would have assets of 500 in the form of deposits at the old banks matched by liabilities in the form of their customers' deposits. It is tempting to suppose the money stock has risen by 500 since total bank deposits have risen by this amount, for there used to be 1,000 deposits at the old banks while now there are 1,000 at the old ones plus 500 at the new ones. However, it was explained in Chapter 3 that money stock measures exclude deposits held by one bank at another – although the only bank there with deposits belonging to other banks was the central bank – so the measured money stock would not rise here as the only bank deposits to include are the 500 at the new banks and the 500 non-bank deposits at the old banks.

Now the crucial point to grasp is that the new banks can begin to expand by creating deposits and so can start raising the money stock. How can they do this? Suppose they were approached by customers who between them wanted to borrow 100. The new banks could raise their liabilities by giving these people deposits of

100 merely by writing larger numbers in these depositors' accounts. The new bank balance sheets would match this rise of 100 in liabilities by including a new asset of 100 in the form of loans. The process has thus increased the deposits of the new banks by 100 and it has raised the money stock by 100. This stock now includes deposits of 600 at the new banks and the 500 non-bank deposits at the old banks.

The money stock will not fall again no matter how these new bank loans are spent provided they are not withdrawn in cash, for that would result in the new banks demanding cash from the old banks who would then react to lower cash holdings by a multiple contraction in their liabilities. If the loans are spent in favour of other new bank depositors, then total new bank deposits stay at 600 and so the money stock is clearly unaffected. If the loans are spent in favour of old bank depositors, then new bank deposits would fall to 500 but non-bank deposits at the old banks would show an offsetting rise to 600. Incidentally, in this latter case the old banks would reduce the deposits with them of the new banks by 100, so new bank assets would fall by this amount to match the fall in their deposits.

Now some loans are bound to be spent in favour of old bank depositors, so new bank deposits at old banks are sure to fall a little from 500. But the new banks can carry on expanding until these deposits are very small since the new banks use such deposits only for their clearing needs. Thus the introduction of the new generation of banks could lead to a substantial rise in the money stock. This need not be the end of the story. More new banks could be set up with clearing deposits at the old banks. Conceivably, still more could be set up with clearing deposits at the new banks, and so on!

It follows that the authorities are likely to seek to control all banks in some way no matter whether or not they have deposits at the central bank which they use for clearing purposes. In the UK, one simple method of limitation in the requirement that all banks must have a cash ratio deposit at the Bank of England equal to 0.5 per cent of total eligible sterling liabilities, even if they have no further deposits there to use for clearing purposes.

The example outlined above can be used to show how such a rule is effective. Suppose, for simplicity, that the old banks had been required to keep deposits at the central bank equal to 5 per cent (not the UK's 0.5 per cent) of their liabilities and kept negligible extra deposits for clearing purposes. What might happen when the new banks were established? The authorities could require all banks to keep deposits at the central bank equal to 5 per cent of eligible liabilities where these might be defined – not so very differently from the UK – as equal to a bank's total liabilities minus any assets it has in the form of deposits at other banks; but suppose for convenience that assets in the form of deposits at the central bank are not deducted in the calculation. In this case, the establishment of the new banks with half the depositors from the old banks could leave the new banks with zero eligible liabilities, for against their total liabilities of 500 can be deducted assets of 500 held in deposits at old banks. The old banks would have had total liabilities of 1,000 and all these would be eligible because these banks have no deposits at other banks to be deducted from the 1,000; remember their central bank deposits of 50 are not deducted. Thus the old banks would have to retain their deposits of 50 at the central bank.

Of course, the mere establishment of the new banks did not raise the money stock. What would happen now if the new banks made loans of 100 and thus raised their deposits? The initial effect would be that their liabilities would rise by 100 while their balances at other banks would stay the same. Thus their eligible liabilities would now equal 100 so they would have to deposit 5 at the central bank. They would open accounts at the central bank and instruct the old banks to transfer 5 into these accounts from the deposits the new banks hold at the old banks. The old banks would lose deposits of 5, as the new bank deposits with them fell, and they would lose assets of 5 as the central bank reduced old bank deposits there in favour of the new banks. The old banks are left with liabilities of 995 and central bank deposits of 45. They are thus below the 5 per cent rule and must contract their liabilities, by selling securities or reducing their total advances, until these liabilities are 900. This reduction reduces the money stock by 100. The result then, is that any expansion by the new banks must be offset by contraction by the old ones. The money stock is again under control and will stay constant, even though the competition created by the new banks may lead them to expand at the expense of the old ones.

It is worth adding two points to this analysis. First, since the additional tier of banks has not altered the money stock, so it will not really effect attempts to control that stock using the methods outlined in Chapters 4 and 5. Secondly, banks in the UK that do not have clearing balances at the Bank of England are subject to an additional control beyond the need for a cash ratio deposit. Like all deposit-taking institutions they have to be licensed by the Bank of England. Their continued holding of a licence depends on assuring the Bank that they have adequate stocks of liquid assets. Thus all hold an acceptable percentage of assets in the form of money-at-call to the LDMA. In other words, their expansion, like that of other banks, can occur only when they can increase the size of their call-money. However, it is not easy for banks as a group to increase their call-money since, as an earlier section has shown, the total value of LDMA assets is limited; accordingly, the total value of the LDMA liabilities is limited so there is some limit to the amount they can borrow as call-money.

Having discussed the implications of banks which operate like the UK wholesale or secondary banks, it is now appropriate to look briefly at these banks. Table 7.5 presents a combined balance sheet which can be compared with Table 7.4 to see that the total liabilities and assets of the wholesale banks greatly exceed those of the retail banks, but the wholesale banks have proportionately far more assets and liabilities in foreign currencies than do the retail banks.

This interest in foreign currencies is not surprising once the main groups into which wholesale or secondary banks are usually split are mentioned. These are the 'accepting houses', which are UK banks, and 'other British banks', along with 'American banks', 'Japanese banks' and 'other overseas banks', which are all foreign, and 'consortium banks' which are owned by consortiums comprising some UK and some foreign concerns. The relative sizes of these six groups are shown by Table 7.6. It can be seen that the combined liabilities of the first two all-UK groups are relatively small and account for about 15 per cent only of the total for secondary banks as a whole.

Accepting houses were first mentioned in Chapter 2 in connection with their activities of accepting bills. However, they also operate as banks and are often known by the alternative title of merchant banks. This title reflects the fact that they originated as merchants who saw that the accepting of bills could be a profitable business. Entry into banking was a fairly obvious development. 'Other British banks' is a group comprising all other UK banks that operate as wholesale banks. Most are actually wholesale subsidiaries of the big retail banks. The American, Japanese and 'other

**Table 7.5** Balance sheet for the wholesale banks on 31 October 1986

£m

Liabilities

| | Sterling | Other currencies | Total |
|---|---|---|---|
| UK monetary sector deposits | 47,375 | 92,152 | 139,527 |
| UK public sector deposits | '2,000 | } 21,201 | 57,761 |
| UK private sector deposits | 34,560 | | |
| Overseas deposits | 25,865 | 350,692 | 376,557 |
| Certificates of deposit | 12,402 | 72,302 | 84,704 |
| Notes issued | — | — | — |
| Other liabilities | 5,533[1] | 24,067[2] | 29,600 |
| Total | 127,735[1] | 560,414[2] | 688,149 |

£m

Assets

| | Sterling | Other currencies | Total |
|---|---|---|---|
| Notes and coin | 27 | — | 27 |
| Balances with Bank of England | 352 | — | 352 |
| Secured money with LDMA | 2,483 | — | 2,483 |
| Other loans to UK monetary sector | 35,923 | 82,903 | 118,826 |
| UK monetary sector CDs | 4,853 | 12,341 | 17,194 |
| Market loans to UK local authorities[3] | 1,134 | — | 1,134 |
| Market loans overseas | 12,055 | 0[4] | 12,055[5] |
| Treasury bills | 57 | — | 57 |
| Local authority bills | 8 | — | 8 |
| Other bills | 842 | 2,384 | 3,226 |
| Other UK government securities | 2,174 | — | 2,174 |
| Other securities | 8,183 | 36,705 | 44,888 |
| Advances to UK public sector | 995 | 1,437 | 2,432 |
| Advances to UK private sector | 55,049 | 38,104 | 93,153 |
| Advances overseas | 8,686 | 366,075[6] | 374,761[6] |
| Other assets | 4,717[7] | 10,661[8] | 15,378 |
| Total[9] | 137,538[7] | 550,610[8] | 688,149 |

Source: *Bank of England Quarterly Bulletin*, December 1986, derived from Tables 3.1 and 3.2.

[1] This figure is too small by the amount of 'other liabilities' in other currencies of retail banks.
[2] This figure is too big by the amount of 'other liabilities' in other currencies of retail banks.
[3] Includes only money lent indirectly via other monetary sector institutions.
[4] Actual figure not zero, but amount included in 'advances overseas'.
[5] Excludes foreign currency market loans overseas; *see* note 4.
[6] Includes market loans overseas; *see* note 4.
[7] This figure is too small by the amount of 'other assets' in other currencies of retail banks.
[8] This figure is too big by the amount of 'other assets' in other currencies of retail banks.
[9] Totals subject to rounding errors.

**Table 7.6**   Total liabilities (and assets) of wholesale bank groups, 31 October 1986

| Total liabilities (and assets) | £m |
|---|---|
| Group | |
| Accepting houses | 34,283 |
| Other British banks | 74,500 |
| American banks | 106,439 |
| Japanese banks | 232,245 |
| Other overseas banks | 222,469 |
| Consortium banks | 18,212 |
| Total[1] | 688,149 |

Source: *Bank of England Quarterly Bulletin*, December 1986, Tables 3.3 to 3.8.
[1]Total subject to rounding error.

overseas banks' are essentially subsidiaries of foreign banks set up by their parent companies to undertake banking in the UK. As Table 7.6 shows, most wholesale deposits are held in foreign currencies by overseas citizens. Why would foreigners want to keep foreign currencies in deposits in the UK? They might be foreign-owned multinationals doing business in the UK, or they might simply find interest rates on deposits in the UK tempting.

The overall balance sheet given in Table 7.5 for the wholesale banks is in many ways very similar to the one given for the retail banks in Table 7.4. However, there are some important differences between the two groups of banks. One of the most significant differences – which incidentally does not show up on the tables – is that a much smaller proportion of wholesale bank sterling deposits are sight deposits; the proportion is around 10 per cent compared with 50 per cent for the retail banks (these figures are derived from the same source as the tables). The main objective of wholesale banks is to secure CD deposits and other more conventional time-deposits, perhaps requiring three months or more notice of withdrawal in return for their higher rates of interest. This means they are less concerned than retail banks about a sudden mass loss of deposits, and that in turn means they can indulge with some safety in more long-term loans than the retail banks. Another difference is that wholesale bank advances are generally loans made for fixed terms rather than overdrafts which may be taken out, increased and reduced according to the borrowers' wishes. Also, their loans are generally negotiated at fixed interest rates while the rates on retail bank advances generally fluctuate in line with other interest rates.

Of course, if the terms on wholesale bank loans are typically longer than the terms on their deposits, then the banks run the risk that when deposits mature their holders will wish to withdraw them rather than renew them, and the banks will be unable to honour their obligations to their depositors unless by good fortune a new round of deposits is made. This problem becomes more serious the less well matched the terms of deposits and loans are. The banks must weigh the advantage of a poor match – which is likely to be a tempting difference in interest rates – against the disadvantage of possible embarrassment. There are times, though, when the banks may actually be very keen to lengthen the terms of their loans and shorten the terms of their deposits. This could happen if they expect interest rates to fall. In such circumstances, they will want to keep deposits as short-term as possible, in the hope of renewing them before long at lower interest rates, and they will want to make as many long-term loans as they can while interest rates are still high. The wholesale banks need also to think about balancing their assets and liabilities in different currencies. If, for example, they have far more dollar assets than liabilities and the value of the dollar falls, then the banks stand to make substantial losses.

Another feature of the balance sheet shown in Table 7.5 is that wholesale banks, taken as a group, have very substantial deposits from the UK monetary sector, which effectively represent loans to them by UK banks, and also substantial assets with the UK monetary sector, which include substantial deposits at UK banks. This apparent anomaly is largely explained by the fact that at any point in time, such as the day concerned in Table 7.5, some wholesale banks were busy borrowing from other banks, while others were lending to them. Thus wholesale bank X might be persuading retail bank A to open a deposit at X, that is in effect to lend to X, while wholesale bank Y might be persuading retail bank B to accept a deposit from Y on reasonable terms.

Why might X and Y be acting like this? It might be supposed the most likely explanation is that X's few depositors with sight deposits have been net spenders while Y's have been net recipients. However, net changes in sight deposits at wholesale banks are typically very small and can usually be handled by the very small deposits held for the purpose at the clearing banks. The most likely reason for X's behaviour is that someone has asked A for a loan while A has insufficient funds in its own balances at the retail banks to use; rather than turn a borrower away, X is trying to borrow the funds needed to enable it to make the loan. As for Y, it might have suddenly been offered a large deposit at a time when it has no prospective borrower; rather than turn funds away, it places them in its balance at a retail bank at the most favourable interest it can secure. Of course, loans can also be made between two wholesale banks as well as between a wholesale bank and a retail bank.

It will be seen that X and Y are dealing with shortages and surpluses by means of inter-bank sterling deposits, in much the same way that retail banks with shortages and surpluses and are able to reduce or expand their holdings of call-money. While the use of call-money is called the traditional money market, the use of inter-bank deposits is an example of so-called parallel money market. It was seen earlier that the retail banks could themselves use a parallel market, that is avoid using the traditional money market, by selling or buying CDs, and the same option is also open to wholesale banks. It may be noted that parallel markets exist in other items, notably inter-bank Euro-currency deposits and Euro-currency CDs. In principle, the banks could actually also buy and sell conventional securities on the stock exchange, but this is unattractive, partly because the securities traded there are generally some way from maturity – or may never mature – and thus tend to fluctuate quite widely in value (as explained in Chapter 2), and partly on account of the lags between the transaction and the subsequent settlement or transfer of money. Parallel money markets deal in items where settlement occurs on the same day as the transfer.

There are two final points to note about wholesale bank balance sheets. First, their deposits at the Bank of England seldom exceed the 0.5 per cent cash ratio deposits they need. On the day concerned in Table 7.5, these banks' eligible liabilities were £78,258m (though this is not shown on the table) and their Bank of

England deposits were actually a mere 0.45 per cent of this amount, that is £352m (as shown in the table); this low level is possible because, as with the retail banks, the cash ratio deposits required are set twice a year on the basis of average eligible liabilities over the past six months. Secondly, the wholesale banks have negligible assets of notes and coin. They manage with little in the way of notes and coin because their depositors seldom want to withdraw cash. This is partly because these banks' concentration on large wholesale deposits means that deposits with them are usually spent by cheque; and it is partly because their deposits are largely in foreign currencies which depositors would find fairly useless in the UK if they did demand cash withdrawals!

# Non-bank financial intermediaries

This short final section looks at NBFIs. These were considered in some detail in Chapter 3. It will be recalled that, like banks, they are financial intermediaries in that they seek to make profits by borrowing funds and then lending them at higher rates of interest. Unlike banks, their liabilities are not generally acceptable as a medium of exchange and so do not count as money.

It was explained in Chapter 3 that NBFIs could be divided into two groups, those whose liabilities chiefly take the form of deposits and those whose liabilities do not. The first group of NBFIs contains building societies – which were discussed in Chapter 3 – finance houses and the National Savings Bank. Finance houses use funds raised through deposits to provide hire-purchase loans to consumers and businesses who wish to borrow funds to buy consumer durables or capital equipment. The National Savings Bank operates through Post Offices. Despite its name, it is not a conventional bank at all. It was established with the aid of providing a widely trusted and accessible place for people who want to place money in interest-earning deposits, and it uses money placed in deposits with it to lend to the government, principally by buying government securities. The second group of NBFIs comprises life insurance companies and pension funds along with investment trusts and unit trusts, all of which have been mentioned in earlier chapters.

Another point mentioned in Chapter 3 is that the creation or extension of a system of NBFIs does not automatically alter the money stock. However, that does not mean that the creation or extension is of no concern to the monetary authorities. It was shown in Chapter 4 that if NBFIs were established which took deposits that seemed reasonable substitutes for bank deposits, then the demand for bank deposits could fall. Such a fall would lead to a reduction in interest rates, and – unless the $M_s$ curve was vertical – it would also bring about a small fall in the money stock itself.

This view of the impact of the creation of NBFIs can be looked at in another way. Some of the funds they attract or lend to borrowers will come from people who – in the absence of NBFIs – would have lent their funds directly to borrowers. This is perhaps most clear in the case of the non-deposit taking NBFIs. For instance, most people who buy unit trusts would probably have done something more interesting with their money than leave it in a bank deposit if these particular NBFIs did not exist. On this basis, non-deposit-taking NBFIs can be seen as a convenient mechanism for transferring funds from lenders to borrowers, but they may have little effect on the amounts borrowed or lent and hence seem unlikely to have much effect on interest rates or the economy at all.

In contrast, deposit-taking NBFIs may well attract funds from people who would otherwise keep their money in bank deposits, probably bank time deposits. These NBFIs can then lend money which would otherwise not have been lent, and by increasing the amount of funds available for lending they are likely to put downward pressure on interest rates. In the context of monetary control, therefore, it is deposit-taking NBFIs which are the really significant ones, and they are dominated by the building societies. These societies' activities are regulated by the authorities, but they are becoming more and more like the activities of the banks. Perhaps, one day, the building societies will come to be regarded as banks.

It is perhaps worth concluding this chapter by reassuring the reader that the analysis of monetary control and interest rate determination given in Chapters 4 and 5 would need little adaptation even if some (or all) deposit-taking NBFIs became regarded as banks and their liabilities became regarded as money. Suppose that before the NBFIs were recognized as banks, the $M_d$ and $M_s$ schedules intersected to determine an equilibrium interest rate of 10 per cent and an equilibrium money stock of £1,000m. Suppose the NBFIs had deposits of £500m. A change in definitions to include those deposits in the money stock would clearly have no effect on interest rates, though it would raise the measured value of money stock. In fact, there would be new $M_s$ and $M_d$ curves which would intersect at the original 10 per cent interest rate, but at a new money stock of £1,500m. The $M_s$ curve would shift to the right to include the £500m supplied by the NBFIs while the $M_d$ curve would shift to the right by £500m to include the NBFI deposits that people want to hold. (Of course, it must be added that if the building societies were regarded as banks, then it would be because they had been allowed to act more like banks, and in that case they might be able to expand their liabilities beyond £500m. As a result, the new money stock would exceed £1,500m and interest rates would be subject to downward pressure.)

# 8

# Monetary control in practice

Chapters 4 and 5 described the basic principles of monetary control in a closed economy while Chapter 6 indicated the main qualifications which need to be made in an open economy. This final chapter seeks to give a brief outline of the developments and changes in monetary control in the UK during the present century.

The first section looks at monetary policy until the 1960s and the second section looks at policy in the 1970s. The final section – the sixth – looks at more recent developments. In order to understand these developments, it is necessary to refer to a whole range of monetary targets; these are considered in the third and fourth sections. It is also necessary to relate changes in the money stock to the government's borrowing needs, or, more precisely, to the public sector borrowing requirement (PSBR). These relationships are explained in the fifth section.

## Monetary policy from the 1900s to the 1960s

The key to understanding UK monetary policy at the beginning of the twentieth century and, indeed, throughout most of the nineteenth century, is to recall that the UK was a champion of the gold standard. Accordingly, monetary policy was really dominated by the desire to maintain a fixed value for sterling. The implications of the gold standard will be recalled from Chapter 6. If the UK experienced a balance of payments deficit, then the Bank of England's holdings of gold would fall. Also, the money stock would fall and, consequently, interest rates would rise. The rise in interest rates should have led to a fall in spending so leading in turn to downward pressure on prices. A fall in prices would make home commodities more competitive so, hopefully, leading in time to a fall in imports and a rise in exports. This would ease, and in time perhaps remove, the balance of payments deficit. A further and more rapid effect of the rise in interest rates would be a flow of foreign capital into the UK and this, too, would ease the deficit.

Now it is clear that the adjustment processes stemmed from the rise in interest rates brought about as a direct consequence of the deficit and the induced fall in the money stock. It is also clear that a deficit was a serious situation since, if it persisted, there could be a substantial drop in the country's gold reserves. Thus the authorities would seek to remove the deficit as quickly as possible. They could help matters by seeking to accentuate the rise in interest rates, and they could do this by reducing the money stock even more rapidly than it would have fallen in the absence of official intervention. The main method of reducing the money stock and so raising interest rates was to raise the rate at which last resort lending facilities were made available, this rate being known as the Bank Rate. This method was often reinforced by open-market sales of securities.

Of course, a major objection to the whole gold standard strategy was that any tendency for a country to have a balance of payments deficit necessitated a longish period of high interest rates and reduced spending, thus also reducing employment levels. This objection became much more serious in the UK in the 1925–31 period when the UK returned to the gold standard with the pound being given the same gold price that it had had before the war. The trouble was that this value for the pound was unrealistically high in 1925–31, so that UK industry was very uncompetitive. The reason the pre-war value was too high was that UK prices had risen greatly in the war, no doubt as a result of the increases in demand caused by the high levels of government spending needed to fight the war.

To see the problem with an over-valued pound, suppose that before the war £1 had the same value in gold as $4.87. A UK commodity with a price of £100 would cost US citizens $487. Now if UK prices rose by, say, 50 per cent between 1914 and 1925, then that commodity would have a price of £150 in 1925. Since the UK and US then fixed the gold prices of their currencies in 1925 such that £1 once more had the same value as $4.87, US citizens then had to pay $730.50 for the item which had previously cost them $487. Not surprisingly, exports fell. Also, imports rose as US goods were now relatively cheap. It will be appreciated that the return to the gold standard with sterling at its pre-war level caused balance of payments problems for which the standard remedy was to promote increased interest rates causing a decline in spending. One effect of this remedy was that it created higher unemployment, and unemployment in the UK was always above one million in the late 1920s.

The problems came to a head in 1931 when unemployment had reached two million and, at the same time, there was a balance of payments deficit leading to a substantial outflow of gold from the UK. It was felt unacceptable to raise interest rates, so the UK left the gold standard. No longer was the Bank of England obliged to sell gold in return for sterling. At the same time, the value of sterling fell substantially in relation to other currencies. In 1932 the Exchange Equalization Account was established. This was entrusted with the country's reserves of gold and foreign currencies which it used, as described in Chapter 6, to keep the value of sterling at the level currently desired by the authorities. Until the 1970s, at least, concern focused on sterling's rate against the US dollar.

The fall in the value of sterling in 1931 at once improved the balance of payments situation. This permitted a fall in Bank Rate. This rate had been 4 per cent or more throughout the 1925–31 period but was reduced to 2 per cent in 1932. Of course, this easing of Bank Rate paved the way for monetary expansion and lower interest rates generally. One initial fear was that monetary expansion would cause inflation, perhaps very rapid inflation as had occurred in Germany in the 1920s, but this did not happen. The chief reason was that the UK monetary expansion was relatively modest at a time of high unemployment whereas the German expansion had been very rapid at a time of low unemployment.

As it happens, Bank Rate stayed at 2 per cent from 1932 to 1951, except for a short period at the start of the Second World War. The analysis of Chapters 4 and 5 might seem to imply that a stable Bank Rate – that is a stable rate at which last resort lending will be made available – will lead to a stable money stock and stable interest rates, but this is so only if there are no factors causing shifts in the $M_d$ and $M_s$ curves discussed in those chapters. In fact, rising incomes and modest price rises caused $M_d$ to shift to the right, but the authorities took steps to shift $M_s$ also to the right in pursuit of a policy of 'cheap money' or low interest rates. Their success in maintaining low short-term rates is indicated by the rate on Treasury bills, which fluctuated from about 0.5 to 1.0 per cent in the 1932–51 period, while their success with long-term rates is indicated by the yield on consols, which fluctuated between about 2.5 and 4.0 per cent. Of course there would have been problems in securing low interest rates if the balance of payments had moved into much of a deficit – or at least there would have been problems in these circumstances given that the authorities wanted to keep sterling at its new post-1931 value. Fortunately, the balance of payments situation remained sound.

The arguments in favour of low interest rates changed during the period. In the 1932–39 period, the main argument stemmed from the high level of unemployment, for it was hoped that low interest rates would stimulate investment which would lead to an expanding economy with more jobs. This argument became less important as time passed though, because unemployment fell quite rapidly. In the 1939–45 war period, one advantage of a low interest rate policy was that it reduced the cost of the substantial borrowing which the government had to do, and another was that it ensured that firms whose activities were crucial to the war effort could afford to borrow the sums they needed. However, maintaining low interest rates necessitated increasing the money stock, and the danger of a rising money stock aggravating inflation was met, with only partial success, by imposing controls such as rationing on non-essential spending.

Finally, in the 1945–51 period, the arguments for low interest rates were to promote post-war reconstruction and to try to prevent large-scale unemployment recurring in the wake of demobilization. The main problem with pursuing the policy in the post-war period was that by stimulating investment it increased the general level of demand and added to inflationary pressures. There was already substantial inflationary pressure because there was a large pent-up demand for consumer goods while industry was structured towards military goods. The main counter-inflation forces used were the maintenance of some rationing controls and an attempt by the government to run a surplus of taxation over spending – with a view to paying off some of its massive debts – but these forces were not sufficient. Indeed, despite the further measure of a wage freeze and a devaluation against the dollar in 1949, rising prices ensured that the balance of payments remained in an unsatisfactory condition. There was no option by 1951 but to end the cheap money period.

1951 marks a turning point because Bank Rate rose above 2 per cent for the first time since 1932 – aside from a short period in 1939 – and it reached 4 per cent in 1952. A 2 per cent rise may seem modest, but it did reflect a doubling of Bank Rate. It also reflected the fact that interest rate control of the money stock was being used once again. It should be noted, though, that the prevailing view in the 1950s seems to have been that while interest rates had a pronounced effect on the balance of payments, they had little effect on spending levels; at least they were thought unlikely to have any effect for some time and then only if they were sustained. It followed from this view that changes in the money stock and interest rates were not thought likely to have much effect on the overall level of demand in the economy, and so attempts to alter output levels generally relied on fiscal policy rather than monetary policy.

This view of monetary policy was largely endorsed by the 1959 report of a committee chaired by Lord Radcliffe. However, the Radcliffe report did not suggest a total abandonment of monetary measures to control spending levels. Rather, it promoted the view that what was needed was control over what was termed liquidity rather than control over the money stock. Liquidity was taken to include holdings of liquid assets such as securities and also the liabilities of the NBFIs as well as those of the banks. It was explained in Chapter 4 that an expansion of NBFI activity could help to negate any interest rate effects of money stock falls, so the report was doubtless correct to focus some attention on them. In practice, control over the liquidity available to spenders was largely confined to direct controls over bank lending, but there were also controls over the hire purchase loans for the purchase of cars and consumer durables that were offered by finance houses (one of the NBFIs mentioned in the last chapter) and also over issues of new securities by companies.

This trend for credit limitations continued in the 1960s, largely – perhaps wholly – in order to contain demand and so to prevent prices rising enough to lead to balance of payments problems, for the government was committed to maintaining a fixed value for sterling. To give just one example of credit limitations all banks were asked in March 1965 to restrict their increases in lending to 5 per cent over the next 12 months. An interesting development in the 1960s was the imposition of credit limitations on finance houses as well as on banks. This extension was made partly to help reduce the funds available to borrowers, and partly because of a growing recognition that it was unfair to restrict lending by banks more than lending by NBFIs who, of course, are rivals in the intermediation field. Another development in the 1960s was the use of special deposits to help control the money stock by the means outlined in Chapter 5. The concept of such deposits had been introduced in 1958, but the first call was made in 1960, and some special deposits were required throughout the 1960s except for a period of two and a half years between 1962 and 1965.

The UK economy seemed in the 1960s to be suffering from two problems. One was low growth, and to rectify this the monetary authorities wanted to keep interest rates fairly stable at low levels. The other was the balance of payments which tended either to be in deficit or in danger of moving into a deficit. It was explained in Chapter 6 that under a system of fixed exchange rates such as the UK then had, the authorities have little choice but to keep the money stock at whatever level is necessary to keep interest rates at whatever level is necessary to keep the exchange rate at the target level. It could be argued that the authorities were tempted to keep the money stock too high and interest rates too low, and that this led to the persistent deficits that resulted in the 1967 devaluation. It could also be argued that the target exchange rate of £1 = \$2.80 was itself too high.

The 1967 devaluation was slow to produce results, and to prevent a further devaluation the UK borrowed large sums of foreign exchange from the International Monetary Fund (IMF) in the late 1960s. These loans were accompanied by a major new factor in monetary policy, the setting of monetary targets. The IMF naturally wanted to ensure that its loans would be repaid, so it wanted to be sure that the UK balance of payments would improve. In turn, it wanted to ensure that the UK would not suffer undue price rises which would make it less competitive. Accordingly, the IMF sought assurances that money stock growth would be kept under control. Thus in late 1967 the UK assured the IMF that the money stock growth rate in 1968 would be kept to the 1967 rate. However, it became clear to the IMF that a money stock target was unsatisfactory. This was because the recorded growth in the money stock might be low in a period when there was really an expansionary monetary policy if, at the same time, there was a balance of payments deficit! Accordingly, the next assurances to the IMF, made in 1969, had to refer to a target for domestic credit expansion (DCE). As explained in Chapter 6, increases in DCE broadly equal increases in the money stock plus the balance of payments deficit.

## Monetary policy in the 1970s

The 1970s saw two major developments. First, from 1972 onwards sterling was allowed to float. This at once meant, as explained in Chapter 6, that the authorities had in principle more freedom to pursue the monetary policy of their choice. Secondly, from late 1971, radical changes were made to the system of monetary control. These were presaged in a Bank of England paper called *Competition and Credit Control* (CCC) that was published earlier in 1971. Much of the thrust for the new measures stemmed from a desire to promote competition between the clearing banks and other financial intermediaries. It was felt the previous reliance on credit ceilings had been unfair to the clearing banks on whom the ceilings had chiefly been imposed. The balance was to be improved by ceasing to use ceilings as a measure of control – except as a very last resort – and also by imposing reserve ratios on the larger finance houses and also on all wholesale banks. Instead of credit ceilings, control was to be exercised principally by open-market operations and calls for special deposits. CCC also sought to promote competition between individual clearing banks. There had been little competition beforehand, partly at least because there was little point in competing for deposits when levels of advances were individually controlled. Again, the abandoning of ceilings was to be a key feature in promoting competition.

In keeping with the CCC spirit of stimulating market forces, the authorities became reluctant to use interest rate control with an imposed Bank Rate. Instead, they wanted interest rates to be determined by market forces. As part of this philosophy, Bank Rate was abolished in 1972 after a life of 270 years. Of course, the Bank of England still stood ready to offer assistance to the discount houses, and the rate at which it was always prepared to do so was henceforth known as the Minimum Lending Rate (MLR). However, instead of being laid down by the Bank of England, as Bank Rate had been, MLR had an air of being determined by market forces since it was set each week at 0.5 per cent (rounded to the nearest 1/16 per cent) above the discount rate on newly-issued Treasury bills.

Despite this formula for MLR, the authorities still had control of it really, for the rate on newly-issued bills depended on the bids for them made by the discount houses. If the Bank wanted low bids and a high MLR, then it could secure this either by demanding special deposits from the banks or by a big open-market sale of secur-' ities, for such activities resulted in the clearing banks demanding repayment of money-at-call from the discount houses, and a reduction in funds for them resulted in lower bids for bills!

This description suggests that MLR could be varied, but that it would be varied only as part of a package of monetary control measures, so it seemed that interest rate control was no longer to be the dominant control method. In practice, though, interest-rate control did act as the main method, albeit supported by the others. Indeed, the formula approach for MLR was effectively abandoned in 1978 whereupon it became virtually the same as Bank Rate. To ensure that the discount houses, and in turn the banks, responded to changes in MLR, the Bank of England regularly took action which resulted in the banks having a slight cash shortage which was made good by repayments of call-money from the discount houses who then had to borrow at MLR. In this way, the system was made particularly sensitive to changes in MLR.

The problem with the CCC measures was really that the money stock began to rise rapidly. For instance, it rose by 60 per cent in the two years from December 1971. Many explanations have been offered. One argument is that the removal of credit ceilings meant that the banks were now more able to compete with NBFIs, so some of the increase was no doubt attributable to bank lending rising while NBFI lending fell; to the extent that this was so, there was little cause for alarm. Another possibility is that the removal of credit ceilings simply enabled the banks to expand to meet a previously frustrated demand for loans. Also, stimulating competition between the banks was perhaps likely to encourage aggressive expansion. In addition, there was perhaps inadequate control over the total borrowing and lending levels of the discount houses which meant there was inadequate control over the level of advances that they could be given in the form of call-money, thus reducing one restraint on the total lending levels of the banks (for the CCC rules meant bank liabilities could usually be raised if call-money assets rose). Further, there was perhaps a suspicion that the authorities were fearful of the increases in interest rates that would occur if they sought vigorously to restrain the growth in the money stock, for higher interest rates would reduce spending yet unemployment was at a post-war high; and it may be noted that inflation was rising so that nominal interest rates were already very high despite the monetary growth. Again, the floating of sterling naturally meant there was far less constraint on monetary growth as a result of balance of payments considerations. Another factor, considered further in later sections, was that a huge increase in the PSBR added to the difficulty of controlling the money stock.

Eventually, though, the authorities did respond to this money stock growth, and money stock expansion was restrained in 1974–76, though it became rather more rapid later in the 1970s. Two devices were used to increase control over the money stock. The first of these has already been mentioned. It was the decision in 1978 to stop using a formula for MLR. This enabled MLR to be raised as far above current market rates as the authorities wished.

The second – and perhaps more important of these devices – was the scheme of supplementary special deposits – known as the 'corset'. This was used on a number of occasions between 1973 and 1980. When in operation, the scheme sought to limit the rate at which the banks could increase their interest-bearing eligible deposits, that is to say their interest-bearing deposits held by non-bank depositors. Banks which exceeded the target rate of growth in these deposits were obliged to deposit extra cash at the Bank of England in the form of 'supplementary' special deposits. These supplementary special deposits had the same restraining effect on bank lending that normal special deposits had. However, the effectiveness of the scheme can be doubted. For instance, the banks might reduce the interest rate on deposits, hoping some depositors would merely switch from interest-bearing ones to non-interest bearing ones. At the same time, deposits on NBFIs would seem relatively more attractive, so their activities might rise to offset any fall in the activities of the banks.

By the end of the 1970s, the key economic problem facing the authorities was that of inflation. A major part of their counter-inflation policy was the decision from 1976 to announce targets for monetary growth. The reason for this, and the various targets available, are considered in the next two sections. At the same time, growing importance was attached to the need to control the PSBR in order to reduce monetary growth. The relationship between the PSBR and the money stock is explored in a subsequent section. The final section considers the most recent developments in monetary control.

## The case for monetary targets

The last section has shown how monetary policy over much of the century has been concerned with securing satisfactory interest rates. Broadly speaking, a satisfactory level of interest rates has been taken as one which was as low as possible, in order to promote economic growth, consistent with avoiding balance of payments crises. Now concern with the balance of payments diminished substantially after sterling was floated in 1972, and in the late 1970s and 1980s governments became less pre-occupied with promoting growth than with restraining inflation.

It can be seen, then, that the traditional reasons for concern over interest rates have declined. Nevertheless, it might still seem odd that attention focused more on the money stock than on interest rates. After all, both the Keynesian and monetarist models mentioned in Chapter 4 suggest that insofar as changes in the money stock do affect the economy, they do so principally by altering interest rates. So if, for example, the authorities are seeking to establish a particular level of total demand in order to achieve some particular rate of employment or inflationary pressure, then it might be assumed that they would set out to achieve whatever level of interest rates was necessary to secure the chosen level of demand. Of course, that in turn might require achieving some particular money stock. But why would the authorities announce their target in money stock terms rather than in interest rate terms?

Most answers to this question refer in one way or another to inflation, but it is useful to begin with one answer that makes no particular reference to inflation. To set the scene, suppose that the authorities find that the interest rate levels produced by the present money stock have led to satisfactory levels of demand and output, and suppose the authorities would like output to remain at its present level. Next, suppose that one component of the demand for output – investment perhaps – is rather volatile, so that even at constant interest rates its level tends to fluctuate, perhaps moving in line with fluctuating expectations by businesses.

What would happen to output if investment fluctuated and the monetary authorities persisted in keeping the money stock constant? A rise in investment would lead to more spending, higher output and increased incomes and so would raise the demand for money; with a constant money stock, interest rates would rise and this would cause some offsetting fall in total expenditure. What would happen to output if investment fluctuated and the authorities instead decided to keep interest rates constant? A rise in investment would raise the demand for money, as before, but now the money stock would be raised to keep interest rates constant so that now there would be no offsetting fall in expenditure. It can be seen the rise in investment would cause output to rise more if the authorities adhered to an interest rate target than if they adhered to a money stock target. Conversely, output would fall more when investment fell if the authorities adjusted the money stock to prevent interest rates falling, for they would thus prevent any offsetting rise in investment that the falling rates might have created. It seems that sticking to money stock targets will promote more stability in output than sticking to interest rate targets.

However, this is not quite the end of the story. Suppose that the demand for output was stable but that the demand for money was not, so that one component of the demand for money – the speculative motive, say – tended to fluctuate even at constant interest rates, perhaps moving in line with fluctuating expectations about future levels of security prices. What would happen to output if money demand fluctuated and the authorities persisted in keeping the money stock constant? A rise in the demand for money would then lead to higher interest rates and hence to a lower demand for output, so reducing óutput itself. What would happen to output if money demand fluctuated and the authorities instead decided to keep interest rates constant? A rise in money demand would be followed by a rise in the money stock so keeping interest rates, the demand for output and output itself constant. It follows that adhering to an interest rate target is more appropriate in this case.

The upshot of all this analysis is, broadly speaking, that interest rate targets are more appropriate than money stock targets if money demand is more volatile than output demand. In general, the feeling in the 1950s and 1960s was that money demand was very volatile, so it seemed best to focus attention on stable interest rates. In the late 1960s, though, Friedman and others argued that money demand was much more stable than previously thought, and although later research suggests that the money demand in the UK is not especially stable, it is sufficiently stable for the authorities to place more emphasis on money stock targets than used to be the case.

Turning to inflation-related arguments for monetary targets, it is useful to begin by noting an identity which lay at the heart of the quantity theory of money that was espoused in pre-Keynes days. This is that $MV = PT$. Each side of this equation shows the total monetary value of transactions in a period of time. The left hand side shows the money stock, $M$, and the average number of times that each unit of money changes hands in the period, that is the velocity of circulation, $V$. The right hand side shows the number of transactions, $T$, and their average price, $P$. What happens if $M$ rises? Clearly $V$ must fall and/or $PT$ must rise. The quantity theorists assumed $V$ to be constant and so believed that $PT$ would change in proportion to the change in $M$, though they gave little explanation of the transmission mechanism by which changes in $M$ caused $PT$ to alter. Actually, they also thought that economies tended to settle down at roughly full employment levels so that the number of transactions, $T$, was fairly constant. Accordingly, they thought that the chief result of a change in $M$ would be to cause a roughly proportional change in $P$.

This theory was challenged by Keynes in the 1930s. Developing the analysis captured in the diagrams of Chapter 4, he argued that a rise in $M$ – or, more precisely, a rise in the money stock caused by a rightward shift in the $M_s$ curve – would cause interest rates to fall. He conceded that this should cause some rise in investment and so some rise in demand, thereby raising $P$ and/or $T$, but he thought investment was unlikely to rise much. He also argued that the demand for money was interest-elastic; in other words, he thought the fall in interest rates would cause more money to be held in 'idle' speculative balances that might not be spent for a considerable time. Thus $V$ was likely to fall. Accordingly, he argued that the rise in $M$ would actually lead more to a fall in $V$ than to a rise in $PT$. He also suggested that if, as was often the case, unemployment was less than full, then any effect there was on $PT$ might be felt more on T than on P. These views held sway in the 1950s and 1960s. The Radcliffe Committee, for instance, believed V to be very unstable. In general, it was thought that increases in M would probably not affect P much, so there was little fear of their effects on inflation. On the other hand, there did seem to be something to be said for increases in M to help keep interest rates low; low rates might not encourage investment much, but in an era when output was rising slowly, any encouragement was to be welcomed.

Keynes's views were in turn challenged in the 1960s and 1970s by the monetarists, championed by Friedman. Friedman argued that the demand for money tended to be interest-inelastic, so that a rise in M led to little or no increase in idle balances and so did not lead to much fall in V. On the contrary, the inelastic demand for money meant that a rise in M led to large falls in interest rates which he argued had a substantial effect on the demand for output. Thus the effects of changes in M would be felt chiefly in PT. Moreover, he has argued that, in the long run anyway, economies tend to settle at a particular level of employment – a level of 'natural' unemployment rather than full employment – so that the effect would be concentrated on P. Naturally there has been much empirical research to see how far the world actually corresponds to Friedman's picture. The results have been mixed, but there has been more than enough support to justify government concern over changes in the money stock in periods of inflation. Notice that this concern leads to monetary targets being expressed as aims to secure a particular rate of growth in some measure of the money stock, not as an aim to secure a particular fixed level for that measure.

Inflation has provided two more reasons for focusing on monetary targets. First, it is arguable that what matters in interest rate terms for spending decisions is the *real* rate of interest, or rather the *expected* real rate of interest. Suppose that a firm is considering borrowing £1m for three years and is offered a loan at a *nominal* interest rate of 10 per cent. The firm will obviously be more tempted if it thinks prices will rise at, say, 9 per cent over the next three years, than if it thinks they will rise at 2 per cent, for the real burden of interest charges and subsequent repayment will be much lower in the former case than in the latter. The trouble for the authorities is that they can manipulate the money stock to secure a particular level of nominal interest rates, for these rates can be observed. But they cannot observe people's expectations, so they never know what the expected real interest rate is! In other words, the relevant interest rates are ones which cannot be measured and so cannot be set as targets. It must be conceded, though, that monetary targets, too, are not totally free from this sort of problem. The effects on output of a decision to hold monetary growth over the next year to, say, 5 per cent might be much more drastic if inflation was 25 per cent at the beginning of the year than if it was zero.

Secondly, and very important in practice, is the role of inflationary expectations on pricing policies and wage demands. Businessmen setting their prices and trades unions formulating their wage demands are naturally much influenced by the extent to which they think the general level of prices will rise in coming months. If it is widely thought that there is something in the monetarists' view that inflation is greatly influenced by changes in the money stock, then an announcement by the government that it is going to permit only a very limited growth in the money stock might well reduce the amount of inflation expected. This, in turn, could reduce the extent to which businessmen and unions now feel it appropriate to raise prices or wages.

# Monetary and liquidity aggregates

It is one thing to decide that it is appropriate to set a target rate of growth for monetary expansion. It is another to decide which particular measure of monetary expansion should be used. In the interests of simplicity, earlier chapters have talked about 'the' money stock as though there is only one possible measure. In fact, there are seven different published statistics. These are described in this section. The decisions about which of these measures have been used as targets in recent years are discussed in the final section of the chapter.

The composition of the seven published measures is indicated by Table 8.1 which

**Table 8.1**  Monetary and liquidity aggregates on 17 September 1986

£m
000

| Aggregate: | M0 | M1 | M2 | £M3 | M3 | PSL1 | PSL2 |
|---|---|---|---|---|---|---|---|
| Notes and coin: | | | | | | | |
| in circulation with public | 13.0 | 13.0 | 13.0 | 13.0 | 13.0 | 13.0 | 13.0 |
| held by banks | 1.6 | — | — | — | — | — | — |
| Banks' operational deposits at the Bank of England | 0.2 | — | — | — | — | — | — |
| UK private sector sterling deposits at banks: | | | | | | | |
| non-interest-bearing sight deposits | — | 24.8 | 24.8 | 24.8 | 24.8 | 24.8 | 24.8 |
| interest-bearing sight deposits | — | 31.1 | | 31.1 | 31.1 | 31.1 | 31.1 |
| interest-bearing time deposits under 2 years original maturity | — | — | 40.8[1] | 70.8 | 70.8 | 70.8 | 70.8 |
| interest-bearing time deposits over 2 years original maturity | — | — | — | 2.2 | 2.2 | — | 2.2 |
| UK private sector deposits in other currencies | — | — | — | — | 24.9 | — | — |
| UK private sector retail deposits at building societies | — | — | 80.8 | — | — | — | 80.8 |
| National Savings Bank ordinary accounts | — | — | 1.7 | — | — | — | 1.7 |
| Other deposits and shares with savings institutions | — | — | — | — | — | — | 34.5 |
| Money market instruments held by private sector[3] | — | — | — | — | — | 2.7 | 2.7 |
| Certificates of tax deposit | — | — | — | — | — | 3.5 | 3.5 |
| Total[2] | 14.8 | 68.9 | 161.2 | 141.9 | 166.8 | 145.9 | 265.1 |

Source: *Bank of England Quarterly Bulletin*, December 1986, Tables 11.1 and 12.
Notes: [1]Includes retail deposits only
[2]Some figures in the source differ slightly
[3]Net of liquid assets held by building societies

shows figures for 17 September 1986. Before discussing the seven aggregates, two general points need to be made. First, it should be emphasized that the components of these measures are changed slightly from time to time. Secondly, the figures for deposits in Table 8.1 do not correspond to those in the tables of Chapter 7, for those earlier tables omitted figures for some very small banks which are covered here.

The measure which comes closest to the concept of the money stock used in previous chapters is 'sterling M3' or £M3. As Table 8.1 shows, this essentially comprises all sterling bank deposits held by UK citizens plus cash held by the public. £M3 omits bank deposits held by banks, as do all the other measures. This point can be confirmed by seeing that although the table includes private sector deposits, it does not refer to any monetary sector deposits. The only difference between £M3 and the money stock concept used in earlier chapters is that £M3, again like the other measures, omits public sector deposits. This particular omission has been made only since March 1984 and is not important since public sector deposits are a very small proportion of the total as Tables 7.4 and 7.5 showed. Another measure, which should not be confused with £M3, is the one termed M3. M3 is rather larger than £M3 as it adds to £M3 all UK private sector deposits denominated in foreign currencies. M3 is actually the only measure to include foreign currency deposits.

M1 is a much narrower measure than £M3 since M1 includes sight deposits alone, thus omitting time deposits. The table shows that £24.8bn worth of sight deposits carried no interest while £31.1bn carried some. The argument for a money measure that omits time deposits is that, in principle at least, these deposits cannot be used immediately and so are not available as a medium of exchange. Indeed, it was explained in Chapter 3 that time deposits can be viewed as near-money rather than money. It can be seen that by focusing on deposits which can be used immediately, at least without some penalty, M1 really concentrates on deposits held for transactions purpose. However, it is arguable that M1 is not a wholly satisfactory measure of transactions balances. On the one hand, it includes wholesale sight deposits which are generally thought to be seen by their holders more as investments, albeit short-term ones, than as transactions balances. On the other hand, M1 excludes retail deposits at building societies and the National Savings Bank, and also interest-bearing retail deposits at banks, yet all of these are generally thought to be seen by their holders as funds available for transactions, despite the fact that they may not always be instantly available for spending, at least without some penalty. M2 is an alternative measure of transactions balances which avoids these alleged shortcomings of M1, for it excludes wholesale sight deposits and includes retail deposits at building societies and the National Savings Bank along with interest-bearing retail deposits at banks.

M0 is even narrower than M1 and measures what is called the monetary base. It is best thought of as a measure of the cash that is – in principle – available to the public. Thus it includes cash in circulation with the public plus cash held by banks. It also includes banks' operational deposits at the Bank of England, that is deposits held there voluntarily in excess of their compulsory cash ratio deposits. Unlike the cash ratio deposits, which cannot be withdrawn because the banks are compelled to hold them, operational deposits can be withdrawn and the banks can ask for cash if they withdraw them. Indeed, this is the way in which they replenish their own cash holdings when needed. Note, however, that although M0 measures the amount of cash the public could obtain in principle, in practice they could demand and obtain more from the banks. The banks could get hold of more cash by demanding that some money-at-call be repaid by the discount houses, and the discount houses could raise funds by selling bills to the Bank of England in its capacity as lender of last resort. The Bank would credit funds to the houses' deposits there and these funds would be transferred to the banks' operational deposits when the call-money was repaid. The banks would then withdraw some of these larger operational deposits in cash.

As noted earlier, £M3 – like M3 – includes all private sector sterling bank deposits. This approach to the money stock has been supported in earlier chapters on the grounds that, in practice, banks ordinarily allow people to 'spend' time deposits without notice just as they allow them to spend sight deposits; and if both types of deposit can be spent without notice, then they can both be regarded equally as a medium of exchange. However, earlier chapters have not considered whether deposits in the form of CDs should count as money. A holder of a CD who wants to spend the money represented by this CD before maturity must sell it first, so a CD might be regarded more like a security than a deposit. However, a CD differs from a security in that on maturity it will be converted into a bank deposit and no other depositor's deposit will fall when its holder's deposit rises; but when a security such as a debenture matures, then the rise in its holder's deposit will be at the expense of its issuer's deposit. In this sense, CDs can be seen as representing money rather than securities. For this reason, £M3 – and indeed M3 – includes sterling CDs which are covered in the table under interest-bearing time deposits. M3 also includes foreign currency CDs which are covered by private sector deposits in other currencies.

Now it is clear that although a deposit in the form of a CD is a shade less spendable than other sorts of deposit, it still represents a very liquid asset to its holder. However, there are other very liquid assets, albeit not in the form of money, that are not covered by £M3. The purpose of PSL1 and PSL2 is to include these other very liquid assets and so give some estimates of the total liquidity of the private sector, the letters PSL standing for private sector liquidity. Inevitably, the decision about precisely what assets should be regarded as liquid enough to warrant inclusion is a little arbitrary.

PSL1 adds in to £M3 'money market instruments held by the private sector', which chiefly comprises holdings of bills and very short term loans to local authorities, and it also adds in certificates of tax deposit. These certificates bear interest and can be bought by companies from tax offices in anticipation of a tax demand; they are liquid because they can be surrendered in order to release funds for other purposes, although there is then an interest penalty. Against these additions, PSL1 deducts from £M3 the small value of time deposits with an original maturity value of over 2 years; these deposits will, of course, be in CD form.

PSL2 adds back in these time deposits with an original maturity value over two years, and it also adds in the retail deposits at building societies and the National Savings Bank ordinary accounts that were included in M2. In addition, PSL2 includes all other deposits at building societies as well as deposits at savings institutions, principally investment accounts at the National Savings Bank and premium bonds issued by it. Notice that PSL2 nets out the building societies' liquid assets of cash, bank deposits and CDs. This means that PSL2 treats the societies like banks for PSL2 does not include cash, bank deposits or CDs that are held by the banks.

---

Note:  the Bank of England intends to rename some of its measures in late 1987. £M3 is to be renamed M3, the present M3 is to be renamed M3c (the c to show that it includes holdings of foreign currency deposits) and PSL2 is to be renamed M5. PSL1 will no longer be published. There will be a new measure, M4, which adds to £M3 all building society deposits (i.e. the 80.8 retail deposits at the societies plus that part of the 34.5 accounted for by wholesale deposits with them) but nets out the societies' liquid assets. M4 can be thought of as showing what 'the' money stock concept of earlier chapters would cover if building societies were regarded as banks and their deposits as money.

# The money stock and the PSBR

This section seeks to relate changes in the money stock to the public sector borrowing requirement. It is essentially concerned with proving that the PSBR and £M3 are related as shown in Table 8.5 which comes at the end of the section. Readers who do not wish to see the proof can proceed directly to that table and then on to the next section. To follow the proof, it is first necessary to do some manipulations with balance sheets.

It will be recalled that Tables 7.2–7.5 in Chapter 7 showed the items that occur in the balance sheet of the Bank of England's Banking Department, the discount houses and the banks. The total liabilities equal the total assets for each individual concern covered by those tables. It follows that if a monetary sector balance sheet were drawn up showing the liabilities and assets of all these concerns added together, then the total liabilities and assets would once again have to be equal. Such a monetary sector balance sheet would have all the items shown in Table 8.2, though no numbers are shown on this table. For the purposes of Table 8.2 – and other tables in this section – deposits are taken to include items in suspense and transmission and also CDs.

This balance sheet can be simplified in four ways to produce the version shown in Table 8.3. First, the items marked with an asterisk in Table 8.2 can be deleted. This

**Table 8.2**  Balance sheet items for discount houses and banks

| Liabilities | Assets |
| --- | --- |
| * Loans from UK monetary sector | Notes and coin |
| Loans from UK non-monetary sector | |
| Loans from overseas | * Balances at Bank of England |
| | * Secured money with LDMA |
| * UK monetary sector deposits[1] | * Other loans to UK monetary sector |
| UK private sector deposits[1] | * UK monetary sector CDs |
| UK public sector deposits[1] | |
| Overseas deposits[1] | Loans to UK local authorities |
| Notes issued | Treasury bills |
| Other liabilities | Local authority bills |
| | Advances to UK public sector |
| | Other UK government securities |
| | |
| | Advances to UK private sector |
| | Other bills |
| | Other securities |
| | |
| | Market loans overseas |
| | Advances overseas |
| | |
| | Other assets |
| Total | Total |

Notes: [1]Include CDs
*The total value of the liabilities marked with an asterisk equals to the total value of assets marked with an asterisk

**Table 8.3** Monetary sector liabilities and assets – version I

| Liabilities | Assets |
|---|---|
| UK private sector deposits[1] | Notes and coin[3] |
| UK public sector deposits[1] | Loans to UK local authorities |
| Overseas deposits[1] | Treasury bills |
| Net non-deposit liabilities[2] | Local authority bills |
| | Advances to UK public sector[4] |
| | Other UK government securities |
| | |
| | Advances to UK private sector[4] |
| | Other bills |
| | Other securities |
| | |
| | Market loans overseas |
| | Advances overseas[4] |
| Total | Total |

Notes: [1] Include CDs
[2] Equals 'non-deposit liabilities' *minus* 'other assets'
[3] Equals 'notes and coin' held as assets *minus* 'notes issued' as liabilities
[4] Net of any loans to the discount houses

would make both the total liabilities and the total assets smaller, but total liabilities would still equal total assets. Why is this? It is because the starred items cover financial claims which actually occur on *both* sides of Table 8.2 because each of them is a claim that is a liability for one member of the monetary sector and an asset for another member. For instance, the liabilities entry 'UK monetary sector deposits' includes the 'banks' balances at Bank of England'; these are liabilities to the Bank of England and assets to the banks which hold them. Again, 'loans from UK monetary sector' includes 'secured money with LDMA' – that is secured loans to the LDMA from banks; these are liabilities to the discount houses and assets to the banks. In short, removing the starred items simply reflects the removal of items which are internal to the UK monetary sector.

Secondly, 'notes issued' can be deleted. These are issued by the Scottish and Irish banks who, as explained in Chapter 7, must 'cover' their issues with holdings of Bank of England notes. Deleting this item from the liabilities side naturally reduces total liabilities. Total assets can be made to balance by deducting the value of the Scottish and Irish notes issued from the true asset value of notes and coin.

Thirdly, the item 'other assets' can be removed. This will reduce the total for assets. However, total liabilities can be made to balance by deducting the value of these other assets from other liabilities to produce an item termed 'net non-deposit liabilities'.

Fourthly, the items 'loans from UK non-monetary sector' and 'loans from overseas', which appear on the liabilities side solely because they appear on the discount houses' balance sheets, can be removed. This will reduce the value of total liabilities, but total assets can be reduced to balance by deducting the amounts for these items from 'advances to UK private sector' (and also from 'advances to the UK public sector' if this has made loans to the discount houses) and from 'advances overseas'.

**Table 8.4** Monetary sector liabilities and assets – version II

| Liabilities | Assets |
|---|---|
| Sterling deposits of: | Sterling lending[3] to: |
|   UK private sector[1] |   UK public sector[4] |
|   UK public sector[1] |   UK private sector |
|   Overseas residents[1] |   Overseas residents |
| Foreign currency deposits[1] | Foreign currency assets |
| Net non-deposit liabilities[2] | |
| Total | Total |

Notes: [1]Include CDs
      [2]Equals 'non-deposit liabilities' *minus* 'other assets'
      [3]Net of any loans to the discount houses
      [4]Includes holdings of notes and coin

One final point to note about Table 8.3 is that assets are split into three groups for reasons which will become clear in a moment. Now the Table 8.3 presentation can be readily reduced to the simpler one shown in Table 8.4. The adjustments made this time leave total assets and liabilities unaltered and simply involve slightly different terms to include precisely the same items that appear in Table 8.3. Thus on the liabilities side, deposits (including CDs) are now primarily split into sterling and foreign currency deposits rather than into deposits held by the UK private and public sectors and by overseas residents, though sterling deposits are subdivided into these three groups. On the assets side, there is a primary split into sterling and foreign currency assets. The former are divided into loans to the UK public sector, the UK private sector and the overseas sector. These three groups cover respectively the sterling assets in the three groups of assets shown in Table 8.3.

It may seem odd to include notes and coin in lending to the public sector, but it will be recalled from Chapter 7 that when the banks want more notes, for example, then they approach the Bank of England Banking Department which in turn exchanges government securities for notes with the Issue Department. In effect, the Issue Department, on behalf of the government which owns it, swaps one type of claim, namely securities, for another, namely notes. As far the assets as in Table 8.3 are concerned, the value of assets in the form of 'other UK government securities' will fall because this table – like the others in this section – does not include the assets (or liabilities) of the Issue Department; this fall will be offset by a rise in the notes and coin held by the monetary sector. Thus the total value of the first group of assets in Table 8.3 will be unaffected, and so, in turn, will 'sterling lending to UK public sector' in Table 8.4.

Now the totals on each side of Table 8.4 must always be equal. Accordingly, any increase in total liabilities must be equalled by a corresponding increase in total assets. Thus it is clear that any:

    increase in sterling deposits of UK private sector
+ increase in sterling deposits of UK public sector
+ increase in sterling deposits of overseas residents
+ increase in foreign currency deposits
+ increase in net non-deposit liabilities

must be equalled by an:

    increase in sterling lending to UK public sector
+ increase in sterling lending to UK private sector
+ increase in sterling lending to overseas residents
+ increase in foreign currency assets

From this it follows that any:

    increase in sterling deposits of UK private sector must be equalled by an:

    increase in sterling lending to UK public sector
+ increase in sterling lending to UK private sector
− increase in sterling deposits of UK public sector
− increase in net non-deposit liabilities
+ increase in sterling lending to overseas residents
+ increase in foreign currency assets
− increase in foreign currency deposits
− increase in sterling deposits of overseas residents

This, at last, enables something to be said about £M3 which, as was shown in Table 8.1, equals notes and coin held by the public plus the sterling deposits of the UK private sector. It follows that any increase in £M3 must be equalled by an increase in notes and coin held by the public plus an increase in the sterling deposits of the UK private sector. Given the identity noted at the end of the last paragraph, it follows that any:

    increase in £M3

must be equalled by an:

    increase in notes and coin held by the public
+ increase in sterling lending to UK public sector
+ increase in sterling lending to UK private sector
− increase in sterling deposits of UK public sector
− increase in net non-deposit liabilities
+ external and foreign currency transactions (rise in assets less rise in liabilities)

where the item 'external and foreign currency transactions' gives the net value of the final four items of the list at the end of the last paragraph. In order to understand future references to this identity, it should be emphasized that the sterling lending it refers to is, of course, lending by the UK monetary sector.

It is now possible to relate changes in £M3 to the PSBR. In essence, the PSBR shows how much more is spent in a year by the public sector than is received by the sector in revenue other than loans. The public sector covers the central government, local authorities and public corporations (or nationalized industries). The sector's expenditure includes any loans made by the public sector. Now in recent years the PSBR has always been positive, showing that the sector typically spends more than it receives, but it has been negative at times in the past. When the sector spends more than it receives, then it needs to borrow. In practice, it typically borrows a shade more each year than it needs so that its bank deposits end up a little higher than they started. It can be seen, therefore, that loans to the public sector will equal the PSBR plus any increase in the public sector's bank deposits. It follows that the PSBR equals the value of all loans made to the public sector minus the value of any rise in its deposits. This can be spelt out more fully as follows:

the PSBR

must be equalled by:

increase in UK monetary sector sterling lending to UK public sector
+ increase in UK private sector sterling lending to UK public sector
+ increase in UK monetary sector foreign currency lending to UK public sector
+ increase in UK private sector foreign currency lending to UK public sector
+ increase in lending by overseas residents to UK public sector
+ increase in notes and coin held by public
− increase in UK public sector sterling deposits
− increase in UK public sector foreign currency deposits

The only oddity here is the inclusion of the increase in notes and coin held by the public. The simplest way of seeing why this item appears is to realise that the public sector can reduce the amount that needs to be lent to it in order to make its payments if it can make some of those payments in the form of new cash printed by the Issue Department which is regarded as part of the public sector.

It is possible to rearrange the terms in the identity of the last paragraph to show that any:

increase in (UK monetary sector) sterling lending to UK public sector

must be equalled by:
PSBR
− purchases of public sector debt by UK private sector
− external and foreign currency finance of UK public sector
− increase in notes and coin held by public
+ increase in UK public sector sterling deposits

where 'purchases of public sector debt by UK private sector' equals increases in UK private sector sterling lending to UK public sector' and includes, for instance, all

**Table 8.5** PSBR and other counterparts to changes in £M3, July–September 1986

|  | Item | £m 000 |
|---|---|---|
|  | Public sector borrowing requirement (PSBR) | + 3,525[1] |
| − | Purchases of public sector debt by UK private sector | − 1,579 |
| − | External and foreign currency finance of public sector | − 903 |
| + | Banks' sterling lending to UK private sector | + 6,646 |
| + | External and foreign currency transactions of UK banks (rise in assets *less* rise in liabilities) | − 805[2] |
| − | Increase in net non-deposit liabilities | − 710 |
|  | Change in £M3 | + 6,174 |

Source: *Bank of England Quarterly Bulletin*, December 1986, Table 11.3.
Notes: [1]A surplus would be shown by a negative number
[2]Liabilities rose more than asset to produce a negative number

purchases of government securities, National Savings Certificates and premium bonds. Also, 'external and foreign currency finance of UK public sector' includes the 'increase in lending by overseas residents to UK public sector' and any foreign currency lending to the UK public sector by the UK private and monetary sectors, net of any increase in UK public sector foreign currency deposits.

This identity for the increase in sterling lending to the UK public sector can be substituted into the identity for the increase in £M3 given earlier to produce the identity shown below. Note that the substitution results in the increase in notes and coin held by the public being first added and then subtracted, so the increase does not appear in the final result. Likewise the increase in sterling deposits of the UK public sector are first subtracted and then added, so these too disappear. In short, any:

increase in £M3

must be equalled by:
   PSBR
  − purchase of public sector debt by UK private sector
  − external and foreign currency finance of UK public sector
  + increase in sterling lending to UK private sector
  + external and foreign currency transactions
  − increase in net non-deposit liabilities.

This formulation is reproduced in Table 8.5 with some minor changes in terminology. The table shows the actual figures for the third quarter of 1986.

## Monetary control in the 1980s

This final section looks at some of the changes and issues in monetary control that have emerged since the 1979 General Election. In broad terms, it is fair to say that the present government has sought to develop two of the main trends that developed in the 1970s.

First, it has attempted to strengthen the role of market forces and competition in the monetary sector. For instance, in October 1979, the government abandoned exchange controls which had previously restricted the extent to which people could convert sterling into foreign currencies in order to invest their money abroad. Also, in June 1980, the supplementary special deposits scheme – the corset – was abolished. This scheme can be seen as having interfered with competition by penalising most those banks which were most successful in attracting deposits. The abandonment of the corset has meant that monetary control has relied on interest rate control reinforced by open-market operations. There is still provision for the call of special deposits, but in practice none have been required since 1980.

Insofar as interest rate control has been given a greater role, it might seem a little paradoxical to have to record that MLR was scrapped in September 1981. However, this should perhaps be seen more as a change in the way interest rate control worked rather than a major change of substance. The idea with MLR – and indeed with Bank Rate before it – was that the rate at which last resort lending facilities would be made was, as it were, publicized and so well-known. Under the present arrangements, the authorities keep the rate unpublished. When the discount houses want to sell bills to the Bank of England to relieve a cash shortage, they offer bills at a price of their own choosing which the Bank may or may not accept; if it does not accept the offered price, then the houses must offer the bills at successively lower prices until the Bank does accept! The uncertainty attached to this procedure probably encourages the banks and discount houses to run with a greater margin of reserves than before.

Note that the new system of interest rate control has the advantage of giving the authorities more flexibility in that an unpublished rate for last resort lending can be altered more frequently than a published one without too much notice being attracted to an apparent lack of consistency. On the other hand, the present system seems to have the disadvantage that when the authorities wish to raise interest rates drastically in a crisis, then they lack a published rate drawing attention to the fact. This disadvantage was realized, though, and there is provision for an MLR to be announced if the need arises. The need was perceived in January 1985 when the exchange rate had sunk to an all-time low of £1 = \$1.11.

The second 1970s trend that has been developed is the use of monetary targets. As noted earlier, targets were first publicized in the late 1960s, but they were not introduced on a regular basis until 1976. For a while it was thought that M3 might be the best target since it included all money held by UK citizens including foreign currency deposits. However, it seemed that foreign currency deposits were held chiefly by UK businesses in connection with activities overseas and hence that they were of little concern to the UK monetary authorities, so attention was soon focused on £M3 which ignores UK citizens' foreign currency deposits. It is perhaps arguable that the authorities should use a measure which includes sterling deposits held by foreigners, but this has not been done. Between 1976 and 1978, targets were set for both £M3 and domestic credit expansion (DCE) although DCE was then less important than it had been in the fixed exchange rate days of the late 1960s, so from 1978 onwards it was dropped. The same arrangements were maintained after the 1979 election, for £M3 alone was targeted in late 1979 and also in the first statement in March 1980 of the government's new Medium Term Financial Strategy. This set out a target £M3 growth rate range for February 1980 to February 1981 of 7–11 per cent, falling steadily to 4–8 per cent by 1983–84.

From 1982 onwards, however, targets were added for M1 and PSL2, while from 1983 M0 was added in as well. Why was there this proliferation of targets? A major part of the answer is that £M3 actually grew by 20 per cent in February 1980 to February 1981! On its own, this growth seemed to suggest that monetary policy had been lax. However, all other factors – such as the growth of other monetary measures and high real interest rates – suggested that monetary policy was tight. Moreover, it was clear that prices were rising about 10 per cent per annum while output was almost static. Clearly, then, the velocity of circulation had fallen. Equally clearly, the authorities would prefer to have a target whose velocity was more stable.

In retrospect, it seems that there must have been major rightwards shifts in both the $M_d$ and $M_s$ curves during 1980–81. These shifts resulted in a substantial increase in the £M3 money stock without any serious impact on interest rates. The end of the corset could have been a major factor helping to produce these shifts. For one thing, its removal allowed the banks to create more money than they otherwise would, thus shifting $M_s$ to the right. At the same time, much of the banks' extra lending went into mortgages, a form of loan in which they started competing vigorously with building societies. This would have reduced building society lending and so cut the societies' demands for deposits, thereby putting downward pressure on their deposit interest rates. Such a fall would raise the demand for bank deposits, so shifting $M_d$ to the right.

This experience suggested, at the very least, that the demand for money as defined by £M3 could be unstable. If the monetary authorities persisted with £M3 as their target, then they would have to accommodate wide fluctuations in order to maintain stable interest rates. This might have been acceptable except that it was a time of rapid inflation. In these circumstances, the authorities wanted a target which they were happy to let grow slowly and steadily without fluctuations so that they could announce and pursue a policy of restrained expansion. There seemed to be two options. One was to use a wider measure, PSL2 being the obvious one. This included building society deposits and so had risen much less rapidly than £M3. The other was M1, which excluded time deposits, and so most interest-bearing deposits, and was hence less susceptible to changes caused by interest rates on bank deposits altering in relation to other interest rates. For these reasons, both PSL2 and M1 were included as targets in budgetary statements from 1982 onwards.

As it happened, though, there was then a rapid expansion in interest-bearing sight deposits and hence M1! This is one factor that has stimulated interest in M0. Another factor, probably a related one, is that changes in M0 seem in recent years to have been better guides to future inflation rates than changes in the other measures, particularly £M3 (and, more recently, M1). Paradoxically, this could be because the authorities have sought to control £M3 and not M0. It has been suggested by Goodhart (1975, p. 5) that once a measure is used for control purposes then it loses its predictive power. For instance, if £M3 is controlled by restricting bank lending, then NBFI activity may expand so that interest rates fall and spending and output rise much as they would if £M3 were not controlled; but the relationship between £M3 and output will be much weaker in the controlled case. Despite this pessimistic view, M0 was adopted as a target in 1984. As it happens, further unsatisfactory performance by £M3 as a predictor led to it being dropped as a target late in September 1985, only to be restored again in May 1986!

Another measure which has been the subject of attention is M2. Figures have been collected only since 1981, so it is too early at present to see how useful it might be as a target. This post-1981 M2 measure should not be confused with an earlier and different M2 series that was dropped in 1971. The new M2 measure attempts to overcome perceived problems with M1 and £M3. The trouble with M1 is that it is dominated by interest-free sight deposits many of which, if interest rates rise only slightly, may be switched into highly liquid seven-day interest-bearing deposits. Thus a small rise in interest rates can lead to a large fall in M1 which overstates the real extent of any monetary tightening. Likewise, for reasons already shown, £M3 too can fluctuate much more than any likely changes in final spending. Now M2 seeks to provide a measure of transactions balances, and it is thought that changes in this will give much better indications of changes in spending. Of course, there is no way of being certain of correctly identifying which balances are held for transactions purposes and which are not. The initial measure used in 1982 included all non-interest-bearing sight deposits and all interest-bearing deposits on which, in practice, cheques could be made, and it also included any other deposits under £100,000 which had less than a month to maturity; in addition it included publicly-held cash. The composition of M2 was widened in 1983. All shares and deposits in building societies with less than a month to maturity were added then, along with ordinary accounts at the National Savings Bank.

Despite the attractions of targets other than £M3, it is £M3 which the authorities have made most efforts to control. This is not as paradoxical as it sounds. The money stock control measures available to the authorities seek chiefly to influence the level of bank deposits and so act directly on £M3. The effects on other measures are typically indirect. Thus it can make sense to seek to adhere to a target in, say, M1, by manipulating £M3. It could be that the manipulations require or permit wide fluctuation in £M3, the sort of fluctuations which would cause misunderstanding if £M3 were itself the target.

Chapters 4 and 5 discussed four ways in which the money stock could be changed: open-market operations, interest rate control, credit ceilings and changes in reserve ratios. Although the last two methods have been eschewed in the 1980s, it might be thought that the other two would be sufficient. Technically, perhaps, this is so, but there are some sound reasons why the government has found it difficult to restrain the money stock as much as it would like. One type of difficulty is that control measures can have very uncertain effects. For instance, a series of open-market sales to the public would be expected to contract £M3. But if, for some reason, the public simultaneously decided to reduce their cash holdings, or if the banks happened to have higher reserve ratios than they thought desirable, or if the discount houses were not up to their borrowing limits, then the effect on £M3 could be very modest.

Another problem concerns the exchange rate. To restrain £M3 it will be necessary for interest rates to rise. This will attract capital from overseas causing the balance of payments to move into surplus. The surplus should disappear again if sterling is allowed to float freely upwards in value, but the authorities may not wish sterling to appreciate and so they may hold it down by buying foreign currencies on the foreign exchange markets. As explained in Chapter 6, these purchases will then create expansionary pressures on the money stock. In short, the government can choose either a particular money stock target or a particular exchange rate. It cannot easily choose both!

There are further problems in controlling the money stock that relate to the PSBR. These problems can be seen with the help of the relationships shown in Table 8.5. Suppose the government decides to raise its spending levels but not its taxes. This increases the PSBR and, as Table 8.5 suggests, puts upward pressure on £M3. The final effect on £M3 depends, though, on who lends the money to the government, a point explained in Chapter 3. If it is the central bank, then there will be an expansion in clearing bank holdings of cash and, in turn, probably a multiple expansion of bank lending to the private sector causing more rises in £M3. If it is the clearing banks, then there are two possible consequences: either the banks were not fully lent, so that £M3 rises by the same amount as the PSBR, or they were fully lent, in which case loans to the public sector must be offset by a fall in lending to the private sector and £M3 stays constant. If it is the private sector, so that the public sector sells securities to the private sector, then again the rise in PSBR is offset by another item in the table and £M3 is unaffected.

Now it must seem that if the government has a large borrowing requirement, as has been the case throughout the 1980s, and if it wishes to restrain the growth of £M3, then the safest course is to seek to finance the PSBR by sales of government securities to the private sector. However, this option does not particularly appeal to the government even though it no doubt regards it as the best of a bad bunch. The trouble is that it is likely to lead to a rise in interest rates and so is likely to reduce or 'crowd-out' private sector investment. It is worth asking why interest rates would rise. After all, any expansionary effect on bank reserves caused by the public expenditure which had to be financed by borrowing will be offset by a contractionary effect produced when people in the private sector buy the new securities off the government, so the $M_s$ curve should be stable. The trouble is that the new public expenditure will raise incomes and so increase the demand for money, thereby shifting $M_d$ to the right and causing interest rates to rise.

In the circumstances, it is not hard to see why the government would want to cut the PSBR in its effort to restrain the growth of £M3 and so, it would hope, restrain the rate of inflation. However, cutting the PSBR is hard, for tax increases – which are anyway virtually taboo for the present government – are always politically unpopular, as are cuts in public expenditure. Moreover, both cuts in expenditure and increases in taxes have downward effects on employment levels, and these effects are particularly unsatisfactory at a time of high unemployment. Notice, too, that if the government did cut its spending in order to reduce the PSBR, and if unemployment rose as a result, then there would be further financial problems. For then the government's tax yield would fall – as the new unemployed would probably cease paying income tax and would certainly pay less in the way of taxes on expenditure such as value added tax – while other government expenditure would rise, notably unemployment benefit. So the final impact on the PSBR could be modest.

Given that the PSBR is hard to cut and that sales of government debt to the private sector have disadvantages, it is not wholly surprising that £M3 has been allowed to rise at generally higher rates than inflation, as indeed have all other targets. Recalling the identity $MV = PT$, and noting that M – taken here to be £M3 – has risen more rapidly than P, it might be thought that T would have risen with significant effects on employment levels, but alas it seems the main effect has been falls in V. It is not entirely clear why V should have fallen at a time of high real interest rates. In part, at least, it could be that velocity has fallen because inflation has fallen; lower inflation means that people are now less anxious to spend money quickly before price rises occur.

It is clear that controlling the money stock is not in practice as simple as earlier chapters suggested. It is perhaps pertinent to end by this book observing that even if the money stock could be easily and readily changed, the effects on the economy of changing it could be uncertain in both magnitude and timing. The effects would be uncertain in magnitude because the effects on interest rates depend on the interest-elasticity of the demand for money and the effects on spending depend on the interest-elasticity of the demand for goods and services. These elasticities are hard to estimate and no doubt fluctuate over time. The effects are likely to be uncertain in timing because it may take some time for the banks to react fully to, say, restraint and reduce their lending, so it may be some time before the final rises in interest rates occur, and it may then be some time before spending is cut by the full amount, for some projects to be financed by borrowed funds may be too far advanced for the borrowers to feel like cancelling them. It may be added that other lags can arise even earlier in the monetary policy control process. There may be a lag between events occurring which require monetary restraint and data on the events being available. There may be a lag between data being available and problems being recognised. And there may be a lag between recognition and policy measures. The presence of such lags is one reason why monetarists, anyway, argue that economic policies such as monetary policy cannot be used effectively to produce satisfactory short-run fine-tuning policies.

# Bibliography

This bibliography includes items referred to in the text and suggested further reading. For convenience, the works cited are divided into three broad sections.

## A  Development of money (Chapter 1)

Crowther, G., 1940: *An Outline of Money*. London: Thomas Nelson & Sons.
Kindleberger, C.P., 1984: *A Financial History of Western Europe*. London: George Allen & Unwin.
Morgan, E.V., 1965: *A History of Money*. London: Penguin Books.
Smith, A., 1776, republished 1964: *The Wealth of Nations*. Everyman's Library, London: Dent.
Tschoegl, A.E., 1985: 'Modern Barter', *Lloyds Bank Review*, No. 158, October, pp. 32–40.
Vilar, P., 1976: *A History of Gold and Money 1450–1920*. London: New Left Books.

## B  Descriptions of financial claims and intermediaries in the UK (Chapters 2, 3 and 7)

Carter, H. and Partington, I., 1984, 3rd ed.: *Applied Economics in Banking and Finance*. Oxford: Oxford University Press.
Dacey, W.M., 1964, 5th ed: *The British Banking Mechanism*. London: Hutchinson University Library.
Day, A.C.L., 1957: *An Outline of Monetary Economics*. Oxford: Oxford University Press.
Day, A.C.L. 1968, 3rd ed: *The Economics of Money*. Oxford: Oxford University Press.
McKenzie, G.W., 1976: *The Economics of the Euro-Currency System*. London: Macmillan.
Pringle, R., 1975: *Banking in Britain*. London: Methuen.
Revell, J., 1973: *The British Financial System*. London: Macmillan.
Sayers, R.S., 1964, 6th ed: *Modern Banking*. Oxford: Oxford University Press.
Shaw, E.R., 1978, 2nd ed.: *The London Money Market* London: Heinemann.

## C  Control of the money stock – theory and practice (Chapters 4, 5, 6 and 8)

Artis, M.J. and Lewis, M.K., 1981: *Monetary Control in the United Kingdom*. Oxford: Philip Allan.
Bank of England, 1984: *The Development and Operation of Monetary Policy: 1960–1983*. Oxford: Oxford University Press.
Coghlan, R., 1980: *The Theory of Money and Finance*. London: Macmillan.

Dow, S.C., 1982: *Recent Developments in UK Monetary Policy*. Stirling: University of Stirling, Department of Economics, Teaching Paper No. 8.

Dow, S.C. and Earl, P.E., 1982: *Money Matters: A Keynesian Approach to Monetary Economics*. Oxford: Martin Robertson.

Friedman, M. 1956: 'The quantity theory of money – a restatement' in *Studies in the Quantity Theory of Money* (ed M. Friedman). Chicago: Chicago University Press, pp. 3–21.

Goodhart, C.A.E., 1984: *Monetary Theory and Practice: the UK Experience*. London: Macmillan.

Goodhart, C.A.E., 1975: *Problems of Monetary Management: the UK Experience*. Discussion Paper for Conference in Monetary Economics, Canberra: Reserve Bank of Australia.

Kettell, B., 1985: *Monetary Economics*. London: Graham & Trotman.

Keynes, J.M., 1936: *The General Theory of Employment, Interest and Money*. London: Macmillan.

Llewelyn, D.T. (ed.), 1982: *The Framework of UK Monetary Policy*. London: Heinemann.

Newlyn, W.T. and Bootle, R.P., 1978, 3rd edn: *Theory of Money*. Oxford: Oxford University Press.

Pierce, D.G. and Tysome, P.J., 1985, 2nd edn: *Monetary Economics*. London: Butterworth.

Radcliffe, Lord, 1959: *The Committee on the Working of the Monetary System: Report*. London: HMSO, CMND 827.

Zawadzki, K.K.E., 1981: *Competition and Credit Control*. Oxford: Basil Blackwell.

# Index

absolute advantage 1
accepting houses 29, 114, 159
advances 61, 63, 156, 161
  *see also* bank lending *and* banks: and
    creation of money
Allied Irish Banks 150
  *see also* Northern Irish banks
American banks 159
Amsterdam, Bank of 10
assets:
  current 12, 22
  financial 22–4
  fixed 12, 22
  physical 22–4, 76–7, 138

bad debts 12, 80
balance of payments deficit 125, 127–9,
    165–6, 168
balance sheets:
  basic principles 11–13
  for ancient banks 14
  for Bank of England 46–50, 137–42
  for clearing banks 46–50, 51–4, 55–8,
    59–64, 95–6, 98–111
  for deposit-creating bank 18–19
  for discount houses 142–7
  for early English banks 16
  for retail banks 150–6
  for wholesale banks 159–63
bank accounts 18, 59
  *see also* deposits
bank charges 60
bank deposits
  *see* deposits
bank lending 14, 156, 161, 168

  *see also* advances *and* banks: and creation of
    money
bank-notes 15–18, 24, 45, 139–41, 151–2,
    179
Bank Rate 119, 166, 167, 169, 182
bank statements 18, 156
Bank of England:
  and clearing 45–6, 147
  and coin issue 141
  and convertibility 18, 118–19
  and creation of money 50
  and Exchange Equalization Account 124
  as lender of last resort 62, 138, 142, 148
  bankers' balances 100, 127, 138, 152–4
  bankers' bank 45, 47–9
  Banking Department 46, 137–40, 141–2,
    150
  cash ratio 139
  effect of its bond purchases 74–5, 76
  foundation 18
  gold stock 18, 119–20
  government's bank 46–50
  Issue Department 46, 139, 142, 179
  issue of bank-notes 18, 139–41
  nationalization 69
  powers 69, 159
  public deposits 29, 47, 48–9, 122, 127,
    138, 175
  *see also* money stock *and* open-market
    operations
Bank of Ireland 150
  *see also* Northern Irish banks
Bank of Scotland 149
  *see also* Scottish banks
bankers' bank 44–6
bankers' orders 150

Banking Act (1979) 70
banks:
    ancient 9, 13–15
    and creation of money 15, 19, 52–9, 64, 157–9
    and international transactions 115–17, 122–6
    and overseas deposits 115–17, 123–4, 151, 161
    balance held abroad 115–17, 123–4
    cash ratio deposits 63, 152–4, 158, 163
    correspondent 115, 122
    early English 15–21
    foreign currency deposits 131–5, 175, 183
    operational deposits 154, 175
    see also clearing banks, deposits, merchant banks, retail banks and wholesale banks
Barclays Bank 149
barter 2–5
bezant 8
bills:
    accepting 26, 27–9
    and interest rate control 107–11
    and private sector liquidity 176
    as bank assets 62
    bank 29
    commercial 26
    discount rates 27
    drawing 26
    local authority 31
    of exchange 10, 26, 30, 114
    Treasury 29–31, 64, 99, 102, 107–11, 167, 169
bimetallism 8, 119
Blunden, P. 7
bonds:
    definition 32
    index-linked 32
    long-dated 32, 40–1
    medium-dated 32, 40–1
    short-dated 32, 35, 40–1
    see also fixed-interest securities
Bretton Woods system 119–21
building societies 64–8, 163–4, 175–6, 183, 184
Byzantine Empire 8

Caesar, J. 6
call-money see money-at-call
cash 18–20, 45, 48–50, 70, 92, 112, 175
    see also bank-notes and coins
cash drain 53–4, 59

cash ratio:
    and credit creation 53–8, 81, 88–9
    and interest rates 81
    and monetary control 84–6, 91, 92, 100–4
    composition 51
    deposits 152–4, 158, 163
    need for 14–15, 17, 19, 20, 61
certificates of deposits (CDs) 143–5, 155, 161, 162, 176
certificates of tax deposit 176
Charles I, King 11
cheques 18, 20–1, 49, 150
clearing banks:
    and cash ratio rules 84–5, 90, 152–4
    and clearing 45–6, 149
    and credit ceilings 86–8, 91, 104–6
    and interest rate control 90, 110–12
    and last resort lending 88–90
    and money supply curve 77–82
    and open-market operations 82–3, 90, 98–100
    and special deposits 100–4
    balance sheet 59–64
    notes and coin 61, 112
    see also banks and retail banks
clipping 7, 8, 118
Clydesdale Bank 149
    see also Scottish banks
coins 6–9, 13–18, 24, 113–14, 118, 141, 179
collateral 145
comparative advantage 1–2
Competition and Credit Control (CCC) 169–70
consols 32, 71, 73, 74, 107
consortium banks 159
convertibility 18, 118–21
Co-operative Bank 149
copper 6, 7
correspondent banks 115, 122
corset 170, 182, 183
coupon 31, 33
Coutts Bank 149
cowrie shells 5–6
credit cards 72
credit ceilings 86–8, 91, 92, 93, 104–6, 112, 168, 169–70
credit multiplier:
    with Euro-currencies 134–5
    with one bank 50–5
    with several banks 55–9
credit transfers 150
creditors 12, 26
crowding-out 185
Crowther, G. 3, 6

debasement 7, 118
debentures 12, 32
debtors 12, 26
demand deposits 59
  *see also* deposits: sight
demand for money:
  and interest-bearing deposits 74, 76
  curve 73–4, 75–6
  Keynesian view 71–5, 76, 92
  monetarist view 75–7
  precautionary motive 72
  speculative motive 72–3, 75, 76, 172
  stability 94, 172, 184
  transactions motive 71–2, 175, 184
deposits:
  at banks 18–20, 24, 38, 48, 59–60
  at building societies 65–6, 175, 176, 183, 184
  at NBFIs 24, 64–8, 93, 112, 163–4
  demand 59
  foreign currency 131–5, 175, 183
  interest-bearing 74, 76, 81, 100, 106, 107, 110, 133
  overseas 122, 123, 135, 151–2, 183
  retail 149, 175, 176
  sight 59–60, 150, 161, 175, 176
  time 59, 161, 175, 176
  wholesale 157, 175
depreciation 13
devaluations 120, 167, 168
direct debits 150
discount brokers 62
discount houses (LDMA):
  and banking system 147–8
  and banks' cash ratios 100–3
  and credit ceilings 104–5
  and interest rate control 107–12
  and last resort lending 30, 62, 148, 182
  and money-at-call 61–4, 96, 102–4
  and open-market operations 98–100
  and Treasury bills 30–1, 64
  assets 143–6
  controls over assets 98, 146
  liabilities 142–3
discounting 27
dividends 36, 142
division of labour 2
dollar convertibility 120–1
domestic credit expansion (DCE) 129, 169, 183
double coincidence of wants 2–3

economies of scale 2
Edward III, King 7

electrum 6
eligible liabilities 152–4
Elizabeth I, Queen 8
equities 35–6, 40
Euro-banks 133–5
Euro-currencies 133, 162
Euro-dollars 133–5
Euro-sterling 133, 135
European Monetary System 121
exchange 1–5
exchange controls 125, 182
Exchange Equalization Account (EEA) 122, 124–5, 127, 166
exchange rates:
  and gold standard 118–19
  changes and balance sheets 147
  fixed 118–21, 124–8, 130, 135, 165–8, 185
  freely floating 118, 123, 129, 131, 135, 185
  in the 1930s 119
  managed floats 118, 121, 169, 170
  medieval 118
  multiple 126

fiduciary issue 139–41
finance houses 65, 163, 168
financial claims 23–6, 38–40
  *see also* bills, equities, fixed-interest securities *and* unit trusts
financial intermediaries 24, 169
  *see also* banks *and* non-bank financial intermediaries
fixed-interest securities 31–5, 40–3
foreign currency:
  assets 146–7, 159
  dealings 9, 114, 117
  deposits 115–17, 123, 131–5, 175, 183
  liabilities 146–7, 151, 159
  loans 143
  reserves 124–6, 127, 166
foreign exchange market 117
forgery 7
Francis I, King (of France) 7
Friedman, M. 71, 76, 172, 173

gilt-edged securities 32
goats 3
gold:
  and convertibility 18, 118–21, 128
  as money 5, 6
  coins 7, 8–9, 118
  confiscated in 1640 11
  reserves 124, 128, 165

*see also* gold standard
goldsmiths 10
gold standard 118–19, 128–9, 165–6
Goodhart, C.A.E. 184
government:
  effect of borrowing from Bank of England 49–50, 185
  effect of borrowing from clearing banks 50, 185
  effect of borrowing from non-bank public 50, 82–3, 185
  effect of expenditure 49–50, 88, 127, 186
  effect of privatization 82–3, 138
  effect of taxes 82–3, 186
Gresham's Law 7, 8
Gresham, Sir Thomas 7
gross redemption yield 34–5

Henry VIII, King 8

idle balances 172
  *see also* demand for money: speculative motive
inflation 166, 170, 172–3, 184
insurance companies 65
inter-bank loans 117, 162
interest-bearing deposits *see* deposits: interest-bearing
interest payments 31, 33, 142
interest rate control 90, 106–12, 169–70, 182–3, 185
interest rate targets 171–2
interest rates:
  and cash ratios 81
  and cash ratio rules 83–5, 91
  and credit ceilings 85–8, 91, 92, 105–6
  and demand for money 72–3, 75, 76, 92, 112
  and Euro-currencies 133–4, 135
  and expectations 42–3, 173
  and foreign currency deposits 135
  and gold standard 119, 165
  and inflation 39–40, 170, 173
  and interest rate control 88–90, 110–11
  and international money flows 130–1, 136
  and last resort lending 88–90
  and liquidity 38, 40
  and NBFIs 93, 112, 164
  and open-market operations 83, 90, 100
  and overseas deposits 135
  and precautionary motive 72
  and risk 38, 40
  and saving 39
  and security prices 27, 33–5, 36

and special deposits 103–4
and speculative motive 72–3
and transactions motive 72
equilibrium 79–80, 82
low 166–7
need for 38–40
nominal 39–40, 170, 173
penal rate 109
real 39–40, 173
term structure 40–3
'the' interest rate 71
International Monetary Fund 120, 168
investment trusts 36–7, 168
IOUs 15–18
Irish banks *see* Northern Irish banks
Italian banks 9
items in suspense and transmission 152

James I, King 7
Japanese banks 159

Keynes, J.M. 71, 172
  *see also* demand for money: Keynesian view
Kindleberger, C.P. 10, 45

lags 186
last resort lending 21, 62, 88–92, 97, 107–11, 148, 182–3
life insurance companies 24, 163
liquidity 38, 41, 61–3, 168
  *see also* money stock: PSL1 *and* PSL2
Lloyds Bank 149
London Bankers' Clearing House 45, 149
London clearing banks 149
London Discount Market Association (LDMA) 61, 142
  *see also* discount houses
longs 40–3

market loans 61–2
matching 161
maturity 10, 26, 63, 155, 161, 176
medium of exchange *see* money: as a medium of exchange
medium term financial strategy 183
merchant banks 114, 159
metals 5–6
  *see also* bimetallism, gold *and* silver
Midland Bank 149
Minimum Lending Rate (MLR) 169–70, 182–3
mints 6, 7, 8–9, 114
monetary authorities 69, 97
monetary control

*see* monetary policy *and* money stock

monetary policy  165–73, 182–6

monetary sector  142, 151, 155, 162, 175, 177–9

monetary targets  168, 171–4, 183–5

money-at-call:
    and last resort lending  61–2, 140, 148
    and monetary control  98–9, 101–2, 104–5, 107–10
    and money market  147–8
    as bank asset  61–4, 159
    as discount house liability  142

money:
    and bank deposits  18–20, 59–60
    as a medium of exchange  2–4, 5–6, 15–17, 18–20, 67, 175
    as a store of value  4, 38, 73, 75
    as a unit of account  3–4
    demand for *see* demand for money
    desirable properties  5
    items which have been used as money  3, 5, 6–7, 15
    *see also* credit multiplier, deposits *and* money stock

money-changers  9, 114

money demand *see* demand for money

money market:
    definition  61
    inter-bank  155, 162
    parallel  155, 162
    traditional  147, 155–6

money stock:
    and cash drain  53–4, 92–3, 112
    and cash ratio rules  84–5, 88, 91, 92, 98
    and credit ceilings  86–8, 91, 92, 98, 104–6
    and Euro-currencies  134, 135
    and foreign currency deposits  135, 175, 183
    and government borrowing  48–50, 82–3, 185
    and interest rate control  90, 98, 106–12
    and international transactions  121–6, 127–9, 135–6
    and last resort lending  88–90, 92
    and loans to LDMA  102–4
    and NBFIs  66–8, 93, 112, 163–4
    and open-market operations  82–3, 88, 90, 98–100
    and special deposits  100–3
    determination  77–82
    in coin-only economy  14

£M3  69, 175, 176, 180–2, 183–6

M0  175, 183, 184

M1  175, 183, 184–5

M2  175, 176, 184

M3 (pre-1987 definition)  175, 176, 183

M3 (post-1987 definition) *see* £M3

M3c  176

M4  176

M5  176

omits bankers' deposits  48, 157, 175

omits overseas deposits  122, 135–6, 175, 183

omits public sector deposits  175

PSL1  176

PSL2  176, 183, 184

with coins and IOUs  16

with deposit-creating banks  19

*see also* monetary policy *and* monetary targets

money supply curve:
    and cash drain  112
    and cash ratio rules  84–5, 102–3
    and credit ceilings  86–7, 91, 105, 112
    and interest rate control  90, 107, 111, 112
    and international money flows  130–1
    and last resort lending  89–90
    and open-market operations  82–3, 90, 100
    derivation  78, 80–2

Morgan, E.V.  2, 6, 7, 11, 114

National Girobank  149

National Savings Bank  163, 175, 176, 184

National Savings Certificates  25, 38, 93, 112

National Westminster Bank  149

natural unemployment  173

near-money  60, 67, 93, 175

Nero  8

net worth  23

Newton, Sir Isaac  9, 18, 119

non-bank financial intermediaries (NBFIs):
    activities  42, 65–6
    and interest rate control  110
    and interest rates  94, 112, 164
    and monetary policy  168, 169–70
    and money stock  67–8, 93–4, 112, 163–4, 170
    as financial intermediaries  24
    relationship with banking system  66–7, 164, 170
    types  65, 163
    *see also* building societies, deposits, finance houses *and* National Savings Bank

Northern Bank  150
    *see also* Northern Irish banks

Northern Irish banks  18, 150, 151–2, 178

notes *see* bank-notes

open-market operations 82–3, 90, 98–100, 111, 128, 169, 182, 185
operational deposits 154, 175
overdrafts 156
overseas deposits 122, 123, 135, 151–2, 183

paper money 6
    *see also* bank-notes
parity rates 120
pension funds 65, 163
precautionary motive *see* demand for money
premium bonds 25, 176
primary banks *see* retail banks
private sector liquidity (PSL) *see* money stock: PSL1 *and* PSL2
profit and loss a/c 12, 142
public sector borrowing requirement 170, 177, 180–2, 185–6

quantity theory of money 172

Radcliffe report 168, 173
redemption 31, 32
    *see also* gross redemption yield
retail banks:
    and clearing 149
    assets 152–6
    cash ratio rules 152–4
    composition 149–50
    liabilities 150–2
    *see also* banks *and* clearing banks
retail deposits *see* deposits: retail
revaluation reserve 12–13, 142, 143, 147, 152
revaluations 120
risk 14, 37, 38, 40, 41–3, 51, 161
Royal Bank of Scotland 149
    *see also* Scottish banks
Royal Mint 9, 11, 141

save-as-you-earn 25
savings banks 65
    *see also* National Savings Bank *and* Trustee Savings Bank
Scottish banks 18, 149, 151–2, 178
secondary banks *see* wholesale banks
secured loans 25, 61, 145–6
securities 25, 63, 138, 143, 153, 160
    *see also* bills, equities, fixed-interest securities *and* unit trusts
seignorage 6, 118

share capital 12
shares:
    building society 65
    investment trust 36–7
    ordinary 35–6, 40
    preference 32
shorts 40–3
sight deposits 59–60, 150, 161, 175, 176
silver 5, 6, 7, 8, 9, 18
Smith, A. 2, 7, 8
special deposits 100–4, 154, 168, 169
    *see also* corset
speculative motive *see* demand for money
sterilization 126–9, 130
stock exchange 25, 32, 36, 39, 63, 162
supplementary special deposits *see* corset
sweating 7, 8, 118

tale 6, 7
tap issue 30
tender issue 30–1
time deposits 59, 161, 175, 176
    *see also* deposits: interest-bearing
transactions motive *see under* demand for money
Treasury 69, 137, 142
Treasury bills *see* bills: Treasury
Trustee Savings Bank 149
Tschoegl, A.E. 4

Uap 5
Ulster Bank 150
    *see also* Northern Irish banks
unit trusts 37, 51, 65, 163
usury 9–10, 114

velocity of circulation 172–3, 186
Vilar, P. 7

wealth 23–4, 75–6
wholesale banks:
    and money stock 157–9
    assets 159–62
    composition 159
    liabilities 159–62
    nature 157–9
    *see also* banks
wholesale deposits *see* deposits: wholesale
William I, King 7
Williams & Glynn's Bank 149

Yorkshire Bank 149